Murder and Counterrevolution in Mexico

THE MEXICAN EXPERIENCE

William H. Beezley, series editor

Murder and Counterrevolution in Mexico

The Eyewitness Account of German Ambassador Paul von Hintze, 1912–1914

Edited and with an introduction by
Friedrich E. Schuler

University of Nebraska Press
Lincoln and London

Library of Congress Cataloging-in-Publication Data
Hintze, Paul von, 1864-1941, author.
Murder and counterrevolution in Mexico:
the eyewitness account of German ambassador
Paul von Hintze, 1912-1914 / edited and with an
introduction by Friedrich E. Schuler.
pages   cm — (The Mexican experience)
Includes bibliographical references and index.
ISBN 978-0-8032-4963-9 (pbk.: alk. paper)
1. Hintze, Paul von, 1864-1941—Diaries. 2. Mexico—
History—Revolution, 1910-1920—Personal
narratives, German. 3. Ambassadors—Germany—
Biography. I. Schuler, Friedrich Engelbert, 1960-
II. Title. III. Series: Mexican experience.
F1234.H793 2014   972.08'16092—dc23
2014030765

Set in Lyon Text by Renni Johnson.

Dedicated to Michael C. Meyer and William H. Beezley

Contents

Illustrations

Acknowledgments

In the Freiburg branch of the German National Archive, Frau Waibel and Frau Meyer deserve sincere thanks for helping over all those years. Herr Weins was most kind in working with me through the process of publication.

A most profound thank you goes to the entire team at the Political Archive of the German Foreign Ministry, Berlin. This book would not be complete without the regular diplomatic reports and their use, which Frau Sabine Schafferdt so graciously approved. Herr Guenter Scheidemann did everything possible to make the new pictures from Germany available. Both often went "the extra mile." The entire team at the German Foreign Ministry archive remains one of Germany's most outstanding archival support teams.

In Berlin-Lichterfelde, National Archive of Germany, Frau Regina Gruener and Herr Klein were of invaluable help.

I am grateful to the Library of Congress in Washington DC for its efforts to make pictures available. At the El Paso Public Library, Ms. Claudia M. Martinez provided new images of the thus far enigmatic Felix A. Sommerfeld.

The History Department of Portland State University, guided by Tom Luckett and the Friends of History, graciously provided unending support and funds at critical moments.

The final stages of the book became reality because of Bridget Barry at the University of Nebraska Press and because of William H. Beezley. A profound thank you to both of them and to the readers of the manuscript for believing in this project.

I thank Joy Margheim for her most discriminating eyes and splendid suggestions. They made this manuscript a much better document collection.

Gracias to my Berlin Kreuzberg muse who tolerated endless mentioning of the name Hintze over all those years. Vienna Diestra, I thank you for playing with me all those mornings and relaxing me. That way I could do my translations in the afternoon. Please consider becoming a historian.

Editor's Note

Paul von Hintze wrote in German—in a style typical of the early twentieth century—in his diary segments, but he used a more formal tone in his diplomatic cables to Berlin. At times I replaced the language of 1913 and 1914 with contemporary terminology for the reader's benefit. Because the diaries and reports are being translated into English a century after they were first written, I occasionally found it necessary to defer to the vocabulary and literary expections of a contemporary twenty-first-century readership. A much-appreciated copyediting further refined the translation to satisfy English-language expectations. At no time was the original meaning of any sentence changed on purpose in order to please contemporary tastes.

Murder and Counterrevolution in Mexico

Introduction

On January 18, 1911, Paul von Hintze, rear admiral of the German navy, cabled Berlin to accept his nomination as Germany's foreign diplomat to Mexico.[1] The German emperor Wilhelm II had selected Hintze personally to act as his eyes and ears in Mexico.[2] Hintze departed on a steamer bound for Mexico on April 12, 1911, and upon arrival in Mexico City on May 8, he took over responsibility for the German diplomatic legation. Hintze arrived in a Mexico City deep in political turmoil. On May 25 President Porfirio Díaz resigned after nearly thirty years of continuous rule, acknowledging agrarian and regional demands for power and justice. On May 31 Díaz fled to Spain and then to Paris. Francisco de la Barra served as interim president until November 1911.

Hintze's relationship with Wilhelm II gave him relative independence from the formal reporting style preferred by the German Foreign Ministry, and he reported more informal and personal impressions from inside Mexico City. His descriptions paint a new, previously unavailable tableau, showing how the Mexican Revolution was lived, fought, and experienced inside the capital while Emiliano Zapata and Pancho Villa were driving home the message of agrarian revolution from Mexico's periphery. Now, one hundred years later, Admiral von Hintze's descriptions encourage us to step into the streets among the revolutionaries and their rivaling factions. A German historian has called Hintze one of the German empire's most gifted diplomats and foreign policy observers.

This book relies on three major sources. The first is Hintze's diary focused on the coup against President Francisco Madero and the days following Madero's overthrow. It covers the period from February 9 to February 18, 1913. Hintze's first tour, reporting the fall of President Madero, lasted until March 15, 1913, at which point he used a medical leave to stay in Europe, returning to Mexico in early September 1913.

The second, larger diary details dictator Victoriano Huerta's last months in office and preparations for his journey into European exile, spanning the period April 24, 1913, to July 6, 1914.[3]

Third, when necessary, diary entries are supplemented with selections from diplomatic daily reports.[4] They provide a larger context to better understand the unfolding drama in Mexico. On occasion they add opinions from diplomats residing in Washington DC; Santiago, Chile; Madrid; and Tokyo. Mexican foreign relations are always global foreign relations, never just a bilateral U.S.-Mexican exchange.

Until today the slanted writings of the infamous U.S. ambassador Henry Lane Wilson and the diary of Edith O'Shaughnessy, wife of the counselor of the U.S. embassy, have dominated foreign diplomatic eyewitness reporting about what went on in Mexico City among elites and bureaucrats in this period. Now these newly discovered diaries add to the intrigues of Mexican generals, the malice of the British ambassador, Lionel Carden, and the Machiavellian suggestions, but also silences, of Admiral von Hintze.

Hintze's writings suggest that he and British diplomat Lionel Carden were every bit as important as U.S. ambassador Wilson in bringing President Madero down and propping the dictator Huerta up. In addition, the roles of Brazilian and Canadian diplomats must not be forgotten. They were significant contributors in meetings at Niagara Falls, Canada; Washington DC; and Mexico City.

A Summary Biography of Admiral von Hintze

The author of these remarkable diaries was born a commoner, Paul Wilhelm Carl Hintze, on February 13, 1864, in Schwedt, near the river Oder, in eastern Germany. In spite of profound familial hardship he managed to reach Berlin, where he left high school to join the newly founded German navy. Following enlistment on April 20, 1882, he gathered valuable experiences as he served with the East Asian Squadron. This was the squadron Emperor Wilhelm II used to occupy Kiautschou in Shantung, China. History has recorded a famous shouting match between the sailor Hintze and Admiral George Dewey during the war over the Philippines.

FIG. 1. Paul von Hintze in later years. Courtesy of the German Federal Foreign Office.

In February 1903 Emperor Wilhelm II appointed Hintze naval attaché to the Russian court of St. Petersburg. The twelve hundred reports Hintze wrote about Russia singled him out as an unusually gifted individual. Emperor Wilhelm II honored Hintze on February 17, 1906, appointing him wing commander. Two years later he was elevated to nobility and became the emperor's key man dealing with Tsar Nicholas II in all types of military affairs.

Wilhelm II's favor later allowed Hintze, a naval man, to become accepted as an extraordinary ambassador. On January 14, 1911, Chancellor Theobald von Bethmann-Hollweg recommended Hintze be transferred to Mexico, the important neighbor to the United States and also to the emerging Panama Canal. It was also a region where the Japanese navy had begun to patrol.

Hintze's first tour saw the fall of Madero. After an extended stay in Europe, he returned to Mexico and reported Victoriano Huerta's demise.

After the outbreak of World War I Hintze continued to serve Wilhelm II at important posts in Beijing, China, and in Norway. During the 1918 November Revolution in Germany he was elevated to serve the emerging Weimar Republic as undersecretary of state. In this capacity he renewed flirtations between the German army and the newly emerging Soviet state.

Still, in the newly emerging foreign policy culture of Weimar Germany of the 1920s he was no longer a good fit. In 1921 he became head of the Association of Ethnic Germandom Abroad (VDA). In 1924 he was mentioned as a possible advisor to the Chinese revolutionary Sun Yat-sen, but the appointment never materialized.

When Hitler came to power in 1933 Hintze was no longer an influential man. A marriage in 1927 had moved him to the dukedom of Glatz, where he lived in Aigen, near Salzburg. On August 19, 1941, he passed away in Merano, Italy, while resting at a spa resort.

1

An Eyewitness Learns about Revolutionary Mexico

TRANSNATIONAL IMPRESSIONS

Paul von Hintze, a bright, internationally experienced individual who had served in the Philippines as well as at the court of the tsar during the Russo-Japanese War, was utterly unfamiliar with Mexico's culture, politics, and environment. In July 1911 Mexico's political future was open and the government was run by interim president Francisco de la Barra.[1]

July 22, 1911, Mexico City

A REGULAR DIPLOMATIC REPORT

In no way would U.S. citizens repeat the mistake made in Cuba.[2] A protectorate would lead to the eventual economic unification; slowly probably, [a political] union between Mexico and the United States.[3] That would mean the end of German competitiveness in Mexican markets.

On the other hand it is obvious that neither Germany nor Europe possesses any means to pressure Mexico: when Europe is unwilling to take up Mexican bonds, U.S. America is more than willing to do so. When Europe no longer invests in the industry in this country, the United States desires nothing more and will cover the shortfall.

One should assume that the Mexican government is aware of the danger of being absorbed by the United States—by economics or force—or through both means. Some individuals holding government positions are thinking about this—I have reported about this repeatedly. But many Mexicans, specifically of the better classes, concerned about their material well-being, look at an intervention as the lesser evil if compared to the current revolutionary situation. They are working directly to bring about U.S. intervention.

Of course, the large mass of Mexicans hates the Americans. Not because of political reasons but because of fear that any tutelage would threaten their [national] existence. One excellent observer of the country summarized, "They don't want to be hustled."

The local representatives of European powers constantly offer moving laments about the state of affairs. But nobody, except the French chargé d'affaires, suggests active means to counter it. Probably Mr. De Veaux is honest when he heaps complaints onto his government, but, due to its lack of interest, nothing does happen. Other diplomats, in spite of their concerns, unconsciously make themselves into a tool of U.S. diplomacy.

They pressure the Mexican government with threats. Nothing can be more useless, with the exception of sending a demonstration of warships. Certainly such pressures will drive Mexico into U.S. arms. Of course, an entirely different meaning would be created if a dispatch of ships were sent [. . .] in case the . . . situation in the country or during an intervention would force [foreigners] to flee.

This was the only purpose of my report from July 18, to point out the necessity [of sending relief ships], in case of a possible intervention. Therefore I closed it with the request to transmit . . . early news about a possible intervention so that women and children can be brought to safety in time.

If the United States will undertake an intervention without reaching an agreement with other foreign powers or to inform them, then I have to look around here for possible signs in order to be able to act in time.

One indicator can be identified: according to the report of the imperial vice consul in Torreón, there Americans have dismissed their employees as of September 1. And as far as they are U.S. citizens they have asked them to return . . . [home]. A second indicator, as several local diplomats claim to recognize, is the sudden departure of the U.S. ambassador. They remind others that his first, similarly sudden departure in December 1910 was followed as an immediate consequence by the occupation of the border and the mobilization of the U.S. Army.

I personally cannot decide yet if what lies ahead of us is a development in the direction of anarchy or an armed intervention. As far as banditry is concerned, I see signs of recognizing that what is necessary is the harshest action by the interim government as well as among Maderistas. As far as intervention is concerned, I see no need to do so here. The United States could achieve dominance cheaper through waiting. But I have to admit that my knowledge of the people and country is limited and that an intervention might be dictated as much by the current world situation as by domestic U.S. politics. I cannot judge either of them. **Hintze[4]**

July 25, 1911, Mexico City

A REGULAR DIPLOMATIC REPORT

The representative of the Associated Press, Mr. Sommerfeld, is a man of confidence among the Maderoses and enjoys their high esteem.[5] He is German and deserves trust, of course only to a certain degree, as far as I and others observe him up to now. I have been able to interest him in exploring discreetly the mood of the Madero family as far as a treaty of reciprocity with the United States is concerned.[6] Francisco Madero, as a presidential candidate, had spoken with great determination against any reciprocity treaty with the United States.[7] His current opinion is that Mexico's central government cannot survive without the customs income (compare report No. A 47 from July 13). Even though Francisco Madero is the recognized head of the Maderistas, he is not always the one who is the decision maker, especially as far as deals of a difficult nature are concerned. Often they remain undiscovered by him.

Therefore Mr. Sommerfeld recently approached the current secretary of finance with the statement that European and U.S. newspapers had published news about beginning negotiations in the direction of a U.S.-Mexican reciprocity treaty. Rumors connected with this [event] established a link between the Maderoses entering into such a treaty as a price for the direct and indirect support of the Maderista revolution. European financial circles close to him—said Sommerfeld—were beginning to become concerned because of the possibility of such a treaty. He asked the secretary of finance to issue an unequivocal statement: yes or no?

Mr. Ernesto Madero thereupon ridiculed the question of reciprocity between Mexico and the United States, pointing out that the needs of the central government could not be covered any other way than through customs income.[8] He declared himself willing to provide a written statement [to this effect]. The original is attached. [. . .]

As far as "special aspects" are concerned, the rumor means, according to Sommerfeld, that the Maderistas would have to agree to enter into a reciprocity treaty as price for U.S. support.

As the last sentence makes apparent, the secretary of finance in no way wants to consider his declaration a secret. Rather, he makes it available for publication to Mr. Sommerfeld.

It appears to me, from the vantage point that is possible to grasp here, that a news story now would not take place at a good time. It would create a storm against the U.S. press and have the effect of doubling the activity of U.S. representative Hopkins, who has been sent here.[9] Perhaps it also would move U.S. officials to engage in more decisive behavior. Therefore, I asked Mr. Sommerfeld to keep secret Mr. Madero's letter, for the time being. Only when Your Excellency considers the moment right to use it in public will I give the necessary wink to Mr. Sommerfeld. Duly obedient, I await Your Excellency's orders. **Hintze**[10]

On November 6, 1911, interim president de la Barra handed the Mexican presidency to Francisco Madero.

February 12, 1912, Washington DC

A REGULAR DIPLOMATIC REPORT

Mr. Knox told me that his government is very concerned about the situation in Mexico.[11] For the time being the uprising is not a general one but Madero is being belittled and is without power. Mr. Knox hopes that de la Barra will again become president. His government wants to intervene, following congressional approval, only if it is absolutely necessary. Knox is quite certain [his government will] not have to resort to intervention.

The above words are made in an honest way because, here, the difficulties of intervention are completely appreciated. On the other hand some mighty interests are pressing in favor of intervention and, probably, also are fanning Mexican unrest. Moreover, the powerless [Mexican] army will do the same. . . . **Bernstorff**[12]

September 15, 1912, Mexico City

A REGULAR DIPLOMATIC REPORT

On September 17 (filed under date of September 15) the U.S. ambassador, before going on vacation, following a *U.S. State Department order*, handed Mexico a note that sought to receive from the Mexican government a categorical answer to:

I. Which measures she [the Mexican government] intends to take to catch the murderers of U.S. citizens and to punish them.
II. How Mexico intends to counter the existing hostilities against U.S. citizens.
III. How Mexico intends to get rid of the existing revolution, anarchy, and chaos.

The Mexican government issued an answer in a twenty-four-page-long memorandum. . . .

. . . I do not consider the exchange of notes to be either more meaningful or to bring about heavier consequences than the earlier ones of March 1 and April 15. . . .

What is important, in general, is the official declaration of the Mexican government:

Mexico does *not* consider itself liable for damage to life and property of foreigners in times of uprising or due to temporary elimination of government power.

That is counter to contractual and legally existing principles of liability in cases where

A. The government is at fault, or rather government offices exist.
B. Mexico's own citizens receive claim awards.
C. The uprising ends in the capture of government responsibility.

Knowledge of the note . . . came to me in a confidential manner. Following inquiry, the other diplomatic representatives do not know anything about it.[13]

December 1912, Mexico City

A REGULAR DIPLOMATIC REPORT

Ambassador Wilson told me yesterday about events leading up to the February Revolution, in a highly confidential way and under the condition not to talk about this to any of my colleagues:[14]

In December 1912 he held a long conference with President Taft and Secretary of State Knox, [discussing] what should be done in Mexico.[15] After [the Mexican government] answered the September 15, 1912, note partially with evasion and partially with rejection, Washington felt the need to become active.

He—Wilson—suggested: either seize some territory and hold it—or overthrow the Madero administration. President Taft had been open to both, but Knox bristled and spoke against the idea of occupying Mexican territory. Thus—the three—reached the agreement to overthrow the Madero administration.

As for the means to be used: the threat of intervention, dangling of office and honor (what this means is income from bribes). Here [in Mexico] there exist few people who do not have a price. Of most, their price is known. [. . .][16]

January 14, 1913, Washington DC

A REGULAR DIPLOMATIC REPORT

Secretary of State Knox, having returned from his Christmas vacation, told me today that not a single word is true of news stories in the press of an intended U.S. intervention. Nevertheless, a short while ago he explained to the Mexican ambassador that no one here [in DC] is content with the attitude of the Mexican government. Mexico does not provide sufficient security for the life and property of U.S. citizens. Since then, however, the situation in Mexico has improved, and it can be hoped that the local government will not be pressed to take further measures.[17]

January 21, 1913, Mexico City

A REGULAR DIPLOMATIC REPORT

Lascuraín, the secretary of foreign affairs, returned from his trip to Washington and New York.[18] The result of his negotiations with President Taft, Secretary of State Knox, and other leading personalities he describes as: the United States does not want an intervention in Mexico. Nevertheless, the leading officers have indicated to me that they will be forced, against their own will, into an intervention if the continuing murders of U.S. citizens and the continued destruction of U.S. property does not stop. "Therefore we are undertaking a ultimate supreme effort to end it." Also, this has

FIG. 2. Pedro Lascuraín Paredes. Courtesy of the Library of Congress.

been the decision of today's council of diplomats. Movements of troops have begun and individual commands have received new commanders.

The U.S. ambassador has returned and informed me in a similar way about the intentions of his government. However, he added: I have always been relying on your sober judgment and on your clear vision. I have sent a report to that effect to Washington and shall inform our ambassador at Berlin. I want help and hope to get it from you. The British diplomat [Carden] is a good fellow but more optimistic—he added a request to contribute to the "enlightenment" inside the diplomatic corps.[19]

I was taken aback by these undeserved words of praise and I merely offered courteous phrases. However, I hinted, as I had done repeatedly earlier, that in my estimation an armed intervention of the United States is unnecessary because the Mexicans seem to provide themselves with disintegration and the final downfall of their country through never ending domestic feuds and fights.

Repeatedly, I have reported to Your Excellency my opinion. . . . I am not holding back about it in front of the U.S. ambassador because, based on my knowledge of the situation and in the opinion of the best experts of the country, it represents the factual situation. This way I follow Your Excellency's high instructions and stay within their limits. Because it is, in my humble opinion, in our interest to postpone the time [when] and in no way to help the United States, at some time, to take an open hegemonic position. [This has to be done] in such a way that we don't step into open opposition to the United States or its representative.

I have to report to Your Excellency that neither I nor my opinion finds the applause of Germans living in this country. Rather, with a few exceptions, they favor U.S. intervention, even in the German press. Unfortunately, my influence upon the *Deutsche Zeitung von Mexico* is not sufficient because the head of the newspaper avoids the diplomatic legation out of principle, due to a [prior] confrontation with the former diplomat Count von Wangenheim.[20] The other newspaper, *Der Wanderer* has fallen into general disrespect due to the activity of its former reporter, Dr. Bauer. In order to change its reputation it has become entirely bland. It is alleged to face bankruptcy.

I have repeatedly reported the arguments in favor of U.S intervention in the opinion of our countrymen in Mexico. They are focusing on their personal interests, not the interests of German exports. Besides, a certain number are familiar with the United States because they came here after unsatisfactory experiences there. Some also took out U.S. citizenship papers and have taken public positions as Germans here in Mexico only because right now it is of no advantage to be U.S. citizens.

In *confidence* the British diplomat tells me that he bluntly told the U.S. diplomat: England holds important interests in Mexico, investments in property: mining, railroads, estates, petroleum wells, etc. Besides, [England holds] important trade interests. This property and trade are making it impossible for Great Britain to remain indifferent toward a U.S. intervention. England will do everything in its power to avoid such intervention. Mr. Montgomery Schuyler, the local U.S. chargé d'affaires who is still present[21]—I know him well from early postings—describes the U.S. position vis-à-vis Mexico as follows: The best thing for us would be a strong government in Mexico. The next best is a very weak government, such as the present one—so, we might be satisfied. **Hintze**[22]

FIG. 3. Félix Díaz. Courtesy of the Library of Congress.

2

The Path to Madero's Assassination

AN HOUR-BY-HOUR ACCOUNT

By early 1913 dissatisfaction with President Madero had reached the breaking point, and generals attempted to topple him. In February Manuel Mondragón and Félix Díaz freed General Bernardo Reyes from Mexico City's Tlatelolco prison. After General Lauro Villar, protector of the National Palace, was severely wounded in an attack, Madero replaced him with Victoriano Huerta.[1]

February 9, 1913, Mexico City

5:00 P.M.

1. Today, at lunch, Díaz grabbed the Citadel.[2]
2. The largest part of the garrison and the police declared themselves in favor of Huerta.[3]
3. The president and his diplomats are inside the National Palace.
4. López Figueroa negotiates with Díaz inside the Citadel.
5. The prisoners of the Santiago military prison are free, in contrast to those in the penitentiary and in Belém, who are still inside the prisons.
6. This evening street fights can be expected to resume.
7. All Germans have been advised to stay within their houses. And those who believe they are not safe should come to the legation.[4]

7:45 P.M.

1. The president of the republic and his cabinet have left the National Palace.
2. Gen. Huerta has taken over as commander of the National Palace.

3. People are saying that negotiations between Huerta and Díaz are underway.
4. We repeat the warning to stay at home and, if one feels insecure, come to the legation.

February 10, 1913, Mexico City

1. The diplomatic corps asked government and rebel [troops] not to undertake any military activities that could damage foreigners or foreign property.
2. Since neither the government nor the rebels want to guarantee the protection of life or property—repeating justifications given earlier—the police and self-defense forces of communities of foreigners have to rely on their own existing organizations.

   Already the U.S. and French colonies have mobilized their organizations. It is well known that the imperial German legation is open for everybody—as a place of refuge but not as a place to [conduct a] military defense, since this would be against international law.
3. In case Necaxa is cut off, preparations have been made to maintain streetlights.[5] But there would not be enough electrical power to keep the houses lit.
4. The news that the Zapatistas are occupying Tlalpam is wrong, according to the best source.[6]
5. Tonight hostilities are not expected, but probably tomorrow.

February 11, 1913, Mexico City

8:30 A.M.

1. In the morning I visit the National Palace.[7] On the way I find the troops of General Ángeles[8]—infantry—in the Avenida del Cinco de Mayo. Ángeles's Rurales are located on the Zócalo along with troops and mounted police.[9] In the National Palace are *guarda bosques*, artillery and infantry. Upstairs are the secretary of foreign affairs, the governor of the Federal District, and the president of the republic. The latter says, "I have four thousand to five thousand troops here against Díaz's one thousand."

   Huerta commands as usual: slow, considerate. He wants to encircle the Citadel with as little bloodshed as possible.[10] He—the president—had believed everything was over, as he reentered the

FIG. 4. Artillery soldiers of Félix Díaz at the southeast entrance of the Citadel. Courtesy of the German Federal Foreign Office.

National Palace on the ninth, about 9:30 a.m. (at 8:00 in the morning he had left Chapultepec accompanied by a few cadets and the presidential guard).[11]—Then somebody told him that Díaz was moving toward the Citadel . . . . [sic]. In the evening, using a car, he moved out through the back of the palace and picked up Ángeles from Cuernavaca.[12] The plan was to surround the Citadel and take it with as little bloodshed as possible.

Huerta, with Ángeles, is supposed to be on the way to check the position.

The president appears alert, mentally as well as physically. Asked about Blanquet, [he says], Blanquet is advancing.[13] He has not been able to be here because a few bridges have been burned. He—the president—has just received a telegram from him [stating] that he is showing in a most enthusiastic way his "declaration of loyalty."

The exchange of fire begins. I withdraw [inside].

2. The U.S. ambassador insists he knows that:

a. Díaz has between twenty-five hundred and three thousand men in the Citadel.

b. Madero has between four thousand and five thousand men.

c. Blanquet will not come.

I ask the U.S. ambassador to instruct the anticipated U.S. warships to protect German life and property. The ambassador says, immediately, he will instruct via cable the appropriate U.S. consuls. U.S. warships are numerous in Central America. He demanded some from the north that are particularly fast.

3. Ricardo García Granados arrives because of de la Barra's order to determine whether the diplomatic corps is willing to mediate between Díaz and Madero.[14] The representative answers: he does not doubt it will, if this desire is expressed with the appropriate vigor. However, Díaz's representative, a German with the name Herrman, came on February 9 and expressed in a brusque tone that the diplomatic corps should ask Madero to step down—and later, Díaz rejected outright the diplomatic corps' demand "to keep order on the streets in the area where foreigners live." He rejected it outright, citing as reason that he did not have enough troops available.

Ricardo García Granados reports that de la Barra and Alberto García Granados were making efforts to obtain mediation.[15] But since gunfire has been exchanged since ten o'clock, their [efforts] are considered hopeless.

Ricardo García Granados says that today, February 11, at eight o'clock, he was visiting the Citadel: Díaz had placed there about twelve hundred men. This explains Díaz's behavior; he apparently does not feel himself strong enough. On the one hand, he does have personal courage, but he is not the *right man for this situation*: he is lacking grit.

On February 9, in the evening, Huerta had let Díaz know that he "was hoping to reach an understanding with him." Díaz fell into this trap. Now it becomes apparent that Huerta has used this understanding only as a pretext to gain time in order to bring in troops.

4:30 P.M.

1. The personal physician of the president, Dr. Gutierrez de la Lara, informs by telephone: Maderistas under Robert have taken Belém and the Parque de Ingenieros.

Huerta is well.

The commander of the Seventh Cavalry Regiment is dead. News about the destruction of a rural regiment is false.

Inside the Citadel the artillery is finished.

Pretty heavy losses.

4:55 P.M.

2. Woern informs that Zapatistas have attacked Peña Pobre in the night from February 9 to 10. But they have been beaten back by Rurales and his [Madero's] private house army. He and his family are in excellent shape in Tlalpam. *No Zapatistas in Tlalpam.*

5:15 P.M.

1. Capt. Malpica telephoned report:[16] General Blanquet has not yet arrived with his troops.

5:35 P.M.

2. I was able to overhear the following from a special source:

Huerta is well. He has not been shot. Calle Balderas has been almost entirely destroyed through fighting. General Blanquet has not yet arrived and has not been inside the city. López Figueroa visited Díaz, not as a negotiator for a faction but as a traitor: he is supposed to have been executed. Probably the [electric] lights will be turned off.

SINCE 5:20 P.M.

3. The exchange of gunfire weakens.

5:40 P.M.

4. From Adolfo Basso: troops are expected from Puebla and Oaxaca.

General[s] Caus, Maas, and Delgado have arrived. They are on the side of the Maderistas. Also, Blanquet is expected. He has to march on foot since some bridges have been burned.

5:48 P.M.

1. In Belém, artillery fire is beginning once again.

FIG. 5. Destruction at the intersection of Rinconada and San Diego. Courtesy of the German Federal Foreign Office.

6:10 P.M.

2. Break in the exchange of gunfire. Sunset. It is dark at 6:20.

6:30 P.M.

3. The British diplomat telephones: since the morning of February 11, de la Barra and his son have been inside the British legation. Yesterday, February 10, de la Barra wrote to the president and offered his mediation. At midnight he received the response (in writing): Madero will negotiate with Díaz only under condition of unconditional surrender. All news that is arriving there (British legation) appears rather beneficial for Díaz. For example, Maderista artillery is out of ammunition and, already, Díaz's troops are advancing toward the National Palace. But latest news contradicts this. At the U.S. embassy no news.

6:38 P.M.

4. Bacmeister reports by telephone: Huerta is dead, also Delgado. The rumor is circulating that Maderista troops lack enthusiasm to fight after the fall of their leader.

FIG. 6. President Francisco Madero. Courtesy of the Library of Congress.

7:02 P.M.

5. The British ambassador reports by telephone: the Federales have destroyed the roof of the Citadel and have killed nearly all of the artillerymen with their quickfire [guns]. The Federales are preparing to attack the Citadel. (The informant is not quite certain when.)

7:10 P.M.

6. The French diplomat says: Pottere is reporting by telephone that three-quarters of the Citadel has been destroyed.[17] Díaz broke

FIG. 7. On the roof of the Citadel. Courtesy of the German Federal Foreign Office.

through at the northern side but returned: Pottere claims to have received this news from Lascuraín.

7:18 P.M.

7. Pottere telephones: Lascuraín observed the Citadel from the tower of the church on Calle Orizaba. He says that destruction could be observed on the roof. He—Lascuraín—is supposed to have said in addition: the Maderistas have occupied the houses on the three sides surrounding the Citadel, and an attack is being prepared. In contrast, at the U.S. embassy, it is being assumed that all is well for the Felicistas.

7:47 P.M.

8. F. Sommerfeld says, after returning from his visit to the older Madero family inside the Japanese diplomatic mission: The Citadel is being surrounded from all sides by Maderistas. Ángeles had led the attack from the Hotel Braniff. Huerta is alive and eager to fight. Near Salazar, the bridge has been burned; therefore, Blanquet has to march (21.5 km). Tonight troops are expected to arrive from Puebla and Queretaro.

9. After inquiry Dobroschke reports:[18] located at the corner of Calle
   Bucareli and Avenida Chapultepec is one platoon of entirely drunk-
   en Díaz soldiers who are refusing entry to Calle Bucareli or in direction of Belém. Two Mexican civilians are with them. How many soldiers? It is impossible to estimate due to complete darkness.

7:58 P.M.

10. From Bacmeister:[19] fifteen infantry wagons have arrived from Cu-
    ernavaca and are being unloaded.

8:30 P.M.

11. From Bacmeister: at 7:00 p.m.: the president's wife reported that
    Huerta is well.

8:45 P.M.

12. From Viau: at Calle Bucareli, a Felicista outpost; many drunks; *al-
    legedly* Belém has been cleared by Maderistas.

9:00 P.M.

13. From Coyoacán, Consul General Kosidowski:[20] all is quiet in Coyo-
    acán; nothing [heard from] Zapatistas.
14. F. Sommerfeld reports from the *National Palace*: Lieutenant de Lara
    from *estado mayor*: reinforcements have arrived; more are expected.
    At noon, news from Blanquet that he is on his way.
    Mr. Bacmeister telephones at 6:30 p.m.: undersecretary Pani is
    living with him, an old friend of his family.[21] In confidence Mr. Pani
    has informed him that about half an hour ago General Blanquet ar-
    rived here (from Toluca) with about three thousand men, and with
    him *Madero*. Mr. Bacmeister also claims to have overheard a tele-
    phone conversation between Mr. Pani and Gustavo (Ernesto? [*sic*])
    Madero. Mr. Pani asked him to remain quiet about it since it re-
    ferred to the arrival of Madero and Blanquet. Today in the Nation-
    al Palace Mr. Pani negotiated with Lascuraín. Blanquet's troops are
    supposed to have been tired and, therefore, will move into action
    only tomorrow morning.

FIG. 8. Government troops at Independence Street. Courtesy of the German Federal Foreign Office.

Mr. Meyer (from the rowing club) reports that he knows *for sure* that Ángeles's troops are located inside several trains near Contreras. Please keep source confidential.

February 12, 1913, Mexico City

7:45 A.M.

1. I visit U.S. embassy. The ambassador states: Díaz has sent to them two U.S citizens who were fighting on his side. They claimed Díaz could hold out in the Citadel for thirty days. Díaz was expecting reinforcements from Chalco and Jojutla, where the garrisons have risen up in his favor. The Maderistas are supposed to have experienced large losses. Their attacks from the Citadel are supposed to have been beaten back four times.

    U.S. citizens who were living in the city center are supposed to have reported to the embassy: abandoned cannons left behind by the Maderistas were standing in Independencia and Victoria Streets. Whether or not Blanquet has arrived, he—the ambassador—did not know.

On February 11 the ambassador sent a note to the president:

1. To call attention to serious conditions now involving lives and property of noncombatant foreigners.
2. [To call attention to] uncivilized and barbarous warfare in the heart of town.
3. U.S. consulate hit by bullets, embassy too: strong protest against [this].
4. Hopes the president will find ways to stop such procedures in the interest of humanity. So far: no answer.

2.[22] Following requests for an official statement from the ambassador, requested by me, the latter cables the consulates in Tampico, Veracruz, Mazatlán, and Acapulco: the expected U.S. warships are supposed to protect German life and property.
3. The ambassador does not have contact with his consulates inside of the country. The exception: Tepic. There, nothing noteworthy [to report].
4. According to news (not verified) from Guadalajara—the ambassador states—the garrison ([commanded by] General Tellez) there has risen in favor of Díaz.
5. North of the Paseo de Reforma, between the British mission and the Colonia Station—three federal cannons, not covered by infantry, are firing toward the Citadel.

9:30 A.M.

6. The firing of artillery toward (5) is beginning. For the time being it is not being answered from the Citadel.

10:15 A.M.

At merchant Veerkamp's house:[23] one or two grenades have hit the kitchen and the room where administrator Stahlecker is residing. They have caused great destruction. Nobody has been hurt. At this time twenty people are living in the house. They are keeping to themselves in the rooms on the lower level and remain quiet. The corner of Independencia and San Juan de Letrán (also Porter's Hotel) has suffered greatly. Also, a grenade entered the restaurant opposite of the German House (Berger's German House, not the house of the German community). There a German (Albert Weinheimer) is living, and he remains unhurt.

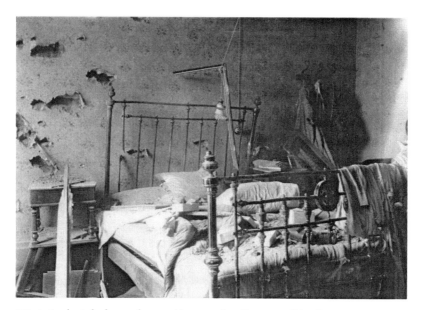

FIG. 9. A private bedroom damaged by grenades. Courtesy of the German Federal Foreign Office.

10:30 A.M.

Pablo Viau:[24] since this morning, eight o'clock, Belém is in the hands of Félix Díaz. Prisoners have been freed. Viau has learned the news from one of them; four hundred Belém volunteers have switched sides to Díaz. Just now Navarrete has organized an artillery corps.[25]

10:45 A.M.

Telephone company reports that, following government order, the use of telephones by private people has been prohibited. Bacmeister could still be reached under the pretext that he wanted to talk to Pani. However, he does not know anything new.

12 NOON

All is quiet in the neighborhood; only a few shots.

12:15 P.M.

Veerkamp's household reports following inquiry (apparently the use of telephone by private people is once again allowed):

FIG. 10. The Belém prison. Courtesy of the German Federal Foreign Office.

12:30 P.M.

One Mr. Feil (of Badische Anilin Gesellschaft)[26] has just arrived from Puebla; there everything is quiet; troops are in favor of Díaz; General de la Llave had intended to enter Puebla but a city delegation prevented this, stating it was not necessary.—Alleged cease-fire.

12:45 P.M.

Carlos Dittmer: nothing new to report about the battles; however, he broke his arm when he slipped inside the room this morning; no doctor available.

12:45 P.M.

Once again heavy cannon fire from the direction of Belém is beginning.

1:30 P.M.

Flores returns; following an order from higher-ups, telephone company must not accept telegrams addressed to those inside the country.

2:30 P.M.

Once again heavy machine-gun fire begins.

FIG. 11. Inside the Citadel's machine shop. Courtesy of the German Federal Foreign Office.

February 12, 1913, Mexico City

10:00 A.M.

1. I visit the U.S. embassy. I am joined by the Spanish and the U.S. diplomats (the British diplomat agreed in writing to all steps that would end the current state of affairs); we go to the National Palace. There we conferred with the president and the secretary of foreign affairs. The ambassador protests against the uncivilized conduct of war in the name of humanity, life, and property of foreigners. We object to risking peaceful life and property in the midst of a large city through grenades and other gunfire. President answers that endangerment has been created by the fire of the rebels, *not* his; but he is doing everything possible that is available to him to protect civilian life and property; that he issued such a proclamation to the population and also wrote to Díaz in this regard. U.S. ambassador informs him that Washington has sent warships to Mexican ports and that he was looking at the current situation with great concern; however, he says nothing about troop transports. The president assured us that the Citadel would be taken tomorrow evening; already one corner of

the Citadel has been destroyed through gunfire. Only a small coup has taken place in Oaxaca. The Twenty-First Battalion and the Leales de Veracruz have defeated it within two hours: otherwise opposition against Díaz's revolt has been reported from all parts of the country. Only a single grenade has hit the National Palace, killing a guard and wounding two soldiers. The U.S. ambassador states that we think it is appropriate also to complain to Díaz against inhumane conduct of war; the president is not opposed to it. Lascuraín protests "because Díaz could interpret this as weakness of the government." However, facing the attitude of the president, he gives up his objection.

Remark: inside the National Palace the majority of mounted *aspirantes* squadron remain prisoners; they were the ones who had revolted. General Blanquet is supposed to be approaching.

2. Díaz has been signaled through a U.S. citizen who is serving with him that the same diplomatic chiefs as mentioned above would want to talk to him; thereupon a one-hour-long cease-fire was agreed to between him and the government. However, when our car passed the corner of Bucareli and Avenida Chapultepec the guards standing there fired, disregarding the white flag. Southern entry has been occupied with two field cannons, next to which lay many cartridge shells. I passed through those, entering the southern entry into the garden. There are about 150 rogues behind piles of stones; they cower there, most of them without weapons. In spite of agreed-upon stoppage of fire, gunfire starts anew. There is an honor guard at the southeast entrance and people in gray field uniforms; some forest rangers. On the left a kind of mechanical repair workshop is being maintained. A gang of criminal hoodlums surrounds that door, yelling, "Viva Félix Díaz!" They are held back only with great effort by the honor guard.

General Díaz enters; a small black man [*sic*], only poorly controlling himself. The ambassador repeats the objection against inhumane conduct of war and adds, the United States government has sent men of war to all Mexican ports, besides soldiers and marines in transport [ships] to Tampico and Veracruz. They will land when circumstances require such a step and will march on the capital. Díaz desperately swears he has no ambition. At this moment General Mondragón enters and demands, without much formal ado, to be present at the meeting;[27] Díaz asks him to do so [remain], with visible satisfaction. Díaz continues: he is only obeying public opinion; the country is in favor of him. He could have marched against the National Palace right away; he had not done so in order to spare life and property. Inside the Citadel, he says, he is maintaining fifteen hundred men and outside a field regiment of 150 men: *he is in control of the situation but* maintains a defensive position because he wanted to spare life and property. However, the Federales have relentlessly attacked him and forced him to answer. He could not allow any limitation of the firing zone as long as the Federales attacked from all sides. I suggest restricting from gunfire the [areas of the] city located west of the Citadel, where the foreigners are residing. Díaz: he would have been happy to do so if that would have been agreed upon on the first day; now such agreements are difficult to make. People are shooting at him from Chapultepec (incorrect!) and from Colonia (correct!)—that obliges him to answer. In the meantime the firefight continues. Díaz orders: take cover and not respond—and he declares: there, we saw proof of the lack of good faith of the government, which is failing to keep its promise not to fire for one hour. As we stand up, Díaz utters with slightly trembling voice: he would very much like to see the diplomatic leaders as mediators. Mondragón interrupts during the talks several times. He lists all the troops that allegedly have switched to his side, but he fails to state their strength.

Díaz gives the impression of someone with a not very intelligent character and one that is more impulsive than strong; Mondragón gives a suspicious appearance. The relationship between the two is apparently not very good; Mondragón is trying to dominate Díaz. Results of this visit: Díaz is in poor standing. He talks about one thousand men who have risen up in his favor in states and are in the process of approaching, but he does not want to say from where.

3. The president sends the chief of the department of infantry to apologize for the gunfire during the agreed-upon hour. The British diplomat and I urged Ambassador Wilson to answer: no harm done, everything is all right—after he was first trying to make a big deal out of it.

4. Lascuraín gives assurances that the government would gain control over the situation within the shortest time if given a free hand: Díaz

has been locked up for four days without water and food, *he should capitulate*. The gunfire will continue in order to demoralize his men. Now the government has six thousand people; [it] does not need to wait for Blanquet.

The U.S. ambassador suggests a limit on the exchange of fire so that foreigners are not being affected and adds: he is not in a position to judge whether this is possible. Thereafter I am asked about it and say, one could try not to shoot from and to the west side of the Citadel; such limitation would keep Roma and Juárez and the communities of foreigners outside the range of fire and all foreigners could withdraw to there.[28] Lascuraín promises to propose this restriction; I have the impression that he is not serious.

4. British diplomat reports that Calero (besides de la Barra) has taken refuge with him. He stated that the government wants to arrest him and shoot him. I visit communities of Roma and Juárez.

7:15 P.M.

5. Mr. Herman, allegedly a German national, the well-known friend of Félix Díaz, visits me. Allegedly to offer his services; in fact, in order to hear what the agreement with Díaz might consist of. He asks if now Díaz appears to be full of vigor. In the first days of the uprising he had looked flat, unmotivated, and depressed. Answer: because of the short period of the discussion I have not been able to gather knowledge about this.

6. Summary of the day: on the morning of February 12 the U.S. ambassador, without doubt, had been willing to use a sharper tone against Madero. Once Madero had informed him about the state of affairs he used a milder one. He changed his position completely when the visit to Díaz showed him *how poorly informed his sources were about the forces*. After that he even declared to Lascuraín that, naturally, he thought it desirable to limit military undertakings. Meaning the sparing of life and property of foreigners. However, as a nonmilitary person, he could not judge how far this would be possible.

10:00 P.M.

7. At exactly 10:00 p.m., after a heavy firefight, a cease-fire signal was trumpeted. Almost immediately the fire stopped on both sides. During the night only a few single shots from the guns and cannons.

February 13, 1913, Mexico City

8:30 A.M.

1. Beginning of artillery fire soon followed by gunfire. Captain Burnside, military attaché, says that the Federales have gained territory.[29] He attributes the slow advance to a lack of ammunition.
2. Yesterday two trains left from Veracruz for Mexico City with all the remaining ammunition for the Federales. In Veracruz, calm and waiting.
3. According to the opinion of the U.S. embassy, the entire country remains waiting to see the outcome.
4. Allegedly German nationals should live in the Calle Ayuntamiento. According to H. Weise and Abels these people have long moved out.

11:00 A.M.

1. Calle de Liverpool occupied by Rurales. They are coming from the Avenida Chapultepec and advance slowly.
   They are Rurales No. 30, from Oaxaca.
2. In the Calle Ayuntamiento there are only three houses where Germans are living. No. 133, the Colorado House, had been cleared before the beginning of the battle; Seelbach, No.168, has been warned by Abel; on Monday afternoon the soldiers stood on the roof of the house; Welton, No. 111, is German American; there, on Monday, German nationals Wolanke and Hemken sought refuge.
3. The news arrived at the U.S. embassy that warships will arrive on Saturday (February 15).
4. The Spanish diplomat, according to Wilson, works on Lascuraín to move Madero to resign (this is not in agreement with earlier word from Cólogan, for example, word from yesterday).[30]
5. The Austro-Hungarian representative has learned from a "U.S. lady"—he does not know where she resides—that uprisings in favor of Díaz have happened in Mazatlán, Guadalajara, and Toluca.
6. According to Wilson, this morning four U.S. citizens were killed in a church; some Germans were hurt; Schuyler—the embassy's counsel—declared the latter a fantasy. That is correct.

7. U.S. ambassador Wilson says the National Palace is now being attacked by two cannons from the Citadel. He fears government troops will be driven out of there and then would withdraw to Chapultepec.

1:30 P.M.

Gunfire stops.

2:20 P.M.

The Rurales No. 30 have been beaten back in Liverpool, including a number of wounded soldiers; they are positioning themselves at Dinamarca and in Liverpool. When I asked one, he told me they have no orders, no food, and nobody is concerned about them. Telephone call to Sommerfeld: one should give food to these people.

8. The U.S. ambassador reports as incorrect news that he is supposed to have released, which Díaz is supposed to have told him: two thousand men for him [in support of Díaz] have arrived at San Lazaro from Puebla. A few less trustworthy U.S. citizens had told him that a few Felicistas had occupied San Lazaro Station and the *escuela de tiro* [shooting academy]; from there they would be shooting at the National Palace. He doubts this news.

4:30 P.M.

9. At 11:00 a.m.one of Huerta's negotiators was sent to Díaz. Engineer Joaquín Maas, son of General Maas, is asking me for an automobile because his had been driven away without him.[31] I referred him to Moor Car Rental. Maas says the situation is bad, no party wants to give in; he wondered if the diplomatic corps did not want to motivate the government to give in?

4:00 P.M.

10. F. Sommerfeld reports from Chapultepec that today fifteen hundred Rurales would arrive from Guerrero, led by Figueroa; otherwise he has no news. The Federales in Tacubaya possess two hundred thousand grenades and have found four large and two small cannons.

FIG. 12. Felicista soldiers and the women who took care of them, outside the Citadel. Courtesy of the German Federal Foreign Office.

5:00 P.M.

11. The Thirtieth Corps of the Rurales is withdrawing to the Paseo.

6:15 P.M.

12. The U.S. embassy received information that the presidential train has been readied; there is fighting in Calle Nuevo Mexico to Letrán; the president is supposed to be depressed (source, U.S. citizen Whiffen); General Huerta is supposed to be drinking cognac.

6:15 P.M.

13. Mr. Briede says that Garito, a biological son of Porfirio Díaz, has told him that generals were negotiating on the basis of forcing Madero to step down.[32]

8:30 P.M.

14. Sommerfeld reports from Chapultepec: he has no news about the situation (a bad sign).

9:00 P.M.

15. Both sides stop gunfire; Citadel in complete darkness; so are Paseo and Alameda; illuminated are the cathedral, the building of the Mutual, and the Correo post office only.

February 14, 1913, Mexico City

AT 7:00 A.M.

1. Heavy gunfire begins.

7:30 A.M.

2. I visit the southern positions of the Federales (a few cannons); from there to the German school. There all is quiet; two pieces of shrapnel (7.6 cm) have fallen into the garden, two bullet holes [made by] Mauser machine guns in the auditorium (the majority of the inhabitants of the school were still sleeping). Principal Dobroschke states that since yesterday the school has no longer been the target of gunshots.

8:00 A.M.

3. I try to talk to Lascuraín; he had stepped outside.

9:00 A.M.

4. I [go] to Chapultepec; at the racetrack I encounter advanced post of Federales. I cross the Paseo, move toward Calles de Rhin. There two people have just been wounded. I talk to General Ángeles. He says that all he has to keep the enemy in check are his cannons. He claims not to have any hope that his projectiles could do much damage. Their method could be described as slowly drawing close to the Citadel with as few losses as possible. Battalion No. Seventeen was covering the cannons, also a few Rurales. I have the impression that these troops have been stationed here in order to counter a possible move to the west (toward Chapultepec). Ángeles reacts to remarks about why no attack is taking place, saying he would have to take into consideration his soldiers, and they are not German soldiers.

FIG. 13. General Felipe Ángeles's cannons. Courtesy of the German
Federal Foreign Office.

11:00 A.M.

5. Today at British legation about forty refugees; also Calero; today,
February 14, de la Barra returned to his house.

6. At the Japanese legation I encounter the family of Madero's father;
they say that they've left the German legation because of the consul's prohibition against using the telephone.

7. The owner of the Hotel Juárez, Otto Paglasch, appears at 9:00 a.m.
and informs me: yesterday (or the day before) he had paid a friendly visit to General Díaz inside the Citadel; now he has been warned
that the government is after him. He was seeking protection. When
I point out to him the carelessness of his visits to Díaz, Paglasch answers, "After all, I should be able to visit my friend!"

The gentlemen Wunderlich and Obermeyer report that Rudolph
Groth (Sommer Herrmann & Co.)[33] also visited Díaz in the Citadel.
He was alleged to have greeted Díaz with, "I greet the future president." Whereupon Díaz is supposed to have answered, "Don't say
that but use: a patriot." Groth himself described the event in this way.

8. The house servant appears from the Diener house (Havre 52), where provisions are stored for the German colony. He reports that the house has been occupied by federal soldiers. Weise and Wunderlich go to the house and there I meet them. Through the troop commander an effort to have the house cleared is successful.
9. Mr. Beveridge, the engineer of the Mexican Telephone Company, promises to establish, if at all possible, a telephone line to the diplomatic legation.
10. The British diplomat presents a telegram from his government which says that under no circumstances should he expose himself to any dangers. If the diplomatic legation is not safe he should leave it; under all such circumstances the British government will make the Mexican government liable for any mishap that he, his personnel, or his relatives would experience. *Warships* are on their way
11. Gunfire stops at about twelve o'clock.

12. The house of the president's father in Calle Liverpool goes up in flames; apparently arson; also, neighboring houses catch fire but they are extinguished.

13. Mr. Herman, known friend of Díaz, arrives. Supposedly being sent from the U.S. embassy to ask me for a passport to pass through hostile lines; this pass could bring him and deputy Galvan to Díaz: this Galvan (previously a *científico*, then a Maderista) now calls himself an independent (a wild one) and stated to the U.S. embassy that he wanted, after talking to Díaz, to work toward calling together Congress. Then possibly Congress will demand that Madero give up his office or depose him.

   I refuse to issue to him the passport. It is needless. I ask him how one should present oneself in public as a member of Congress during a war. And then I told him how the diplomatic representatives had gone inside [the Citadel] to see Díaz (even under fire).

FIG. 14. Madero's father's house after the arson attack. Courtesy of the German Federal Foreign Office.

4:40 P.M.

14. I learn that de la Barra, located at Calle Dinamarca No. 50, called for a car to drive there [to the Citadel] with a mission. I offer him an automobile and, since it flies the German flag, to accompany him, *after* de la Barra has declared that the president had asked him to take over negotiations. He had visited Díaz following the announcement of his visit and the assurance of safety—which was *completely* given to him.

However, I found him not very willing to yield. He had taken over this mission after General Ángeles, in the British legation, had hinted that an end of hostilities is desirable (see my impressions from today's talk with Ángeles). In his well-known manner, de la Barra praises his patriotic goals. I point out to him that Díaz also has reason to give in. In a sense, the citadel would be possible to take immediately, if one *was determined to do so.*

An automobile near Alameda calls de la Barra back to Camacho's house, where the Senate has convened (so says de la Barra).[34] Note: de la Barra dismisses any activity or intervention by the Chamber of Deputies. I told him about this (Galvan-Herrmann), probably because he does not trust the majority of Maderistas in the Chamber. De la Barra, off to Camacho's house, promises updated news about the result of his negotiations with the Senate inside the palace. It is noteworthy that the Senate is *not* meeting in the National Palace—where it usually meets—but has convened at Camacho's house: its anti-Maderist point demonstrated. The prediction proves correct: the decisive revolution will be the military one.

9:30 P.M

15. Sommerfeld calls from Chapultepec and reports: this morning the president sent de la Barra to Díaz with the task of demanding that he not shoot at the communities of foreigners. Díaz dismissed it firmly out of hand. Besides, the president *and the generals* are determined to maintain the attack further. Any talk about stepping down was far from reality. General Blanquet is supposed to have arrived in Tacubaya with fifteen hundred men. They did find a telemeter besides ammunition and *cannons*.

I reported that a lack of motivation was beginning to dominate the military; the men no longer wanted to attack. Thereupon Sommerfeld answered, "Precisely, this is the most terrible reality!"

February 14, 1913, Mexico City

1. A Spanish diplomat, *on his own* account, goes to see the president of the republic asking him to resolve the question: suggesting he step down. The president refuses. The ministry cancels his appointment. General Huerta enters, saying, "Mr. President, I see that my services do not carry your favor because you are negotiating with the Spanish representative!" The latter asks him to remain at his post. The Spanish diplomat takes his hat and leaves.
2. In the afternoon the Spanish diplomat goes to Díaz, also on his own initiative, appeals to his patriotism, etc.; finally a great emotional scene: "Long live the mother of the fatherland!" But no tangible result. Only the promise to sacrifice himself for the fatherland.
3. In the morning Lascuraín visits U.S. ambassador Wilson and proposes that he vacate his house with his entire personnel, etc. He is

supposed to move to a different one that is situated in a safe location. The U.S. ambassador refuses. Lascuraín asks about his view of the situation. Wilson says he wants to state as a friend: within a few days he will have three to four thousand U.S. soldiers here; then he will reestablish order. Otherwise only one tool remains: tell the president to get out; and, in a way that is legal, make him and the vice president hand over their powers to the legislative assembly. "Don't call the Chamber of Deputies, but call in the Senate."—Lascuraín (after long deliberation): "I suppose you're right; I shall devote myself exclusively to that purpose, to get the president out."

February 15, 1913, Mexico City

9:30 A.M.

1. The U.S. embassy asks me and the Spanish diplomat to come for a talk. On the way several bullets are shot at my car.

   The ambassador tells us about his talk with Lascuraín on February 14, saying that mentioning U.S. soldiers, etc., was merely a bluff, made with approval of the U.S. government. He proposes that the powers present here—currently United States, Spain, Great Britain, Germany—should demand Madero step down.

   I propose to speak about this suggestion "in a friendly way," without authorization or order of our governments. One should state as the main reason: if Madero does not step down his army will fall apart. Because yesterday (February 14), while driving around, at all posts I encountered the growing unwillingness to fight for Madero. Ambassador and others agreed.

   According to the ambassador's news reports, Chihuahua, Puebla, and others—in short, half of the country—have risen up against Madero. The ambassador himself admits that this news is mostly exaggerated. Furthermore, Mr. Wilson reports that Blanquet has arrived with seven hundred men, not fifteen hundred. Finally, the U.S. ambassador requests the Spanish diplomat assume the responsibility of asking the president and the vice president to step down—through friendly suggestion, the morning of the fifteenth.

2. During the night of February 14–15, the cannons located near the community fire intensely. Also gunfire from the vicinity of Calle Ver-

FIG. 15. General Aurelio Blanquet's troops march toward the National Palace. Courtesy of the German Federal Foreign Office.

sailles and Calle Bucareli. It is being answered with machine-gun fire. The streets are dark because we have run out of carbon pins.

11:30 A.M.

3. News that a battery has been set up near the house of Diener, as well as Bourjeau. I go to see General Ángeles, who orders the battery to be moved. I once again visit General Ángeles to learn about additional relocation of batteries. I hear that Hotchkiss cannons are supposed to be set up near Colonia Station, in order to fire from there down Calle Dinamarca Street into Calle Bucareli Street, where Felicistas have set up a mitrailleuse.[35] I object because the soldiers' poor shooting skills would lob grenades into the legation. After long deliberation General Ángeles gives his word not to set up cannons there. (See point 5.)

1:00–2:00 P.M.

I visit U.S. embassy. He [Wilson] proposed to proceed jointly in order to achieve:

A. a prohibition to set up [gun] batteries in the communities of foreigners in such a way that the foreign missions will be damaged;
B. a cease-fire, in order to let the people who want to leave drive to secure suburbs or to other cities;
C. protests right away against gunfights to and from the foreign communities; right away I communicate it to the National Palace; U.S. ambassador agrees.

4. At the British legation I encounter de la Barra. I tell him: yesterday in the Senate no quorum could be established; today [the Senate] moved into the Palais. So many came—according to yesterday's agreement—to ask the president and vice president to step down. The president did not receive them but asked to communicate with them; he, together with Huerta and Blanquet, were inspecting armed positions.

In his place Ernesto Madero came. He—de la Barra—as well as José Fernandez had asked for Madero's resignation. Ernesto replied that if Madero steps down then another revolution would break out. Three senators—"*Porristas*" [sic] are supposed to have visited to speak against resignation; also one deputy from Zacatecas. The Senate formulated in writing its initiative (without quorum).

1:20 P.M.

5. Heavy gunfire in Calle Dinamarca.

1:35 P.M.

6. Several Hotchkiss grenades hit, one immediately after another, in the legation's garden. One immediately in front of the stairs to the kitchen; a second in front of the house entry. Near the kitchen all the windows and the glass awning above the automobile driveway are shattered; women and children are being taken to the basement.

7. Taking into consideration event (6), during the afternoon the families of Dr. Wislicenus and Mardus, which have small children, are being transferred by car to Tacubaya. There everything is quiet and secure shelter is relatively easily available. For the time being they found a home in the house of Professor C. Reiche, 1a. Gelati 2 [sic].

FIG. 16. Hotchkiss cannons on Ayuntamiento Street. Courtesy of the German Federal Foreign Office.

8:30 P.M.

8. I visit the president together with the U.S. ambassador, Lascuraín, and General Huerta. The ambassador states *that never, based on his initiative, has the question of intervention been discussed in Washington.*[36]

But now Washington DC wants to apply serious corrective means,[37] due to the demands of European powers and U.S. public opinion. I interject, trying to calm the situation: the German government asks the U.S. government to order its warships so that they can provide aid and support in the ports to German residents. The president shows a telegram sent to Taft in which he points to the consequences of an intervention. He promises complete security to the U.S. citizens who have withdrawn to the suburbs of Mexico City. The government is not willing to take any responsibility. As far as damages and loss are concerned, [those are] justified according to international law. Furthermore, the president shows telegrams from inside the country, namely from Chihuahua (Rabago), and Puebla (Pradillo), which announce that the country [*sic*] is quiet. The ambassador counters that an uprising has taken place in Salina Cruz and Tehuantepec; the president says he has no news about this.

The president states that this morning he gave an immediate order about protecting and sparing diplomatic missions and foreign communities, and he ordered a cease-fire, as he learned that some diplomatic missions were endangered. (The diplomat presented him with some grenade shrapnel). He—the president—suggests the diplomatic missions move to Tacubaya, where the situation is absolutely secure.

The ambassador answers: he was authorized to move but would not move even if he were to receive an order to move; he wouldn't leave his embassy unless dead [*sic*]. The president counters: he will issue an order to spare diplomatic missions.

General Huerta wants to undertake preparations for a cease-fire and announce it so that people who want to move out can prepare. I want to arrange a cease-fire in a way that assures the secure use of trains to Veracruz. Also, Huerta wants to arrange military movements in such a way that missions are not damaged.

The president agrees that matters of diplomatic missions, as far as military operations are concerned, should be handled directly by Huerta, with a copy to Lascuraín. President and Huerta leave a good impression.

Initially Wilson presents himself in a brusque tone but with time becomes milder. Wilson says to the president's face: Félix Díaz has always been "pro-American." This is in agreement with a Díaz statement of February 14: " I would rather change my nationality than let this government stand.

SINCE 1:35 [IN THE AFTER]NOON

9. Indeed, gunfire has ceased, the president says: he ordered his troops to do so after he heard that diplomatic missions had been damaged.
10. In the night of February 15-16 very little [gun]fire exchanged. A cease-fire is being agreed upon from early 2:00 a.m. the sixteenth until 2:00 a.m. February 17. The ambassador is being informed about this. He informs *nobody in the diplomatic corps.*

February 16, 1913, Mexico City

1. Early, 8:00 a.m., I visit the U.S embassy. At that time the ambassador was busy. The secretary of the embassy states: a cease-fire

FIG. 17. Government cannons in Victoria Street. Courtesy of the German Federal Foreign Office.

has *not* been agreed upon because negotiations are ongoing. While leaving, by coincidence, I meet the ambassador, to whom I repeat the question. The ambassador declares a cease-fire has been agreed upon until the seventeenth, 2:00 p.m.: you must not believe what [Montgomery] Schuyler tells you.

I send the consul general with car to Colonias Roma and Juárez. I myself drive downtown to order all Germans to move toward security; the legation rents two houses in Tacubaya; one house in Santa Maris [is] to provide space for the homeless, as well as two cars for transport purposes. An announcement is made to all German nationals in Mexico:

(1) After attempts failed to keep gunfire away from the residences of most German nationals, my efforts led to a cease-fire, signed at the U.S. embassy. This will temporarily give nationals of the empire the opportunity to travel to a safe suburb or to Veracruz or another safe location.

(2) We will announce in time when the cease-fire will begin and how long it will last.

(3) Those German nationals who do not reside in locations that are absolutely safe from gunfire are hereby asked officially to take advantage of the opportunity mentioned under (1), affording them security until the end of hostilities.

(4) For those German nationals who could *not* find other secure places or stay with friends, etc., I am looking for two houses in Tacubaya and [plan] to purchase them. The government has assumed a guarantee to keep Tacubaya secure.

(5) Moving to Tacubaya, one ought to take along the German flag, bedsheets, valuables that are easy to transport, and money; perhaps a few pots and pans; mostly as little as possible.

(6) Those who have a car or some means of transportation, or somehow can organize it, will use it to start the departure from the city. The ones who cannot organize this for themselves will be transported with transportation provided by the legation, *as possible*.

(7) Those who do not use the cease-fire and the opportunity to re-move themselves from the consequences of the fight are doing so at their own responsibility.

(8) Damage to property remaining behind can be addressed through claims.

(9) Those who want to make use of the opportunity to move them-selves to a secure place should begin preparations immediate-ly, because when the beginning of the cease-fire is announced, the preparations for departure have to be finished and no time can be lost.

February 16, 1913, Mexico City

1:40 P.M.

2. Felicistas shoot at my car during the attempt to pick up Mrs. Niggl from Calle Bucareli No. 53. I visit the U.S. [embassy] to negotiate the extension of the cease-fire until Monday, 8:00 p.m.

I complain about the shelling by Felicistas to Díaz's representa-tive, a Lic. Fidencio Hernández,[38] at the U.S. embassy, where he meets the representatives of both parties. The parties cannot reach an agreement about the cease-fire, because Díaz's representative

FIG. 18. Advanced position of Felicistas. Courtesy of the German Federal
Foreign Office.

lacks the authority to do so. They return to the citadel. The representative of Gen. Huerta is Gen. Delgado.

The ambassador produces a State Department telegram, according to which the Mexican chargé d'affaires in Washington reported
that the ambassador, here, has threatened the landing of soldiers
and marines (which is correct); that the ambassador " had notified
Madero to resign, through a delegate, in the name of a few members of the diplomatic corps; that Madero had refused the right of
foreign representatives to interfere in domestic affairs and that he
would sooner die than leave his post." I counsel the ambassador to
clarify that Cólogan handed over only friendly advice, without talking about orders from our governments. And I inform him that I will
send cables stating it in this way (which I did).

3. The Belgian diplomatic representative informed that ambassador,
the morning of February 16, in reply to a Díaz representative who
had complained: in spite of a cease-fire the government troops were
digging trenches and fill them with dynamite. In the presence of the
Belgian diplomat he replied, Shoot them down! The Belgian diplo-

mat assured this, giving his word of honor. Indeed, from noon on, the Felicistas have begun to shoot again. Díaz states he had been unable to inform his outposts in a speedy fashion because messengers are running to them under [conditions] of danger.

4. The group of senators daring to step into the street—about twelve to fifteen—once again gathered voluntarily in early morning and tried to bring to the president and vice president the idea of resigning. The president did not receive them.

6:45 P.M.

5. Shooting stopped at 5:40 p.m.

6. I am driving the Marquardt and Hinrichs families to Buena Vista Station; on the way, everywhere, I encounter resistance and firefights because "the cease-fire has been broken": an order has been given to resume hostilities.

7. I am going to the U.S. ambassador to learn about the outcome of negotiations about extending the cease-fire. U.S. ambassador: the armistice is off because the Federales have broken it. And following my repeated and formal question, "Is it a fact that the armistice is off and that all the negotiations are futile?" The ambassador answers repeatedly and expressly, "It is a fact"—And he adds that government troops had broken the cease-fire. Because he had dispatched U.S. citizens there who had convinced themselves that, indeed, Federales had dug ditches and filled them with dynamite. As I am leaving, Schuyler, by coincidence, comes in and remarks that soon it would be seven o'clock—the time when the negotiators wanted to come back to resume negotiations about the extension of the cease-fire.

Outraged, I turn to the U.S. ambassador and confront him with his most recent assurance: "The negotiations have been broken off, no more cease-fire!" With indifference he admits that this is not correct: only he does not know if the negotiators would appear or not. Somewhat ashamed, he suggests that I should return in the evening. I counter:

I see no reason to do so. It needs to be made clear that the U.S. ambassador fails to perform his duties as doyen of the diplomatic corps:[39] not a single member of the diplomatic corps has received

FIG. 19. General Blanquet outside a cantina. Courtesy of the German Federal Foreign Office.

any news from him. However, he continuously claims to act in the name of the diplomatic corps.

The French chargé d'affaires has demanded to be admitted to the negotiations of the Great Powers. Wilson has rejected it [the demand]. The U.S. ambassador claims that Blanquet would not fight[40] against Díaz and four hundred of his troops had switched to Díaz's side. Apparently this is one of those inventions that are being circulated in favor of Félix Díaz.

8. The U.S. ambassador tells me during the afternoon of the sixteenth that since Díaz's uprising began Gen. Huerta has been in secret negotiations with Díaz. He was willing to declare himself against Madero in public, but he fears that the foreign powers would refuse him diplomatic recognition. The U.S. ambassador: I have let him know that I am willing to recognize any government that is able to restore peace and order in place of Mr. Madero's government and that I shall strongly recommend to my government to grant recognition to any such government.

It appears to me that the ambassador deceives himself about Huerta or allows himself to be deceived. A few suspicious person-

FIG. 20. Victoriano Huerta in better health. Courtesy of the Library of Congress.

alities serve the ambassador in his secret traffic with Díaz. He believes their lies because he *desires* that this is so. I pointed out to him that almost regularly the news from Díaz's camp turns out to be wrong—which he admitted.

9. During the night of February 16–17 a few cannon and machine-gun shots [occur]; also some gunfire. Impossible to step into the street.

10. About 7:00 p.m. the troops of General Blanquet move from the Calzada de Veronica to Chapultepec via the city's southwest.

By February 17 it became known that General Huerta was on the side of the rebels. At the U.S. embassy he signed an armistice in the presence of U.S. ambassador Henry Lane Wilson, Félix Díaz, and Manuel Mondragón. The men agreed to bring about a change of government, with Félix Díaz as the future president.

February 17, 1913, Mexico City

Today I direct the following note to the secretary of foreign relations:

Dear Foreign Diplomat,

On the fifteenth of this month I had the honor to draw to your attention the fact that two obus [howitzer] explosives and many cannonballs have fallen within the walls of the German diplomatic representation. In the presence of Your Excellency, Diplomat, I protest to the President of the Republic against this flagrant violation of international law. The President of the Republic has declared that he will issue the most formal orders in such a way that [military] operations should be conducted in such fashion that the foreign missions will not be affected.

On the sixteenth I have learned from a letter from General Huerta addressed to the Ambassador of the United States of America that an armistice has been concluded that should last until two in the morning of February seventeenth. I have done my best to take advantage of this armistice to transport my compatriots to Tacubaya—which had been agreed upon during the negotiation that had opened on the fifteenth with Your Excellency and General Huerta.

Nevertheless, from one o'clock on the afternoon of February 16, shooting began. Coming from Bucareli Street, someone shot at me and my car and someone has refused passage to me in spite of a legitimate pass with the seal of the secretary of foreign affairs and with the signature of General de la Vega. Thus I had to give up my plan to save a German woman who lives at Calle Bucareli 53 and [to help] with the transport to Tacubaya of the home furnishings of my compatriots who live at the city center. I have the honor to repeat in writing the formal protest against all operations that are capable of endangering the home of the German legation or have come down on the diplomat from Norway and the diplomat from Belgium, both of them with their families and those German families that seek asylum, with children and women. [This is] a formal protest against the rupture of the armistice proclaimed on the fifteenth/sixteenth of February. I take the opportunity, Mr. Diplomat, pp. signed von Hintze. To His Excellency the Secretary of Foreign Affairs, Lic. Pedro Lascuraín. Copy mailed to General Huerta.

6:25 A.M.

1. Heavy cannon fire begins from the Paseo de la Reforma toward the citadel. From there it is being answered.

8:00 A.M.

2. Machine guns are being used.

8:50 A.M.

3. I protest to Secretary Lascuraín verbally and in writing against the shooting at the legation and against the violation of the cease-fire. It prevented bringing all Germans to security outside the city, as I had prepared to do. Lascuraín promises to do his utmost but lacks a connection located inside the seat of government.

His automobile is broken and he had a difficult time reaching the palace by telephone. I propose he should take my car—which he accepts. Then I introduce to him additional likely scenarios of troop revolts: because visibly they're fed up [with] fighting. Furthermore, the increasingly likely vision of a mob uprising; finally, that this artillery fire alone can *never* take the Citadel; but only through attack; and the generals, as they have told me themselves, could not get the troops to do so. Because of personal considerations the situation between Madero and Díaz is difficult to handle: because Díaz demands the president's resignation—[a demand] that he, naturally, does not want to entertain. One has to find a middle path that does justice to both of them and spares them. The only military solution is taking the citadel; with these troops it is not possible because no one can bring them to stage an attack. I propose to impose General Huerta as governor of Mexico with the full power to end the revolution in the way he sees fit. Lascuraín takes up the suggestion and asks me to take him to the National Palace. The previously secure Avenida Veronica is now being strafed by overreaching grenades, shot out of the citadel. I meet General Huerta in the palace. I give him a copy of my protest against the breaking of the cease-fire. He *promises* to take care that the mission will not be shot at.

Lascuraín turns to the president and introduces my proposition to him. He returns after some time and hints that, in principle, the suggestion has been accepted. What remains to be decided is if Huerta or somebody else [will be selected]. I state: the minutes are precious and it seems to me that General Huerta is the only one who enjoys the power to act over the troops: to choose another one—even if perhaps more able—would be a grave error.

Lascuraín wants to raise it for discussion. He states that he has just received a telegram from Taft in which Taft declares his opposition to intervention: warships and troops have been dispatched only out of precaution. However, he—Taft—advises [us] urgently to end the turmoil in Mexico City quickly.

12:00 NOON

3. I talked with Commodore Izaguirre and the adjutant of the secretary of war: both declare that it is impossible to end the revolution through military means.

12:15 P.M.

4. General Blanquet has been seen near the U.S. cemetery. There his troops are standing without doing anything.
5. East of Calle San Lorenzo—in San Lazaro—in the area of the prison the heaviest fighting takes place.

1:15 P.M.

6. The firing of cannons stops; it resumes again at 2:35 p.m.

5:00 P.M.

Silence.

FIG. 21. U.S. ambassador Henry Lane Wilson. Courtesy of the Library of Congress.

February 18, 1913, Mexico City

The night from the seventeenth to the eighteenth passes comparatively quietly.

7:55 A.M.

2. U.S. ambassador states: since February 16 he has been trying to establish a direct connection with Huerta. However, each time the general has announced that he could not leave the palace.

For two days, at different times, representatives from both camps gathered with [the ambassador in] the embassy in order to reach an understanding. He proposed as a basis: a government that was led by de la Barra, Huerta, and Díaz would certainly receive the support of the United States of America. One of the delegates, Senator Obregón, proposed in a formal way the question of whether the United States would forgo intervention once such a government was being formed; he answered this question with yes!

General Blanquet's troops switched to Díaz's side. But Blanquet is inside the National Palace. Following the negotiations that took place yesterday, on February 17, he believes that the matter will be resolved by today, noon, February 18. He claims that during the negotiations he is trying to put aside the president and he negotiates only with Huerta. The batteries of the Federales, which yesterday were located at the Colonia Station, have been forced to pull back to Chapultepec (not true). Blanquet's troops are alleged to have occupied Chapultepec (not true). The Felicistas are alleged to have occupied almost the entire Colonias Roma and Juárez and in that process four federal soldiers were shot in front of the Spanish embassy. He [Blanquet] let Díaz know that he wanted to occupy all neighborhoods so that finally peace and order will govern here.

[Wilson] reports "a fierce correspondence" with the president that included his protest against a U.S. State Department report that he, Wilson, had "officially notified the president that he must resign" and [that he] "has always instigated the diplomatic body against a constitutional government." Thereupon Madero wired Taft, [saying that] Wilson "has given satisfactory explanations." However, he (Wilson) has given no *elaborations*. (Most likely the opposite is true).

8:30 A.M.

3. Lascuraín says: Direct negotiations between both parties are ongoing. They are being held inside *the palace*. (Díaz's side is being represented by Fidencio Hernández.) Díaz is supposed to have counted on Puebla turning against the president, but the entire country is in favor of Madero, including Puebla; or it is taking a wait-and-see attitude. Yesterday Felicistas advanced toward the west in the direction of the foreign communities because, there, the Federales had taken into ac-

FIG. 22. The Twentieth Battalion, with women and children providing support. Courtesy of the German Federal Foreign Office.

count [the presence] of foreigners and did not want to fight. But in the east Felicistas have been pushed out of Calle Bolivar and are standing at Calle Ancha. Once again, the Federales took up a position at the YMCA building. Toward the west access to the citadel is open due to the above-stated reasons. Díaz is getting supplies from there; yesterday three large trucks with meat, bread, etc. had been brought from the expatriate community into the citadel. Huerta intended to close the west side as well, but he gave up a heavy bombardment as pointless. All of Blanquet's troops moved yesterday afternoon—February 17—to the Zócalo in front of the palace. From the palace Huerta gave a speech to the troops, whereupon Blanquet stepped into the palace and announced himself to the president. Blanquet's loyalty and that of his troops are truly beyond reproach. As before, the president continues to be optimistic. The idea to appoint a general as governor was once again dropped in reaction to the good news from last night.

He, Lascuraín, Ernesto Madero, and Rafael Hernández, together with Garcia Peña, were functioning as one block inside the cabinet. They were trying to restore the running of everyday business.

4. I resume reacting to (2) and (3): I believe both sides are keeping the U.S. ambassador at arm's length through negotiations in order to avoid the departure of troops.
5. U.S. warships have arrived in Veracruz and Tampico.
6. The U.S. ambassador used an official note to accuse the vice president of the republic, Pino Suárez,[41] of bribing Mr. Gonzalez, an officer in the Rurales, to take Mr. de la Barra out of the British legation and to execute him; also to incite the population against foreigners and to spread the rumor that Calero was residing in the U.S. embassy. The note used expressions of strongest terms.

11:00 A.M.

7. Major Gonzalez Salas states: they have available three to four mortars, but not enough ammunition (clearly spoken, this means: they have none).

11:10 A.M.

8. I visited the president at the National Palace, where I was brought—despite his initial hesitation—by the secretary of foreign relations. The president had just received the Senate, which had tried since last Sunday to persuade him to resign. The president, after listening to the speech of de la Barra, ordered the telegrams of President Taft and those from inside the country read.
3. Following my initiative, Wilson asks about the murder of Gustavo Madero. Huerta declares: all of this has happened against *his* orders.
4. Following my initiative, Wilson asks about the state of relations between Huerta and Félix Díaz. The answer: "Excellent. Today (February 20), in the afternoon, Félix Díaz will position his troops in front of the palace and put them under my command."

Yesterday (February 19) de la Barra had visited Wilson and declared his greatest fear: trouble had broken out between Díaz and Huerta; the work toward pacification is put into question. Wilson dispatched military attaché Burnside in full uniform with a written declaration to Díaz: "if he or the other party does not live up to the letter of the agreement they signed in the embassy on February 18, and which he—Wilson—had a copy of in his safe, he would withdraw from the settlement and make them responsible for the ensu-

FIG. 23. Outside position First Cavalry regiment. Courtesy of the German Federal Foreign Office.

ing consequences" (that means: intervention). F. Díaz is supposed to have given assurances that *no* trouble existed between him and Huerta.

5. Huerta, as he says goodbye to us, states: he always will be grateful for wise counsel.

   Note: Wilson declares that Huerta is supposed to have told him:

A. Gustavo Madero had tried to poison him with cyanide.
B. One day Francisco Madero asked him, as he was walking up and down, to remain at the window opening. He excused himself, having to use the bathroom: just as the president left, four shots were fired at him from the roof—Huerta standing at the window.
C. On the day when Wilson and I had tried to talk to him, he had [been] taken prisoner inside the palace.

Here the diary concludes with two letters. They have not been included in this translation, as they deal with a minor, unimportant issue.

FIG. 24. Mrs. Madero in front of her husband's coffin at his funeral. Courtesy of the Library of Congress.

On February 19 President Madero and Vice President Pino Suárez were forced to sign their declaration of resignation from office. Immediately thereafter Pedro Lascuraín served for less than sixty minutes as interim president and appointed Victoriano Huerta as secretary of interior (*gobernación*). Madero and Pino Suárez became prisoners inside the National Palace.

Three days later, on February 22, at 11:15 pm, it was argued that these two men should be transferred in order to guarantee greater security for them. A Rurales guard, Captain Francisco Cardenas, ushered them out of the National Palace in two cars. Shortly thereafter Madero and Pino Suárez were found dead at the wall on one side of the Lecumberri prison. Captain Cardenas stated the lie that, somehow, the two men had been killed in the crossfire of an attacking mob. In reality they had been murdered.

May 19, 1913, Berlin

In response to decree I 13847 from May 17, criticizing the expenses undertaken to protect Germans during the revolution of February [1913], I report to Your Excellency: . . . repeatedly I had the honor to report to Your Excellency, following repeated inquiries via cable, that the German citizen F. Sommerfeld sought asylum in the German legation at the beginning of the revolution.

Even there, he received threats to his life, and I too received similar threats against his life. It became impossible to keep Sommerfeld secure in perpetuity inside the legation. Some conspirator could have assassinated him through a window, [shooting] from a surrounding roof as he stepped toward the windowsill. Therefore the task was to bring him outside the country. Thus I entered into negotiations with the Mexican government. The government declared Sommerfeld persona non grata[42] and suggested he be brought outside the country in order to free itself from responsibility for his expected murder and in its own interest. [The government] suggested bringing him, guarded by police, to Veracruz. Obviously this method proved not necessarily safe, as has just been demonstrated by the murder of Francisco Madero, Pino Suárez, and Gustavo Madero. Therefore, I proposed to the Mexican government to try the following: I would accompany Mr. Sommerfeld to Veracruz. The Mexican government then made the greatest effort to suggest that I not do that, pointing at the danger that I would find myself in. This only increased my concern.

Thus I arranged with the government to bring Sommerfeld in a special train car to Veracruz and to accompany him onto a German ship. The government countered, promising protection through secret police during the trip and onboard the steamer until it left the harbor. . . . The special train car was necessary in order to separate Sommerfeld from other passengers so that none of them could suddenly shoot him down. In that train car I hid Sommerfeld. I bought a first-class ticket for myself and for my servant. . . .[43]

3

Getting to Know the Dictator

VICTORIANO HUERTA GOVERNS

Victoriano Huerta never stepped down from his increasingly dictatorial position. Every month politicians and the remaining civilian society were more intimidated and broken apart by Huerta's dictatorship. Terror was meted out by his secret police against an ever-increasing number of "opponents." In the end, when even the politicians in the remaining Congress refused to ratify laws benefiting private British companies, Huerta disbanded altogether the Mexican Congress and the last remnants of representative politics. An unprecedented militarization of Mexican civil society followed. Huerta began to head a counterrevolution.

From the first days after Madero was toppled from office, revolutionaries in Mexico's regions had resumed revolutionary war against the dictator Huerta. They came together in a difficult umbrella coalition called the Constitutionalistas.

October 7, 1913, Mexico City

A REGULAR DIPLOMATIC REPORT

Today President Huerta formed his new cabinet.

It is emblematic that it included four of the most important congressmen of the Liberal Party, Moheno as secretary of foreign affairs,[1] Olaguibel as undersecretary of foreign affairs, Lozano as secretary of justice, and Garcia Naranjo as secretary of education. All four are lawyers, journalists, and the best speakers of the Chamber of Deputies.

Repeatedly they have changed their political credo. Under Porfirio Díaz they were *científicos*; that means followers of the group in power and exploiting the state. Under Madero initially they were spectators, until they had convinced themselves that nothing could be obtained from there. Then they became the so-called Independent Liberals. In essence they are professional politicians—seeking office and income.

I do not give much credence to the predominant interpretation that with these appointments Huerta has changed his policy. Huerta's goal remains without change: to stay in power. The sudden preference for the Liberals is mostly an act of revenge against the Catholic Party, which threw him overboard by making Gamboa its candidate. The three new secretaries do not have wealth and are ambitious; they will follow Huerta or disappear.

Moheno, the new secretary of foreign relations, is considered one of the most brilliant speakers in Congress and, indeed, through the power of his word he frequently has been able to sway the Chamber of Deputies to make decisions according to his wishes. If examined by light, his speeches fall in the category that one commonly calls a "composition essay": historical reminiscences of dubious correctness; quotes—often wrong and, frequently, misleading in their use for the existing case; much lyricism and a bit sentimental. And add to that the flowing word that helps to move over the obstacles of "truth and reality"—in short, exactly what is enjoyed in this country; where the idea—also the one emphasized—is taken as an event and the word is seen as action.

Like most newcomers, as secretary of state he is unnecessarily gracious with assurances and promises. He has changed the political program as follows: excellent relations with the United States—and the other countries. This reflects his lively sympathy for the U.S. chargé d'affaires and his admiration for Mr. Bryan! Moheno tells me that Mr. Zamacona, the confidential Mexican negotiator for Washington[2]—Lind's counterpart—has returned bringing along interesting descriptions of the mood [in Washington]. His opinion in summary: the United States intends to maintain the position of watchful waiting.

President Huerta assured the U.S. chargé d'affaires without being asked that, regardless of circumstances, the presidential elections will be held; if Congress would grant the Maderista proposal to move the elections, he would oppose it. It cannot be detailed how he thinks he will go about it. Congress is sovereign and the constitution grants the president of the republic neither the right to veto nor to dissolve Congress.

But Huerta is a man of many means and, at times, flabbergasting disconcertedness as far as the constitution and the law are concerned. Three days ago he provided new proof. The governor of the state of Queretaro, Loyola, had begun a busy campaign in favor of the candidate [team] of Gamboa-Rascon. Hearing the news, Huerta dispatched General Chicarro [to Queretaro] with troops. Loyola was asked to take a vacation, the state's congressmen were arrested. Then—under military guard— they were marched into the assembly chamber and forced to proclaim Chicarro as governor. There is much gossip about it, but [at] its core it remains a fact that cannot change. A sign that, still, the army—and the person who wants to rely on it—can do whatever he wants to do.

Huerta, slowly, continues to crumble: under the pressure of the "U.S. watchful waiting"—demonstrated by troop mobilizations in the north and the U.S. ships in Mexican ports; in addition, due to diplomatic interference in internal affairs that reminds one of Poland's downfall; as well as because of a type of economic deprivation siege of Mexico.

The propertied classes, once welcoming him in February as a savior from Madero's demagoguery, are beginning to turn away from him, out of fear that their property will be lessened or become endangered because of the disintegrating relationship with the United States. Huerta feels that the trust of him in bourgeois circles is dwindling. And only the army remains uninterrupted in favor of him: therefore, from the beginning, he has emphasized a conciliatory tone vis-à-vis the United States. That is a return to some of the principles of Mexico's greatest presidents, Juárez and Díaz: don't have any difficulties with the United States.

The most important leaders among the rebels (the so-called Constitutionalistas) have decided to separate the states of Sonora, Durango, Chihuahua, and Coahuila and the territory of Baja California from the Republic of Mexico, without demonstrating that this decision will have a practical consequence. The Federales are making slow progress in Coahuila; in the other states there is a standstill; in Sinaloa the revolutionaries have achieved some victories. Durango and Sonora, with a few exceptions, are in the hands of rebels.

Today the news comes that Torreón, the most important railroad switching point in the north and by all means a rich and flourishing city, has been taken by the rebels! Entirely unimaginable mistakes must have been committed there, because inside and around Torreón stood superior numbers of federal army troops. In light of this, Huerta's message to the foreign representatives that the revolution has been put down and all that remains is the repression of violent gangs using police is, to say it modestly, courageously ambitious and pales as far as similar protestations by the Madero administration are concerned.

According to reports from the north, the United States, with great determination, has cut off the flow of weapons, i.e., the import. There, according to the same sources, a daily occurrence among the Mexican federal army is fraud, theft. Officers, paymasters, etc. are fading away with army payment boxes or with stolen money, etc.

The United States allows its consuls to deal with all "administrations who claim control, regardless if they are on the side of the government or on that of the rebels."

The Mexican government tolerates this practice. Mexico has called back her diplomats from Brazil, Chile, Cuba, and Costa Rica because these countries have failed to recognize Huerta. Not a single mumbling can be heard that a corresponding punishment vis-à-vis the United States is even contemplated. To the contrary: the president and the secretary of state show themselves eager to shower the U.S. chargé d'affaires, extending courtesies and fulfilling wishes. Therefore he looks into the future with great trust and talks about the understanding that will come soon. He goes even farther than [conditions] suggested; one should show hope that Huerta could be recognized: for only a mule does not change his mind.

As I have said before, I counter suggestions from the Mexicans and diplomats (the Belgium diplomat remarks, "We all believed it") that Germany should play a leading role on Mexico's side in open resistance against the United States. I counter them predominantly by emphasizing Germany's economic interest in Mexico and the danger to its interests due to continued unrest and disorder in the country.

On October 1 the Mexican government received as an advance 10 million pesos [against foreign bonds] from Mexico City banks. It will be counted toward the soon-to-be-floated 50 million pesos of the external 160 million [pesos in] foreign bonds. 4.5 million of them have been spent to pay the national railroad coupons coming due (prior lien bonds and shares of the Antiguo Ferrocarril Mexicano). Whereby the government spared these railroads from being taken over by shareholders and has secured further control. The rest covers an advance taken up as part of the national bank advances.

The financial emergency is great. The government has under consideration the idea of issuing a *new* foreign loan and using as collateral the income of the just-increased tax for raw [unrefined] petroleum (one peso per ton, previously twenty-five cents). It projects as income from this tax nine to ten million pesos per year and hopes to use it to borrow a sum of tenfold this amount.

The opinion about the situation that, with a few exceptions, is shared by Mexicans as well as in foreign circles [is] that: "It has never been *this* bad during the last three years." Today, summing up, I have to say:

1. Huerta wants to remain president in spite of the elections, but he is not sure how he can pull that off when the time comes. And he is not sure that when the time is right circumstances will allow him to do so. Therefore there exists a strong tendency toward reconciliation and understanding with the United States.
2. More urgently than ever before Mexico needs money from abroad. Also, after the last domestic loan—it had to cover payments coming due—the government has control only over excess customs income and the stamp tax, from which it cannot live. **Hintze**[3]

October 20, 1913, Santiago de Chile

A REGULAR DIPLOMATIC REPORT

The local Mexican diplomat, Mr. Mujica, will travel in the next days to Montevideo. Allegedly to wait there for government instructions for the continuation of his trip. The departure appeared to be very sudden. Mr. Mujica did not provide information about the reason. However, between him and the Chilean president a longer talk has taken place. In diplomatic circles, the thinking is that the reason for his departure can be found in the fact that Chile has not yet recognized the government of General Huerta. In military circles, the thought is the possibility that the departure is connected to the expected purchase of war supplies. As a matter of fact, Mr. Mujica repeatedly contacted the local military offices in regard to weapons purchases. However, [his requests] have been denied because, here, only cartridges but not weapons can be handed over.[4]

October 30, 1913, Mexico City

Elections took place in a calm manner and expressed apathy. The majority of Congress is being named by the government and according to the governmental list. Huerta has received the majority of submitted or faked votes for president and Blanquet for vice president. Whether the majority of districts have voted as law demands can be determined only toward the end of November. Right now the government aims to reach an understanding with the United States. It holds out as bait that Huerta might step down from office because the election has been anticonstitution and, based on law, Blanquet will move into the presidency. [Erased in the original:] Even though it is unlikely that this bait will be taken seriously, at this point it could lead to possible cooperation.

The military's prestige is somewhat increased through the successful defense of Monterrey and victory over Villa.

Here [in Mexico City] British diplomat Carden more and more appears in the role of Huerta's adviser. He offers opinions based on his personal experience and blind and raging hatred toward the United States. It appears that he goes further than the British government is willing to follow him. The French [and] Spanish diplomats are waiting to see what happens. The Japanese diplomat is totally holding back.

Postscript to telegram No. 113. Following repeated urging, the secretary of war plans reinforcement of Mazatlán and the commander has in particular been urged to provide protection for Germans. Besides, he declared the place as not dangerous. Based on information available to him, U.S. warships cannot protect every foreigner. This would require landing of considerable U.S. troops. I have concerns about sending such a request to the U.S. embassy. Because, most likely, it will be denied. **Hintze**[5]

November 4, 1913, Mexico City

Military Report about the Stay of Your Majesty's Ship *Hertha* in Veracruz.

Situation in Veracruz

Up until now everything has been calm. Elections scheduled for October 26 and, even given that occasion, no excitement raised its head.

FIG. 25. Pancho Villa and supporters. Courtesy of the Library of Congress.

I have already reported that Félix Díaz has arrived on board of the *Corcovado*. After his debarkation he stayed in the "German Hotel." Its back touches the backyard of the U.S. consulate. A ladder put against his window allowed him secure escape under U.S. protection. From there, after the elections, he was escorted by John Lind—date cannot be ascertained anymore—to a U.S. warship. During the process John Lind, with a revolver, repeatedly threatened Mexican detectives who rushed toward Díaz. At first Díaz stayed on board of the *Wheeling*. The *Tacoma* was supposed to transfer him to Havana the night of October 31– November 1. However, while leaving the inner harbor, the *Tacoma* had an accident and [incapacitated] her propeller, so the *Michigan* had to take over the task on November 1.

Visiting Mexico City

Following the order of Imperial Diplomat Hintze I traveled on October 27, Monday, with two officers to the capital, Mexico City.

At the train station I was welcomed by him and a few gentlemen of the German colony. The Mexican government had sent a secretary of the foreign ministry and a major from the military staff to accompany me.

On October 28, accompanied by these Mexican gentlemen, visits were made in the morning to the secretary of foreign relations and the secretary of war, General Blanquet. At noon, Imperial Diplomat Hintze presented me to the president of the republic, General Huerta.

The personality of Moheno appears very unsympathetic. He is rather small and fat. The fat head sits directly on the shoulders, the wavy black hair standing upright. The color of his face is yellow and pale, the eyes gray-blue; the face does not express emotion.

Secretary of War Blanquet is tall, has a military-like appearance with energetic facial expression and serious, penetrating eyes. His appearance is very measured and dignified.

President Huerta is short, rather trim, completely gray, wears glasses, through which he looks with piercing eyes. While talking, his gestures are very lively. He walks storming forward while pointing the tip of his shoes somewhat inward, and the arms swing back and forth with animation.

It is said of him that he is proud to originate from pure Native American race—when he has consumed lots of alcohol—and that is often the case.

Based on his words, this morning at the Gambrinus he already had taken a few glasses of beer; we were served cognac and champagne. During the introduction the entire cabinet was present.

We were led through rooms where individual armed officers and lower-level officers [were present]. After the introduction we were walked down the hallway to the first door. It proved to be locked.

It still deserves mentioning that the first secretary of the secretary of war, "General" Vidaurrazaga, held a dinner in honor of me, Admiral Hintze, and the other officers. It was attended by about twenty generals and colonels and the secretary of war. The president cancelled after we had waited for him for 1.5 hours.

"General" Vidaurrazaga, following a poorly chosen way of life, has also been experiencing the power of criminal law. It is considered to be a sign of his great cunning and danger that, nevertheless, he has been able to gain this position. One regrets that this man is the confidant of Secretary of War Blanquet, who, in general, is held in good esteem.

Vidaurrazaga was the one entrusted with the—failed—mission to persuade Félix Díaz, upon arriving in Veracruz on board the *Coronado*, to abandon his candidacy for the presidency.

Following presidential instructions the Mexican attaché and gentlemen toured the capital in the presidential car. At the end we visited Chapultepec. Also, in the afternoon we enjoyed a glass of champagne in a noble restaurant of the city. At this event the Japanese colonel Inouye, who had come from Washington DC, also appeared. Allegedly it was for a ten-day pleasure trip—in reality probably to study the Mexican army. There I made the acquaintance of Carlos Rincon Gallardo, chief of the Rurales and the guard of Chapultepec, and the chief of the military school in Coyoacán, a colonel, who had enjoyed his training in the Prussian army with the Riesenburger Kurasiers; Admiral Hintze had invited him. They were the only officers of all the people I have met who have actual experience as soldiers, based on German concepts.

The Political Situation

The political situation is so extraordinarily complicated that I do not presume to say anything about it.

Most Germans in Mexico see the revolution as a fight of U.S. capital against the republic, which deserves support from the European side. It is assumed that European money would truly be used for the well-being of the country, but that is not the case. Everybody who has access to public money steals and robs and enriches himself.

The Mexican Army

Of its theoretical strength of one hundred thousand men, according to calculations of the imperial diplomat, only sixty-five thousand men are truly in existence. But it is already supposed to be very difficult to reach even this strength. There exists, as a German eyewitness told me, a far-reaching gang impressment system. Also, the prisons are being emptied out. On the streets many teenage boys can be seen. There is a serious lack of officers. Such an army, of course, is inferior. In the north the rebels are supposedly, according to Germans, at times very well equipped and rather disciplined troops. In particular, General Carranza's troops are noteworthy.

Near Torreón, according to official news, a general and four hundred federal soldiers have fallen in battle. The situation is supposed to be that this general celebrated his [Catholic saint's] name day and distributed alcoholic drinks among people. He himself became drunk in the circle of his girlfriends. At night the general was slaughtered with his girlfriends and his entire troop—just as during the Trojan War.

All Germans that I talked to, honestly, regret that German capital behaves with such restraint; yes, even rejecting the rich Mexican raw material wealth. Among Germans there is agreement that gains will be made here, in particular, when the introduction of a financial control system is accomplished. British (Pearson) and Canadian capital are not supposed to have hesitated to secure themselves generous investments, mainly in the oil fields. [. . .][6]

November 9, 1913, Mexico City

A REGULAR DIPLOMATIC REPORT

The following information reached me in high confidence: Huerta painted the following plan for facing renewed U.S. demands: at the end of November, Congress declares as invalid the presidential elections and schedules new ones within three or four months. In the meantime Huerta changes his entire cabinet, taking in a successor at an appropriate place, one that he has chosen. Huerta steps down, selected successor automatically will become interim president according to constitution, and he names Huerta secretary of war. During the next elections Huerta will be a candidate. There is no opposition to him running inside the union,[7] according to the report of the U.S. chargé d'affaires.

In case of war, Huerta floods the south of the United States with guerrilla bands. In light of the military weakness of the nation, until a sufficient force has been mobilized, only the blocking of the northern border and the ports can be expected. The war inside the country will be handed over to the rebels because it is unlikely that the latter will join Huerta during U.S military activity. Such semi-conduct of war is more dangerous to our interests than open war, and also from the long-term perspective.[8]

November 13, 1913, Mexico City

From talks and observations I gained the impression that the British diplomat personally would like to see a warlike entanglement of the United States with Mexico and therefore strengthen Huerta's back.

Lind's first and main demand is now to declare invalid the congressional elections because Great Britain wants to determine its oil concessions with the help of this Congress and its favorable laws.

In contrast, Huerta demands guarantees for himself, and himself as candidate during the next presidential elections, coming three or four months after his resignation. Therefore Lind proposed that two confidants each—representing the government and the rebels, with him as referee—put to rest domestic conflicts.

[...]

Today Washington cabled Lind [about] the intent of withdrawing its diplomatic representative; other steps will follow. Please [wire] your opinion. Lind could be moved to recommend postponement for several days with respect to the pending negotiations.

Huerta's following continues to melt, especially among the "decent" people.[9]

On November 11, 1913, in Washington DC, the representative of British prime minister Edward Grey arrived from London and met with the representative of U.S. president Wilson. Wilson's representative asked the British government not to provide any more aid to Huerta. Sir Lionel Carden, in Mexico City, was asked to abide by the request.[10] Carden chose to be selective about following the request.

November 14, 1913, Washington DC

A REGULAR DIPLOMATIC REPORT

Today Bryan expressed himself [in a] very pessimistic [fashion]. Lind's departure from Mexico City should be seen as break of diplomatic relations with Huerta, since this government has nothing more to say to him. In contrast, on a semiofficial level, negotiations take place with Venustiano Carranza. The arms embargo is about to be lifted. Because of this measure and the fact that Huerta no longer receives money from Europe, Bryan hopes for a collapse of the Huerta regime. [...][11]

November 20, 1913, Washington DC

A REGULAR DIPLOMATIC REPORT

Today the chief of [the] General Staff [Wood] asked me into his office. There, sometimes in the presence of his aide, Capt. McCoy, for more than one hour, he described the situation in Mexico to me.

The main topic was the question of oil, which he had touched on previously. General Wood considers it so important, in connection with the Panama Canal, that it alone would represent a reason for intervention. Proof of the interest that the local military administration pays to this question is that Gen. Wood covertly arranged to receive confidential information through an engineer from the Pearson Group who is personally loyal to him.

Of course, I cannot vouch for the correctness of the content. However, I want to describe it quickly, as follows:

1. The Cowdray concessions date from Porfirio Díaz's tenure. Madero fought against them and Huerta supported and expanded them. They include freedom from all export fees. This alone equals an annual profit of $15–$20 million in favor of the British. Such profits should increase significantly in a few years.
2. In fact, the arrest and dismissal of the Mexican Congress can be traced back to its unwillingness to endorse the British concessions.
3. Huerta cooperated with British money (Lord Cowdray) and perhaps is still doing so.
4. Cowdray's oilfields—the ones brought into production—have an annual yield of 106 (!) million barrels. To this one needs to add sixty-three wells that have not been brought into production. In the meantime, drilled, finished oil wells are kept under pressure in order to keep the yield of oil in unison with the available means of transport. Cowdray is constructing forty tankers (10,000 t). Of those, twenty are close to completion.
5. Out of this follows that the oil riches of the Cowdray concessions alone surpass those of Russia, those of the entirety of Mexico, and with great likelihood, all of those of the United States.
6. Some time ago the German government signed an oil-delivery contract with Pearson for eighty million barrels.
7. As of late the Pearson Company calls itself the "Mexican Standard Oil Company Ltd."

General Wood considers the British push for oil concessions in Mexico, Colombia, and Ecuador to be of a quite threatening character for the Panama Canal (namely, based on the same reasons mentioned in military report No. 198 [final observations]).[12] The United States' sense of self-preservation as a world power demands an intervention soon in Mexico. One should not have to wait for it much longer. [. . .]¹³

November 25, 1913, Washington DC

The incomparably favorable geographic situation of the United States results in the foreign policy of the United States always being of little concern to U.S. statesmen. Regardless of whether Republicans or Democrats are at the head of the government, motives of domestic policy are always what exercise the decisive impact on its way of acting.

Here the current situation, as far as Mexico is concerned, is described a lot like the situation before the beginning of the Spanish War [of 1898]. Then President McKinley also postponed the decision, day after day, in order not to stand against public opinion. And even after the explosion of the *Maine* he could not reach the decision to declare a war. Until Senator Hanna came to him and declared categorically: the Republican Party will lose during the next elections if the president does not finally act now. Often historical analogies are deceiving; and therefore also in this case, the intervention in Mexico can be avoided. In this case events like the explosion of the *Maine* will not occur.

To me President Wilson appears to be leaning toward the use of weapons rather more than McKinley [had been willing to].

In the meantime public opinion demonstrates unusual restraint and the Mexicans avoid, consciously or unconsciously, anything that could provoke the United States.

Even the Hearst newspapers, which want to bring about intervention, are not in the position to present many reports about the destruction of U.S. life or property. Without exaggeration, all those who voted for President Wilson tend to lean away from the idea of intervention. His opponents— the corporations, railroad companies, kings of petroleum, etc.—all try to bring into play everything to bring about intervention. Also the army— although politically without influence—strongly fans the flames, as Your Excellency has been able to learn from the military attaché's report. The army and the prointervention press are dreaming about a war for oil, with a sharp tip directed as much against Great Britain as against Mexico. However, such noise is more useful to hold President Wilson back.

Because he knows that he cannot win over his enemies, even if it ruins his relationship with his friends.

On top of everything, Secretary of State Bryan is unequivocally against intervention. [He is] an idealist of the purest kind and—from the point of view of bourgeois morality—an exceptional man. He is incapable of leading the foreign policy of a country because he does not have an understanding of the concept of "power." He truly believes one can guide people [to take political positions] . . . by appealing to their good instincts. In all seriousness he uses the word "liberalism" when he talks about Carranza's followers because they call themselves Constitutionalists. They, he says, are the representatives of the oppressed classes that one must help. Mr. Bryan would be troubled that his former ambassador, Wilson, declared in public that U.S. oil interests are standing behind Carranza.

Until now it was believed here that President Wilson and Mr. Bryan would soon separate. Both, in the meantime, however, have recognized that such a separation would lead to the division of the Democratic Party. And neither of them, in three years, would have any chance to be elected president, a goal that both are seeking to reach.

Therefore the gentlemen have to make their peace with each other and they are welded together. Should it come to an intervention in Mexico, Mr. Bryan will comfort himself by calling it the exercise of police authority for the improvement of mankind.

The current situation is certainly not enjoyable from the point of view of our economic interests, but it is preferable to the eventuality of U.S. intervention. Even if President Wilson remains firm and achieves his policy of treating Mexico just the same way he treats Cuba, the United States would skim the very best part from Mexico after the intervention.

A local politician who recently pointed out to me the selflessness of the United States vis-à-vis Cuba finally admitted that earlier his countrymen had no economic interests, even though now they dominate the island economically.

Unfortunately, these days Europe cannot influence U.S. policy because it lacks the power. . . . In that regard Great Britain appears to be more timid than ever, following Sir Lionel Carden's putting his foot in his mouth with a statement embarrassing his government.[14]

Lord Cowdray is being completely disavowed by the local embassy. Therefore we must be content with the role of spectator and wait to see whether the well-being of the Democratic Party demands an intervention or not. If it does, the United States will, I fear, bring about a significant strengthening of all local imperial tendencies. Army and navy should be expected to be strengthened and to gain influence. Until now the very best thing about the United States was that they had no idea how strong their power is, nor did they know how to use it. **Bernstorff**[15]

On the twenty-fifth the U.S. chargé d'affaires received via cable the following instruction (approximated translation from an excerpt):

The following note has been presented to all the present embassies here, except Turkey and Mexico. A copy has been sent to our missions abroad as well as Lind:

Paragraph 1. The goal of the policy of the United States is to establish calm and order in Central America and to maintain it.

Paragraph 2. Usurpation, such as was done by General Huerta, is disturbing peace and order. The United States cannot simply watch a usurper kick down the constitution and law. After he has crudely damaged both to usurp power, he changes and signs contracts and concessions for his personal advantage.

Paragraph 3. The United States wants to isolate General Huerta through all means, except war, to undermine his credit in the country and abroad. To brand his acts as unlawful—in short, to force him through all moral and material means without impatience or irritation to step down and to withdraw—

Paragraph 4. Only if all previously stated moral and material ways should fail will the United States see itself forced to turn to the use of armed force. In this case the United States will inform in advance the other powers of such an aggressive step; no such action seems to be immediate.

Paragraph 5. It is the United States' firm decision to step in against revolutionary disruptions of the political or social order in Central America so that commercial and social relations are normal between the other countries.

Paragraph 6. The United States is not pursuing any interest of its own—be it territorial expansion or trade advantages—but will be here as elsewhere the champion of the open door.

Paragraph 7. The United States not only undertakes care for the life and property of U.S. citizens that might become endangered but also accepts the responsibility for the lives and properties of other foreigners.

Communicate this to your government. [...]

General Huerta talks about carrying the war to the United States; thirty thousand men in gangs to make raids into Texas, Arizona, and New Mexico. Certainly such bands could penetrate at some point along the long border. But how long could they live in a foreign country without local knowledge of the area, without sympathy of the people or their own espionage service? Raids might provide an interesting incident and material for newspapers, but they will not have lasting influence on the outcome of the war. At the moment I imagine the United States will tire of the long-lasting guerrilla war, because they realize—as Lind puts it—that it is a nasty job, and [they] will reach an agreement with the exhausted Mexico.

But I can also imagine that they, once shaken awake through some setbacks or through the lack of decisive success, will muster all their power make an incredible effort and create great military might. Once it exists it will not soon be abolished. [...]

The ideas that I can see at this point of limited knowledge affirm to me the frequently presented idea that reaching an understanding between the United States, Mexico, and the local German interests is still the best option.[16]

On November 7 Lind moved for the last time to Mexico City to ask Huerta to step down and to inform him that the U.S. government will not recognize the Mexican Congress staffed with his supporters that Huerta put in place. Without result Lind returned to Veracruz on November 13, 1913.[17]

December 5, 1913, Washington DC

A REGULAR DIPLOMATIC REPORT

Mr. Wilson's message about Mexico is well known to Your Excellency. From Mr. Bryan's [speech] today it emerged with clarity that the local government now completely identifies with Carranza. Mr. Bryan described the latter as a decent person with ideal points of view, even though his methods are "somewhat Spanish." Mr. Bryan expects Carranza to topple

Huerta in a few months, and [Carranza] then will be in the position to pacify the land without the United States having to interfere. **Bernstorff**[18]

December 18, 1913, Mexico City

[...] the Lazar Banking House, London, has loaned twenty million pesos to the Mexican government. The Parisian group [composing] the sixteen-million-pound-sterling loan syndicate is in the process of handing over, in exchange for bonds on this loan, twenty-seven million pesos to pay the interest on the foreign debt, due January 1. Thus the threatened financial collapse of the Huerta government has been averted.[19]

January 5, 1914, Mexico City

A REGULAR DIPLOMATIC REPORT

The Japanese delegate informed me that his government has asked him to be governed by complete openness toward me.

He said about his instructions: it is Japanese policy "to concentrate all its efforts to win the friendship of the United States." That is the goal; in this policy Mexico is only an exploitable object. Until now Japan has played only the role of spectator and has left to the United States a completely free hand, in the expectation that—regardless of intervention or not—Japan could exploit the conflict between the two neighbors in favor of its friendly negotiations with the United States.

Mexican secretary of state Moheno has approached him with suggestions about joining forces, but it is impossible to negotiate with this man. And President Huerta offered some ideas to him about the same topic, which would be, from the Japanese perspective, rather crazy.[20] It is impossible to negotiate with the current power holders. He was wondering about the busy optimism that the British diplomat showcases and could not share it: in his opinion Huerta will last at the most only two to three months.[21]

January 11, 1914, Mexico City

A REGULAR DIPLOMATIC REPORT

On January 11 the British government asked her representative to come to London because "the situation is so delicate that oral discussions will be necessary." They will send a chargé d'affaires here. The British diplomat considers this the beginning of a reorientation of British policy here, in the sense of a more energetic action against the United States. To me it appears to be a withdrawal. I request an interpretation from Berlin. **Hintze**[22]

January 13, 1914, Mexico City

A REGULAR DIPLOMATIC REPORT

Sir Lionel Carden received, about January 9, a.m., from the Foreign Office the request "to come home as the situation is so delicate that it requires verbal discussion; we are going to send Thomas Beaumont Hohler as chargé d'affaires."[23]

In strongest confidence Sir Lionel emphatically told me: I am the only one with whom he would talk about it: he welcomes the possibility of personally enlightening Sir Edward Grey through discussion.[24] And he is sure that important members of the Foreign Office agree with him about the need for a timely step against the expansionist policy of the United States. Otherwise one suddenly will face a United States that is overwhelmingly powerful on land and sea.

On this occasion, for the first time, Sir Lionel opened up to me: this could be the occasion for the British and Germany to join forces. Previously, as is well known, he had emphasized that Great Britain moves ahead *alone* [in Mexico] and needs to. I have answered, however, [saying] how desirable British and German cooperation would be and that this idea has been known to me for a long time. Applied to the present case, I could not quite see that England ever stepped closer to the idea, but my knowledge would not be entirely up to date to speak about this competently. [. . .]

With the exception of me and Mr. O'Shaughnessy,[25] nobody seems to think it is correct that Sir Lionel Carden is being called home. Already it is being discussed in the newspapers; following the rejection of the idea stated by Carden and London, not even the Mexican government [believes them].

It cannot be denied: the fact is, this is a tough blow for the Huerta government. Carden went through thick and thin for it, partially putting second the wishes of his countrymen. And besides, it is the very famous laurel leaf of British diplomacy, which here could achieve much without losing face.[26]

January 15, 1914, Mexico City

A REGULAR DIPLOMATIC REPORT

The British ambassador explained to me that Baron Makino has told him that Japan has no special interests in Mexico because its trade with Japan is only one million yen.[27] The Japanese government, politically, will remain completely neutral.[28]

January 25, 1914, Mexico City

A REGULAR DIPLOMATIC REPORT

British diplomat reads me Sir E. Grey's cable, having the following essential content:

Interested financial circles see Huerta as cause of state bankruptcy and existing anarchy. To avoid further losses, they suggest elimination of Huerta through intervention of Great Britain, France, Germany, etc., etc.

Apparently the telegram contains, furthermore, an order to explore [this suggestion] with French and German representatives; the French diplomat has approved intervention with firearms by the three powers, without paying attention to the United States. I expressed as my personal opinion that Sir E. Grey could not possibly have meant armed intervention; that any part of a conceivable intervention by the three powers could not possibly circumvent the United States; that for me cooperation in friendship with the latter appears as the most promising form of cooperation; that Huerta could be moved to resign, if treated in good form and under the condition that [his] life, property, and influence are secured during further political developments.

After discussion of this opinion the British diplomat dropped the [idea of] armed intervention with the French diplomat under the above condition and, in essence, cabled: Huerta would probably give in to friendly intervention under above condition. Most important is a U.S. agreement of friendly cooperation. **Hintze**[29]

March 6, 1914, Mexico City

A REGULAR DIPLOMATIC REPORT

British diplomat has received instruction to join front with U.S. ambassador here and hopes for cooperation. U.S. diplomat is ordered to work with British diplomat. **Hintze**[30]

March 12, 1914, Mexico City

A REGULAR DIPLOMATIC REPORT

In the last months, from time to time newspapers report that Argentina, Chile, and Brazil, united with the United States, will try to work for the reestablishment of peace in Mexico. Once in a while it is being mentioned that the U.S. government has asked for the help of the three South American goverments. [. . .] **Hintze to Bethmann-Hollweg**[31]

March 19, 1914, Mexico City

A REGULAR DIPLOMATIC REPORT

The French diplomat, before his departure for a several-month-long vacation with the possibility of not returning to this post, asked for an audience with the president of the republic. It was granted and scheduled for March 9.

Mr. Le Faivre arrived on time. The president never came. After long, futile waiting, the French diplomat was furious and left and departed on March 1 without having seen the president.

The British chargé d'affaires, Thomas Beaumont Hohler, had asked for an audience before starting his term of office, which was scheduled for Popotla, a suburb, on the spot where president Huerta is building himself a house and where he spends most of his time in a construction shack. After 1.5 hours waiting in this very inhospitable environment Mr. Hohler could never learn why the president did not come and whether he even [planned to] come. The British chargé d'affaires thereupon left Popotla and the next day informed the secretary of foreign affairs about the result of the audience.

The U.S. chargé d'affaires is granted appointments but the president does not come. According to O'Shaughnessy, therefore, he follows Huerta with his car and looks for the president in a café, restaurant, or cantina (that is what the lowest pubs are called). If he is lucky he takes care of business with him there: release of incarcerated U.S. prisoners, protest against forced loans. Mr. O'Shaughnessy in confidence tells me that it is impossible for him to touch upon political affairs with the president. As soon as he starts Huerta evades him and the conversation is led toward women and cognac: "I know that you have a lover; my agents recently have seen you leave their houses, etc." [. . .]

Four times in the week before his departure, the British diplomat asked for and received an appointment for an audience, without the president ever showing up. Finally he met him by chance at his private secretary's office.

Also, I had arranged an appointment for March 9 in the National Palace. I wanted to urge the president again [to remember] his promise, given in December 1913 and since then repeated, to pay back the loan forced on Germans in Guaymas. I waited three-quarters of an hour while the private secretary of the president kept me company. Then the president called, apologizing, but he could not come because he is ill. Probably he was drunk.

On the following day, March 10, 6:00 p.m., the president visited me in the legation; however, I was not at home. He left word that he would come back on March 11 at about the same time or would welcome me at the National Palace. I called the palace March 11, at 5:30 and 6:00 p.m., asking if the president was present and received the answer: no!

Thereupon I waited in the legation until 7:00 p.m. He did not come. A few days later, meeting him, I kidded the president about the reliability of his agreements; he excused himself with stomach trouble.

It is a waste of time to insist in front of the president on correctness; also, circles around him state that it is impossible that he will internalize even the most rudimentary customs of civilized comportment.

In the meantime one is forced, off and on, to try to catch him because his diplomats do not work. Some because of negative feelings, or on the other hand because Huerta leaves them no freedom. He talks about his diplomats as "pigs, which he would most immediately prefer to spit on." It cannot be denied that Huerta begins to show traces of megalomania. He is protected against the madness of the alcoholic; Indians rarely succumb to this disease, because of their heavy misuse; instead they fall mostly to becoming fools.[32]

March 24, 1914, Washington DC

A REGULAR DIPLOMATIC REPORT

Mr. Bryan tells me today that newspaper reports about negotiations between Lind and Huerta are invented. The factual situation is unchanged. Bryan still hopes that Villa will capture Torreón,[33] and thereby the Constitutionalists [will obtain a] decisive victory. **Bernstoff**[34]

March 24, 1914, Bern, Switzerland

A REGULAR DIPLOMATIC REPORT

The chief of the Swiss General Staff told me in high confidence that the local military department is negotiating the sale of old cannons and some ammunition to Mexico with the company Schroeder in Antwerp.

Payment offered in Mexican state coupons, which Switzerland rejected at first. Now it turns out that British and French banks—which ones, Mr. von Sprecher did not know—have accepted a larger amount of these coupons. Two mill. pound[s in] Mexican bonds have been deposited in the local cantonal bank through a Mr. Leroi, representative of the French cartridge factory Cartoucherie Francaise; the name sounds something like that. The weapons and ammunition factories are very much interested in the business. The representative of Mr. von Sprecher has gained the impression that the business is in particular encouraged by the British and that Great Britain therefore provides great service to the Huerta government. In case this news is of any interest to us, I could learn more perhaps through local financial circles? **Romberg**[35]

March 25, 1914, Mexico City

A REGULAR DIPLOMATIC REPORT

Per decree, President Huerta has ordered the militarization of officers and the teacher corps and has ordered that the pertinent civilians wear military uniforms while working and carry military titles. Another decree names diplomats as major generals and undersecretaries of state as colonels—for the duration of their time in office. These decrees have been received without enthusiasm; inside the army, it is well known, they are causing bitter criticism. [. . .]

The meaning of Huerta's decrees is: to put above everyone possible the *ordenanza militar* and to pull them out of [the protection] of civilian law with its securities and cumbersome process.[36]

April 8, 1914, Mexico City

A REGULAR DIPLOMATIC REPORT

The government received telegraphic news that Torreón had to be evacuated due to lack of ammunition; [the government] hopes that it can retake it in the next days; it keeps the news secret. **Hintze**[37]

FIG. 26. U.S. president Woodrow Wilson delivers his speech to the U.S. Congress. Courtesy of the Library of Congress.

April 11, 1914, Washington DC

A REGULAR DIPLOMATIC REPORT

After President Wilson connected the Panama Canal toll and the Mexican questions, both topics dominate the local political situation completely; it has become impossible to treat those in my [. . .] report as separate items.[38] As far as Mexico is concerned, in general it is believed that in the near future important decisions will be made. The situation will become more and more intolerable here; however, I assume that President Wilson will wait for the vote in the Senate before taking next steps. Still, one cannot say with certainty whether Mr. Wilson will be able to break the resistance of the [Senate]; however, the senators are in a difficult position. On the one hand they are under the influence of Mr. Wilson's towering personality and are inspired by his wish to avoid a serious break inside the Democratic Party, which would make likely a Republican victory during fall elections. On the other hand it cannot be denied that the resistance against lifting the fee exemption for U.S. shipping companies is growing steadily in the entire country.

Two replacement elections in the House of Representatives that took place last week show this decisively. In Massachusetts the Democratic candidate won, but he considered it wise to express himself in favor of no fees for the coastal shipping business in all of his speeches. In New Jersey a

Democratic candidate was even beaten, and mostly because his Republican opponent strongly exploited the question of the Panama Canal toll. [. . .][39]

On April 9 Huerta's forces in Tampico, in a misunderstanding, had temporarily arrested nine U.S. sailors. In reaction, Admiral Henry Mayo, commander of the U.S. fleet, demanded a Mexican apology in the form of a twenty-one-gun salute to the U.S. flag on Mexican soil.

General Huerta refused. But he let the prisoners go, offered a written apology, and expressed words of regret. As demand for the public honoring of the U.S. flag remained unmet, President Wilson saw himself forced to ask the U.S. Congress on April 20, 1914, to authorize the use of force to produce, if necessary, the demanded act of Mexican contrition.

April 20, 1914, Washington DC

A REGULAR DIPLOMATIC REPORT

President Wilson, to lively applause, read to Congress and the galleries his message. It reports the situation in quick fashion and says that the Tampico incident was not a single event. Therefore the president had to demand public satisfaction so that such incidents are not repeated.

He had no intention to conduct a war with Mexico. U.S. strictures were directed only against Huerta, who, without legal justification, calls himself president. At the very end Wilson asked for authority to use the armed might of the United States in order to receive appropriate satisfaction.

Today or tomorrow Congress will pass the requested resolution. It is expected to be given unanimously. At least, that is how the mood was that I just saw in Congress. **Bernstorff**[40]

On April 21 U.S. blue jackets and marines landed in Veracruz and occupied Mexican port facilities.

April 22, 1914, Mexico City

A REGULAR DIPLOMATIC REPORT

The secretary of state called on His Excellency, the German ambassador, at 7:15, April 21, 1914, to say that Admiral Fletcher had, today, through a misunderstanding, exceeded his instructions and notified the captain of a German merchant ship not to leave the harbor of Veracruz with ammunitions of war consigned to or for General Huerta.[41] Admiral Fletcher has been instructed to call upon the captain of the ship and present an apology and explanation.

While the United States hopes that the ammunition intended for General Huerta will be unloaded at the Veracruz customshouse, so that after landing the U.S. government may detain it, still the U.S. government does not claim the right—as a state of war does not exist—to interfere with the ship's departure or to exercise control over said ammunitions of war unless they are delivered at a wharf or customshouse controlled by the United States. The secretary of state, by direction of the president, offered through the German ambassador the apology and explanation that Admiral Fletcher was instructed to offer to the captain of the ship.[42]

April 23, 1914, Hamburg

A REGULAR DIPLOMATIC REPORT

One part of the weapons on the *Ypiranga*, in particular Winchester guns and cartridges, had originally been loaded onto another ship in New York with Odessa [Russia] as the destination. And from there onto a Levante steamer, and there on the *Ypiranga*.[43]

By April 25, 1914, the *Ypiranga* would arrive in the port of Veracruz, carrying ammunition and weapons.

A REGULAR DIPLOMATIC REPORT

House Joint Resolution 251, 63rd Congress

Joint Resolution Justifying the Employment by the President of the Armed Forces of the United States.

In view of the facts presented by the President of the United States in his address delivered to Congress in joint session on the 20th day of April 1914, with regard to certain affronts and indignities committed against the United States in Mexico:

Be it resolved by the Senate and House of Representatives of the United States of America in Congress assembled, that the President is justified in the employment of the armed forces of the United States to enforce his demands for unequivocal amends for certain affronts and indignities committed against the United States.

Be it further resolved, that the United States disclaims any hostility to the Mexican people or any purpose to make war upon Mexico. Approved April 22, 1914.[44]

This was an ex post facto action because U.S. forces had occupied Veracruz a day before.

4

Toppling the Mad Tyrant

A DAY-BY-DAY ACCOUNT OF AN ORDEAL

Friday, April 24, 1914

At 8:00 a.m. the train is supposed to leave for Coatzacoalcos with refugees of all nations, except U.S. citizens.[1] Turns out that the idea of Coatzacoalcos [as the destination] existed only inside the Foreign Ministry; the secretary of war always thought only about the Ferrocarril-Mexicano line [traveling between] Mexico-Soledad-Veracruz. About thirty Germans are traveling. The day before they registered at 7:00 p.m. with the travel committee.

Many U.S. citizens are attempting to travel under the protection of the German flag. For example, one miner named Wienzer from El Oro with wife and six children, but he cannot prove his citizenship and apparently is a U.S. citizen. In the same way a certain Kissel with two women, of unknown origin, who speaks only broken German; he maintains he has served but does not know where; he states he has been at the legislation [*sic*; he meant "legation"] on April 23 at 7:30 p.m.—that is untrue, because if he refers to the *Gesandschaft* [embassy], it was staffed until 11:00 p.m. Both were rejected [and told] to go to the train at their own risk. Both were rejected by the Mexican officer in charge because they are U.S. citizens and because they are not on the legation's list. I vouch for a Seelbach family based on the assurance of Mr. Heynen.[2] The train does not leave not until 3:00 p.m.; on board are twenty-three Germans, most of them [from the] middle social classes. At night the train remains in Orizaba in order to give the women and children an opportunity to sleep. There are 162 English on board. The rest are French, Austrians, Italians, and Mexicans. Based on information from the British legation, more than 100 British departed on the morning of the twenty-third and more than 150 the evening of the twenty-second. The Mexican officer in charge rejects everyone who is not on the list from the legation; also all U.S. citizens who incorrectly travel under the German or British flag.

9:30 A.M.

The telegraph service stops. The cable to Galveston has been interrupted. On the twenty-third the train, including the refugees who left for Soledad at eight o'clock in the morning, is being sent back by General Maas. On either leg no German was on board. "Deutz" is a U.S. citizen who had been believed to be a German.

11:30 A.M.

I visit the Foreign Ministry and win permission for a new train to go to the east coast on April 25; furthermore, I sign a letter of protection for the threatened German C. Heynen. Furthermore, [I arrange] the nonconfiscation—which had been threatened—of machine guns and the weapons of the self-defense organization; finally, [I] stop the searches of German houses for weapons.

López Portillo is entirely demoralized.[3] He admits that news about rebels joining with Huerta had been a fraud.[4] He was convinced that Carranza had reached an understanding with the United States. Now he recognizes the United States' political plan:

The north will be given to the rebels. . . . In the center [the United States] . . . will attack. Even if the Tampico incident would not have occurred, the United States would have used a different event to start trouble. There exists a *state of war*; the Mexican note from April 20, 1913, should be understood this way.

Huerta insists he will be able to hold out for one year without supply of money or war matériel. López puts his hopes on *Ypiranga* incident.

3:00 P.M.

[The German] von Bluecher declines to lead the self-defense organization for military reasons. Von Papen takes over.[5]

The English diplomat has a telegram from Spring-Rice:[6] "Bryan attempted to reach an agreement with Carranza, but the latter protested against occupation of Mexican territory."

Carden explains the Mexican government would remain firm in keeping U.S. citizens who want to leave Mexico. Also, Carden remarked about great demoralization.

FIG. 27. Emiliano Zapata with his staff. Courtesy of the Library of Congress.

I wire to transmission office: a cable has been cut by the United States west of Veracruz (line drawn in air). I telegraph Coatzacoalcos using the land telegraph and demand information whether wire service is working from there.

I visit López Portillo: military reasons demand train departure early [on the] twenty-sixth, not twenty-fifth. News is incorrect alleging that Pánfilo Natera has signed on with Huerta;[7] neither has Zapata. The amnesty pardoning all political criminals has not shown success hoped for. Fact is that the rebels insist on their insurrection, and this will play into the hands of the United States.

Apparently the U.S. plan consists of isolating the government of General Huerta. In the evening: departure from city. Rainy weather, thus all is quiet.

Saturday, April 25, 1914, Mexico City

The train with fifty Germans on board that left on the evening of the twenty-second has made it successfully to Tejeria. From there, for about 1 km, the rails have been taken off the bed. Once the rails resumed [were replaced], a train appeared under the leadership of British admiral Craddock, who brought the refugees to Veracruz.[8] The train that left Mexico

City on the morning of April 25 has also arrived in good state. On board were no Germans, only a German-American named Deutz. Deutz states they had been exposed to all kinds of rude treatment. Deutz is being sent back because he is a U.S. citizen.

I visit the boardinghouses and houses serving food where Germans without means reside. I provide information about the situation and about the possibility of leaving town or finding safety in the city.

1:30 P.M.

I visit the Foreign Ministry. The secretary of state says Huerta is absolutely calm, even though the news is very bad. Since all wire services are controlled by the United States, no possibility exists of approaching the European powers to end the conflict. I say that I wired the *Dresden* to ask if it could establish connection with any cable service. But no answer.

In the future military and police would accompany demonstrations and the press would be muzzled. Government troops at Torreón are supposed to have been beaten back; already they are stationed at Saltillo; General Velasco has been hurt. General Peña fell in battle. The military situation there is supposed to be hopeless.

The president lifted the prohibition preventing U.S. citizens from leaving the country so that the public's ill will will not hit all foreigners without exception. President received news from Veracruz that U.S. troops have shot women and children. These reports are published daily in a bulletin.

However, Secretary of Communication Lozano and Huerta do not favor inciting the press, but [in the end] Huerta is supposed to have given in.[9]

In the city, revolutionaries are intensely industrious—distributing rumors—but they lack weapons and organization. The governor of the Federal District is alleged to be prepared to squash unrest. All in all López Portillo talks very much with trepidation. I express my doubt about the possibility of resistance because the government lacks weapons, money, and soldiers. Public opinion is turning against it.

3:00 P.M.

Orizaba Hirsch, who had departed from Veracruz on Wednesday, brings the attached report about the occupation of Veracruz. It states that it represents a theatrical coup. The proclamation of Admiral Fletcher is indicative: to inspect the administration. Fletcher executed the coup before

Badger arrived with the large fleet.[10] Hirsch states that twelve thousand men are stationed from Veracruz to Tejeria. Twelve thousand men are supposed to still be on the ships; all infantry and artillery, no cavalry.

The *Ypiranga* is supposed to be tied up at wooden quay with refugees on board. The railroad brought them to about Tejeria. The destruction of the rails was executed rather incompletely for about 2.5 km. Near Soledad, a new train accepted them. Arrival in Mexico City on Saturday, April 25, at noon. In Veracruz all is calm.

3:40 P.M.

Siemens-Schuckert Company notes that the government was about to confiscate its forty Protos automobiles. I accompany representatives going to the garage of General Vinegas, *jefe de los transportes militares*. After I speak to him, he declares the confiscation to be an error or a lie; he rescinds all respective orders.

I arrange with Vinegas that the train should travel to the east coast each morning. I go to railroad station Buena Vista; I ask for the opening of the order of General Vinegas, which declares that the train should depart early April 26.

I visit Mexicans of distinction. They are a group of about fifty Mexicans: patriots of important rank stating that the moment has come to propose abdication to Huerta in exchange for some satisfaction of his vanity (he steps down for the benefit of the nation); guarantee for his life; and assurance, or rather payments, of a few millions. A junta composed of new men is then supposed to make peace with the United States. And at that point it would be desirable to hear opinions from the diplomatic corps. I emphasize that the diplomatic corps can act only discreetly and in [the spirit] of friendship in favor of Huerta, as well as Mexico, in hours of highest trepidation. Mexicans who are involved emphasize that the revolutionaries in the city lack organization and weapons.

I visit the English diplomat. *He has entirely changed his position*: Huerta should abdicate. The United States should be confronted with the demand that all governmental acts should be legalized. In no uncertain terms, that means legalization of all concessions for the British that Carden has received for his rabid backing of Huerta. The moment is close when one should speak with Huerta, [saying,] "It would be folly to stick to a course that is no longer useful."

He complains that Washington DC did not recognize him as deputy diplomat: "I am up in the air." I visited López Portillo, who reports failed attempts to win over the rebels.

7:30 P.M.

Information that the train should run early on the twenty-sixth at 7:00 a.m.. I arranged with railroad manager Morcom that departure should be dragged out to eight o'clock, because it is impossible to inform German passengers [about the change in time] now.

April 25, in the morning, a demonstration at Escuela Agricola honoring Germany. I am out and about. The Mexican government takes away the weapons held by the English and French communities; the ones they had lent them for self-defense. This reveals how useful it was, then, to buy weapons for the German community.

April 26, 1914, Sunday, Mexico City

7:00 A.M.

The train with refugees is supposed to depart. About thirty Germans and sixty-seven British are coming. The train to Soledad leaves at 8:30 a.m. I send along a German flag for the train carrying the Germans.

During the day I try to speak to Mexican secretary of state. Allegedly [he] is with the president. However, I learn that the president removed himself and remains impossible for his secretary of state to locate. At twelve I visit the *jefe de los transportes militares* and receive approval for Monday, April 27, for two trains: one at 7:50 a.m. via Interoceanic to St. Francisco (north of Antigua), and the other at 7:00 a.m. through Ferrocarril Mexicano to Soledad. It was announced in the German house.

3:00 P.M.

News arrives that, temporarily, the cable can be used. The United States had cut the direct Mexico-Galveston cable in Veracruz. They intercepted the telegrams coming from Mexico and held back those they could not read or that appeared disconcerting. The Mexicans realized this through the usual chatter of telegraph employees and, therefore, cut 1 km of aboveground cable line. Today the aboveground line has been repaired because they realized how much they had damaged themselves.

Informally they reached an understanding with the United States to resume overseas traffic.

I informed the [German] Foreign Ministry about the events of the last few days. In the meantime, from Coatzacoalcos arrives a U.S. secretary of state telegram cable stating that Washington DC does *not* consider current status to be state of war. Expressly, the Mexican government has declared a state of war in a statement in *Imparcial*.

Nevertheless, it did not bring about a necessary constitutional finding through Congress. My Mexican friends want to bring about such a resolution in Congress. I counsel peace.

Since the United States does not want events to be recognized as an act of war, the only possibility remains a statement that Admiral Fletcher acted prematurely without order. First, to prevent the weapons and ammunition of the *Ypiranga* from reaching land; and second, to deprive Admiral Badger, who is leading the largest segment of the fleet, of gaining fame from his action. Thus Washington seems to be trying now to find a formula for the events that avoids the word "war" and its existence. If this is so, U.S. citizens would remain quiet. And in Veracruz both sides would work toward an understanding.

The British diplomat says he has knowledge of a clash between Huerta and Blanquet. I use a personal presentation to the chief of the telegraph office to cable the Foreign Office through *Nürnberg*.[11]

The [Mexican] secretary of state receives an offer of goodwill mediation services from Brazil, Argentina, and Chile and accepts, invoking his own responsibility, because, once again, the president cannot be found. He reaches the president only at four in the afternoon, who, after long resistance, gives his approval.

Monday, April 27, 1914, Mexico City

At 9:30 the representatives of Protos, von Drateln and Grabau, arrive with a letter from the secretary of war that states: president of republic empowers General Vinegas to commission eighteen automobiles. I went with both to secretary of foreign relations. Nobody is at the ministry! Following a phone call, López Portillo arrives at 10:45. After [we] explain the case to him, he calls secretary of war, asking that he stop all further efforts until he has a talk with him.

López Portillo accepts [letter] copy of my objection and letter from secretary of war. He is about to go see secretary of war as British diplomat enters, accompanied by a British commander. He presents a letter [in] a sealed envelope for the president of the republic.

Today just as yesterday: no Germans apply for [places on] trains.

I advised Consul Gertz, in Veracruz, through telegram and letter:

A. Call *Constancia* with refugees to Veracruz at the end of April.
B. Refugees wanting to go to Galveston should embark on *Ypiranga*.
C. *Ypiranga* should ask *Dania*, Tampico, to pick up refugees who want to go to Galveston.
D. *Ypiranga* moves to Galveston and then returns to Veracruz.

Brazilian diplomat: for a long time he has been instructed to take over U.S. embassy in case of break of diplomatic relations. On the twenty-fourth of the month he was quite surprised that the English diplomat had taken over the job. [He is] amazed but also very content about this, because it is a very unappreciated task. Now, however, he received anew the instruction from his government and, at the same time, instructions from Bryan to take over U.S. affairs, and now he would have to believe them. He felt embarrassed to take away the business from Carden, but why had he taken them over?

Already on the evening of April 25 he had received the mediation offer from Brazil, Chile, and Argentina. He had informed López Portillo about it on April 26, who accepted it immediately. Washington also accepted. But negotiations will be held in Washington because here no Chilean or Argentine representatives are present.

Right away López Portillo has conceded to him as "entrée en matière" approval to emigrate for all U.S. citizens. The Brazilian diplomat emphasized he was counting on my participation. I ask for Washington's conditions that here are still unknown. I suspect that one of the conditions will be Huerta's resignation. The Brazilian diplomat feared that this might cause negotiations to fail. I suggest building him "a door of honor richly covered in gold" because, otherwise, he was unlikely to go.

The French diplomat visits me and suggests we work together. He feels, here, German and French interests are identical but not equal to a third power [Great Britain].

The Mexican Foreign Ministry reports that in the future Protos garage (Siemens Schuckert) should be spared from requisitions. Purchases will take place only in exchange for cash.

The extra train for U.S. citizens, scheduled for 6:00 p.m., is not becoming reality.

I visit a few boardinghouses and meeting halls where less-well-off Germans are living.

A well-informed source tells me that Guasque, general inspector of police, has been removed from office, and Huerta entrusted this post to one of his creatures, "a criminal"; that Huerta under Lozano's influence wants to organize plundering and military unrest. On the other hand, news is increasing that a *cuartelazo* is once again being prepared. The latest motto is: "The revolution is inside the city."

Tuesday, April 28, 1914, Mexico City

I inspected the Japanese and German [self-defense] weapons depots. I recognize the danger of Germans who are not protected like the Japanese through the presence of a diplomatic chancellery.[12] In an exchange, I ask the secretary of foreign relations to leave untouched the weapons depot of the German community, of which I gave him a list on April 18. He hands me a letter addressed to the governor of the Federal District, who supports this request. Iturbide gives the respective order to the police. López Portillo tells me:

A. On the twenty-seventh, at lunch, all South American country representatives in Washington gathered in order to back the mediation proposal of the ABC countries [Argentina, Brazil, and Chile];

B. The representatives of the European powers are reported to have convened during the evening of the same day.

C. The rebels continue to lead in war against Huerta (Huerta counters: rebels in the south have switched sides to him, rebels in the north are in the process of thinking about their situation).

D. Mexico's second secretary, who remained behind in Washington, wired that Wilson has ordered commanders to refrain from all acts of hostility; only defensive measures are allowed to be taken.

E. Any kind of a basis for negotiations has not been created; Mexico will not take the initiative but awaits U.S. proposals.

F. The condition: Huerta must go! is alleged to be unacceptable.

G. Bryan is supposed to have stated to the Brazilian ambassador in Washington the respective note only. The people in Mexico City control affairs there; apparently Washington wants to circumvent Huerta's recognition. But this one is a given because the union is, indeed, negotiating with Huerta via mediation.

H. The letter that the British commander presented yesterday contained only private letters for some individuals in the city and no political matters. He asked for support during the expected negotiations.

The French chargé d'affaires is supposed to have heard that Washington has dropped the demand for elimination of Huerta. Later he energetically denies sharing this opinion. The Brazilian diplomat is very weighed down by the responsibility burdening him: the negotiations. At the Brazilian legation news has arrived from Bryan via ambassador to present the removal of Huerta as condition sine qua non without particular demands.

General Vinegas makes available a train to Soledad (Veracruz) for April 29, seven a.m. Several Germans, about twelve, are supposed to travel, among them glassblowers with their families from Texcoco.

Mr. Ayguésparse, through his Mexican brother-in-law, was able to see the president.[13] He explained to him that a solution to the entire conflict would come about through concessions. Huerta took this as if Ayguésparse was speaking about him stepping down and used words and gestures to protest against it: "Honor above everything, sir!" He also has not given the impression that Huerta should leave the capital.

During the night from the twenty-seventh to the twenty-eighth, six military trains have been sent from Mexico and Pueblo. They carried troops and war matériel; perhaps the core of the army that remains to be assembled to fight against U.S. troops.

The National Palace has been filled with war supplies and ammunition, and later also with cannons. I learn from the Mexicans, who are well-informed, that the higher classes (the intellectuals) are waiting for the masses to turn away from Huerta after the initial enthusiasm of the first days. They feel deceived by him.

Huerta feels this chill and wants to win back the masses by releasing some foreign businesses to them for looting; therefore Guasque's removal from office.

Guasque opposed it and the offer of stepping down by Governor Iturbide. The new inspector of police, Quiroz, is capable and willing to do anything; an authentic son-in-law (Fuentes) commands the mounted police, so he is being seen as "in the family."

Wednesday, April 29, 1914, Mexico City

A REGULAR DIPLOMATIC REPORT

I ask the *Ypiranga* to take refugees not to Galveston but to Mobile, Alabama, based on news from consul in Veracruz saying that New Orleans and Galveston have been put on quarantine for six days.

Mobile—at high tide, twenty-seven inches, twenty-two inches at low tide—is easily reachable for the *Ypiranga*. Garcia, the superintendent of the wire-cable office, does me the favor of running by me the telegrams from and to Veracruz. I informed German Foreign Ministry and asked for the acceptance of refugees and care in Mobile, Alabama. I also inform consul in Veracruz and ask him before *Ypiranga*'s departure for examinations by a U.S. Navy doctor and for issuance of U.S. health certificates.

In this sense I informed consul in Tampico and the *Dresden*, also the consulate agent in Puerto México and captain of the steamer *Constantine*. The consul of Colima informs me that two thousand refugees of all nationalities have left on the German steamer *Marie* and the British steamer *Cetriana*.

Brazilian diplomat seeks advice about broken relationship with British diplomat Sir Lionel Garden. For months it has been a public secret that it is true that the U.S. government has remained with the Brazilian government.

That in case of rupture of diplomatic relations Brazil is supposed to take over U.S. representation. When O'Shaughnessy, at his departure (April 23, eleven o'clock in the evening), handed affairs to Carden contrary to this agreement, the Brazilian diplomat Oliveira had wondered but did not say anything.[14]

Already on April 25, in Washington, he was supposed to have received orders from Bryan and the Brazilian ambassador, and he reported back that

FIG. 28. British diplomat Sir Lionel Carden. Courtesy of the Library of Congress.

Carden had taken over affairs. Then he received the reply: O'Shaughnessy has acted without instructions. He is urgently asked to take over immediately the United States' affairs, embassy, and archive. On April 26 this order was repeated. He, Oliveira, however, believed that Carden should have initiated the first step. When Carden did nothing he took heart on April 27 and asked Carden to hand over U.S. affairs to him, producing Bryan's many orders. Carden offered a short reply. He reproached Olivera in the most impolite way.

The British ambassador is supposed to have been asked to request Carden to hand over business to Oliveira immediately. Oliveira complained bitterly about Carden; according to the official announcements that he [Carden] made to him on the twenty-seventh, Carden is communicating with him only through an officer of the chancellery. Also, he has not asked him to at least be present at the departure of the four hundred U.S. refugees who moved toward Coatzacoalcos. Thus Olivera appears inactive and incapable vis-à-vis the U.S. community. When asked by Olivera, I advise he act with extreme correctness and a lot of patience.

The English diplomat tells me in the presence of Rodriguez Parra, *introducteur des ambassadors*: yesterday evening he got rid of his four hundred U.S. "ansciecitos" [*sic*; pant-wetters]. As far as the ones still remaining in the country, "their blood may come on their own heads." He accompanied this description with a gesture of a kick. This caused an expression of great joy from the Mexican, who was not any prettier than his words. Once again the wire cable is interrupted. "A nonauthorized person" brought it back in service at 4:00 p.m. The English diplomat is kept up to date, just like the Japanese ambassador, by his government, and he reads the few telegrams from Washington.

1. Constitutionalists are viewed by the United States with mistrust; about five days ago (about April 24), the United States again prohibited export of weapons and war matériel to Mexico. And also to the rebels.
2. Woodrow Wilson is very relieved by the offer of mediation.
3. Wood is angry about mediation and predicts that Huerta will keep him at arm's length until the rainy season starts and operation becomes impossible.
4. The U.S. Army is lacking 40 percent of its manpower and ammunition, in particular artillery.
5. Woodrow Wilson is supposed to have expressed delight to have received a letter from Villa.
6. Public opinion is against intervention but will support war and administration, if war becomes unavoidable.

In my opinion that hasty acceptance of mediation is one of those tacks that, based on experience, the United States grants itself and can afford, thanks to isolation and strength.

Secretary of foreign relations answers when asked. He says rebels are making joint cause with United States. He claims that Monterrey and Saltillo have not yet fallen. He feels that the United States' first demand will be the removal of Huerta. This demand is unacceptable and nondebatable. López Portillo asked me for advice, how we would behave in the conflict between Carden and Olivera. He is on Oliveira's side. I advised: stay out of it. Don't get involved; wait until Carden receives the order to hand over business, etc., in case it has not already happened; it should happen sometime today or tomorrow, Oliveira states. Already Carden has received the respective order.

In the evening between eight and nine I gave the German colony a one-hour-long speech. I described the particular situation and gave advice for future behavior. It had a calming effect.

The curious fact is that Carden, once again, changes his position. Once again he is more Huertista than Huerta. Yesterday, on April 28, he saw Huerta and *according to his own words* asked him to pretend to enter into mediation negotiations. This way the rainy season would start before the United States could undertake action—such as to advance into the interior. Huerta himself should treat the question of his stepping down in a dilatory and ambiguous way.

In case Huerta engages, the current situation can draw itself out endlessly. Huerta receives from the Light and Power Company and from Pearson's Petroleum Corporation, both British enterprises—partially voluntarily, partially forced—the daily funds to pay police and the few troops that are staying in the capital. During the night from April 27 to 28 a Spanish diplomat cabled, following an urgent request by the Mexican government to tell the Spanish ambassador in Washington who represents Mexican interests there: to take up negotiations. The *condition* sine qua non to take up negotiations is a truce; in particular an immediate one by the United States and the rebels.

Monterey has fallen into rebel hands; in contrast, Saltillo and San Luis Potosí are still in hands of Federales.

Steamer *Constantine* has been ordered from Puerto México to Veracruz. Hohler, the previous British chargé d'affaires, visits me and complains that Carden is entirely back into his old ways and is more Huertista than ever. "He fights any suggestion of mine as he knows that I absolutely differ with him." When he had been chargé d'affaires he had told Huerta di-

FIG. 29. Victoriano Huerta in a suspicious mood. Courtesy of the Library of Congress.

rectly that it is in the British interest to maintain good relations with the current government of Mexico. But it is not in the British interest who governs Mexico or is president there. Huerta understood that entirely. I told Hohler in confidence that Carden's accident lends itself to prolonging indefinitely the current jinxed situation. Huerta might imagine again that he could count on British help. Hohler agrees without reservation and regrets being unable to influence Carden. He does not share anything with him and does not involve him.

The agent of the Hamburg America Line seeks neutralization of the Tehuantepec Railroad.[15] Upon inquiring, I answer regarding this issue. British ambassador is exploring the issue in Washington.

I don't know if Germany has an interest in pulling the chestnuts out of the fire for Great Britain. The respective railroad is one of the reasons for U.S. policy vis-à-vis Mexico and competition with the Panama Canal. I cabled [this explanation] to the Foreign Ministry. Midday, the news arrives through Brazilian ambassador da Gama that the United States accepts the condition of "a total truce."[16] In the afternoon, a telegram from the same, according to which Carranza agrees to stop hostilities under the condition that he is admitted as a party to the mediation meetings. Immediately the Huerta government accepts the condition. It is a sign that it continues to weaken.

In the evening Secretary of Finance de la Lama visits and informs me confidentially that "the order has been given to all sides to stop hostilities."

At nine I talk with the Brazilian delegate. Afterward I went with him to Secretary of War General Blanquet. Initially I pushed him to order by telegram the release of the U.S. citizen Bryant. He had been arrested in Zacatecas, allegedly because of espionage, and is supposed to be executed tomorrow morning (May 1). After his release he is supposed to be made available in Mexico City at the disposition of the secretary of war.

We used this opportunity to talk with Blanquet in confidence. First, we praised in most glowing colors the achievements and steadfastness of General Huerta. Little by little we moved to say that every man has his time in history. After that we used detailed information to prove the impossibility for Mexico to conduct a war: no soldiers, no officers, no weapons, no ammunition, no gold. We suggest in veiled fashion that the United States' foreseeable demand for reaching an understanding would be Huerta's removal. We don't know that for a fact but we have reason to suspect it. Eventually, once the United States steps forward with this demand, it would be difficult for Huerta to give in without being humiliated. However, if he would step down voluntarily, before any such demand has been presented, then he could claim as his own a major patriotic role: he is stepping down, trying to prevent his country from ruin and an unfortunate war. Doing so, he should be clear that he has not been defeated but that he resigned from his post for the good of the nation. He would defend his position with his life but the well-being of his people ranked higher than his own life. Etc., etc., [we] expand in that direction.

Blanquet edged toward this stance very slowly. He understands that action is required before the United States demands Huerta's resignation. The focus needs to be on finding the form to make it easier for Huerta to step down. He repeats, in about the same way, the same arguments that I had explained repeatedly to López Portillo. Proof that the diplomats had already exchanged views about making efforts to [have Huerta] step down. (This is confirmed to me confidentially.)

Later I learn that Lozano, secretary of transport and communication, and Moheno, the secretary of trade, are against it. Blanquet says verbatim: "War does not suit us," and he agrees that Huerta *should go* before the United States makes the demand. We appeal to him, both being comrades of war. And [we] tell him: *he*, Blanquet, would be the right man to get this through to Huerta. Right away Blanquet replied with his own carefully chosen words what he wants to tell Huerta. [He plans] to speak [always using the informal *tu*] with a loud voice that old people tend to use. We replied that we would find out and tell him if, indeed, the United States would demand Huerta's resignation. We assure him discretion and friendship and depart. Blanquet reports: Huerta has to step down "for the public good." He confirms that the total cessation of all hostilities has been ordered by him, the United States and rebels; and the rebels also needed it because of all their incredible losses. Finance secretary de la Lama says there is no future with Huerta.

The Brazilian diplomat and I have the impression that, if necessary, Blanquet would force Huerta to resign. My urging convinces Oliveira to wire Ambassador da Gama, at 11:00 p.m., [to ask] whether the United States demands the resignation of Huerta. He also explains the importance of discrete treatment of all their demands based on the talk with Blanquet.

Today I drive German glass workers from Texcoco to Veracruz; I hand them a safe-passage letter for the representative who will receive them in the United States.

A REGULAR DIPLOMATIC REPORT

[German ambassador Bernstorff to German Foreign Ministry]

Mr. Bryan told me today that Carranza has accepted mediation of ABC powers. Therefore one could look forward to a general truce.

British ambassador received telegram from Sir E. Grey, according to whom ABC states had sought England, Germany, France to pressure Wilson so that he makes concessions. Sir E. Grey rejected it, since interference inopportune because Wilson certainly will insist on Huerta's resignation.

The British ambassador and I agree that any other answer is impossible. Mediation will fail because, under all circumstances, Wilson demands Huerta's removal. Local government wishes war, with the exception of Bryan. However, only a so-called small war with the support of the Constitutionalists. In spite of probable failure the ABC mediation has achieved its main task, to prove to the United States their solidarity. **Bernstorff** [17]

Friday, May 1, 1914, Mexico City

This morning the British diplomat informs the Brazilian diplomat that he will visit him early in the morning to hand him the diplomatic representation of U.S. affairs. Cardoso waits until twelve o'clock lunch. Since Carden does not come, he goes to the Foreign Ministry. As he leaves he runs into Carden, who claims to have just visited him. On the spot Carden hands him the affairs and assures Cardoso of his support.

Cardoso produces from Bryan a thank you to Carden for the temporary takeover of affairs. And he cables to the Brazilian ambassador: with the exception of Carden the entire diplomatic corps supports it. [Carden] was working against him.

The Foreign Ministry informed that Bryan thinks of the mediation as a means to remove Huerta and to install a new government in Mexico.

Brazilian diplomat Cardoso, and Rees, based on the order from Bryan, searches the U.S. embassy for weapons that might be there.

López Portillo reports:

FIG. 30. Brazilian diplomat J. M. Cardoso. Courtesy of the Library of Congress.

1. In the morning of the thirtieth, 10:00 a.m., President Huerta
   officially posts his condition to agree to negotiations: "that the
   United States make the rebels put down their weapons."
2. 5:00 p.m., the answer is supposed to have arrived that rebels
   are willing to do so, under the condition that [Carranza] will be
   admitted as a party to the negotiations. He—López Portillo—
   without commentary, is supposed to have given this cable to

Huerta. He was not willing to take over the responsibility for his decision to move in this potential direction. [Then he reports] that Huerta asked twice to have the cable read to him. Then he exclaimed, "Well, that is exactly what we wanted this morning"—followed by the order to stop hostilities.

3. Yesterday evening, April 30, the council of cabinet secretaries is supposed to have taken place without tangible success. A new council gathering has been called for 9:00 a.m. All secretaries reported to be present—only the president was absent, even impossible to locate. After 1.5 hours of waiting around the president is supposed to have announced, from an unknown location, that he wants to see the diplomats at 1:00 p.m., afternoon.

4. For about three or four days he and the majority of the cabinet have been working toward Huerta's voluntary resignation. Lozano is alleged to have been won over and completely changed sides. A few cabinet secretaries are against it. Nobody has the courage to speak up.

5. He—López Portillo—a few days ago, had received a cable from a leading U.S. citizen, a true friend of Mexico, which states that he sees Huerta's resignation as the only possibility. López Portillo handed the cable without commentary to Huerta, who never mentioned it with a single word.

I ponder the situation. On the one hand Mexico's inability to wage war; and the result of such an unfortunate war: [is] the existence of the Mexican nation and state. On the other hand, the personal interest of a single man who tried his best to give peace to his country. But he shipwrecked in that effort. In a lively fashion, López Portillo declares, "Exactly like that, that is how the situation is." I explained that the problem needs to be defined: to convince Huerta of this election and to free him of the idea that his staying [in office] is in the interest of the Republic of Mexico.

Already, he [has] weakened his usual summary of Mexican interests. On April 30 he specified, "Nobody has the right to interfere in Mexico's internal affairs," when he himself [had] personally sought out the United States and asked it to stop hostilities. Since then he has dropped the principle that he can no longer maintain. The United States or the mediating powers must avoid bringing up the question of Huerta's resignation as an item of negotiation. Because if this happens, Huerta's narcissism would be hurt and he would resist pressure, no matter where it comes from. It would be a different matter if he would declare, out of his own free will: "his goal and that of his government has been to give peace to the country. His effort had not been rewarded with success, therefore he is resigning; . . ."

I said he could and he should reserve for himself all rights in regard to the future: such as being a candidate in the next election and demanding all kinds of guarantees for his life and property. López Portillo agreed and said, "If only you would speak to the president in such a way!" I agree to do it in a friendly way, not as a diplomat, but as an old military man who wants to make it easier for him to find an honorable exit from a difficult situation.

The Mexican government requests as commissioner for the mediations Esteva Ruiz, undersecretary of the Spanish embassy in Washington DC. Not a good choice. Allegedly he is a lawyer but not a diplomat.

On April 30, 1914, the Mexico City and Oaxaca archbishops held a one-hour meeting with Huerta and counseled temperance. After the talk Huerta received the former governor of Sonora, Garcia, with the words, "I have very joyful news for you: the rebels have stopped hostilities."

The cities of Laredo and Porfirio Díaz have been taken by the rebels.[18] (Garcia Cuella). In my estimation, Huerta, after apparently agreeing to negotiations, did so with only one goal [in mind] : to win time. During the cease-fire he hopes to generate money, weapons, ammunition, and an army. This is an idea with a pathological streak.

At 1:00 p.m. the president ordered the cabinet diplomats to gather in Chapultepec for a meeting. López Portillo told me about it. After waiting half an hour a message arrived by telephone that the president was having breakfast in a restaurant at Chapultepec Park and he wished to see the cabinet secretaries there. They all went there. Huerta talked with one or two but he accepted no advice and soon he signaled good-bye. López Portillo approached and told him: as far as admitting the rebels to negotiations—an offer they had received—the answer to this question remains open. Huerta supposedly answered that López Portillo should be so kind as to visit him at 6:00 p.m. to receive the answer. López P. went to the Foreign Ministry to work at 5:00 p.m. Then cabinet members de

FIG. 31. Mexican secretary of state José López Portillo y Roja.
Courtesy of the Library of Congress.

la Lama, Alcocer (ministry of interior), and Lozano (ministry of communication) appeared and asked him, in the president's name, to announce his resignation. López Portillo attributes this demand to the fact that, in the morning, he had talked to Lozano about the expected U.S. condition that Huerta should resign and Lozano carried it right to the president. López [Portillo] expressed his joy to be relieved of his post.

The same evening Cardoso learned that the notes from the mediating powers remain unanswered. [He also learned about] the rebels' admission to the negotiations under conditions Huerta had demanded and the dismissal of López Portillo. He cabled Ambassador da Gama that, from his point of view, Huerta had given his agreement, *indirectly* and informally—perhaps through the Spanish ambassador—and that Huerta was acting in bad faith. And that he thinks the mediation has failed.

In the evening, around 10:00 p.m., legation secretary Velasquez, employed in the protocol section, brings the former deputy to me with a request for asylum. Referring to international law, I explain the limits of my [ability] to grant asylum. But since both declare that henchmen are already on their heels—and as soon as they leave the house they would be murdered, just as were the former deputies Mangel, Rojas, and a third one—I provide shelter for the time being based on the law of nations.

Saturday, May 2, 1914, Mexico City

I suggest the reopening of the mail service, because hostilities have ceased. The Spanish diplomat has a telegram from the Spanish ambassador in Washington stating that, already, representatives of Huerta *and Carranza* are participating in the mediation negotiations. Furthermore, Bryan is supposed to have answered, when Huerta demanded an end of hostilities, that the United States was not in a war against Mexico. They were only occupying Veracruz. Cólogan believes that a catastrophe is imminent, similar to the one of February 18, 1913.

The Japanese representative believes that mediation has failed. He too has a cable from the ambassador in Washington stating that delegates of Carranza have been admitted to the negotiations. The British diplomat [is] once again under Huerta's influence, even though he insists, "I know pretty well how to handle him." He declares López Portillo's firing as completely "silly." He hopes Huerta will appoint Lascuraín as secretary of foreign affairs. In this way the U.S. public will see that Huerta wants to resign and to reestablish the status quo ante before Madero's murder. I answer, "Yes, there are still believers." In addition, Carden reads me a telegram from the British ambassador in Washington, according to which Carrancistas have stopped hostilities and are participating in negotiations. Carden hopes that Villa will not approve of the latter and will split from Carranza. "Here Huerta ought to drive in the thin edge of the wedge!" Sir Lionel praises Velasco's army, which has withdrawn to Saltillo; even though General Salas, undersecretary of war, told me: [the army] is so "demoralized that it is not [even] able to fence."

In short: this is entirely the old Carden and, before his trip to London, inspired entirely by glowing hatred against the United States and, through Huerta, his longing to be able to play a trick against them. He told Huerta to play this card well and the United States would fall for his trick. No doubt President Woodrow Wilson is discontented with the newly appointed Fletcher's coup in Veracruz. He is looking for an opportunity to get out of the situation that has been created by it. U.S. public opinion, he states, is turning more and more against Wilson. Every day of involvement is a windfall for Huerta and a loss for the United States.

I read the situation as just the opposite. Huerta cannot remain [in office]. Carranza's goal, as well as that of the United States, is Huerta's removal. I don't quite see where Huerta could drive in the wedge. Consistently, Carden confuses armistice with suspension of hostilities.

Despite his closeness to Huerta, Carden has been unable to move him to concede the neutralization of the Tampico oil fields. All that Huerta promised was to protect foreign employees *depending on the possibilities*: a promise entirely without substance, and it was meant to be that. The next days will be critical, because the internal struggle will take place over Huerta's forced resignation.

Sunday, May 3, 1914, Mexico City

Finally, in the afternoon, we hear from the consul in Veracruz that yesterday the [steamer] *Constantine* arrived. And this morning the *Ypiranga* left from there for Mobile, Alabama, via Tampico.

Some Germans (von Thadden, Sommer) spread the rumor that the mob murdered a young German on April 27, in the Calle de Gante. The fact that they spread a rumor is proven because when asked the name of this German they could not provide it. . . .

The Mexican side announces that the remnants of the Velasco army led by General Maas are marching south from Saltillo, supposedly in the direction of the capital. From the same source I hear that Huerta wants to send a commission to Washington DC, or rather to Canada, to lead the negotiations. Finally, the same source says that Joaquin Amor, the negotiator for the Zapata government, specified the price for switching to Huerta: a music band and five hundred Mauser machine guns supplied through avenues open to the government. The reaction to these demands was deep silence.

Monday, May 4, 1914, Mexico City

Today, 6:00 p.m., five hundred U.S. refugees depart to the United States via Puerto México. The Brazilian representative declares in the cable to his ambassador in Washington DC that, with the exception of the British representative, the entire diplomatic corps is supporting him. He complains that Huerta imagines that Great Britain is speaking to him; Carden is constantly encouraging Huerta in favor of resistance. Whereas it is only Carden's private opinion. The Brazilian ambassador then cabled that Ambassador Spring had admonished Carden to support the local Brazilian diplomat. Also, Cardoso has been told by Carden that he had been so ordered.

Cardoso showed me telegram No. 13 from May 3 from his ambassador. It states that Carrancistas will participate in negotiations. And telegram No.14, where da Gama says to continue to report immediately about indications and perspectives.

The withdrawal of the United States would change the entire situation. The rebels refused to seize facilities but participate in the negotiations. On the afternoon of May 3 Cardoso met the president at Chapultepec and talked with him about getting the United States out. The president only remarked, "Whatever the outcome of the negotiations I always will be grateful to the Latin American sister republics." Nothing further. Cardoso reported that Secretary of Finance de la Lama talked to the president about his resignation and Huerta is supposed to have answered, "If you don't want to have me anymore, then kill me."

I obtained from the secretary of war safe conduct for the German Heynen, who wants to go to Puerto México. In addition, I recommended to his urgent and kind attention the train that the Hamburg America shipping line requested to transport the passengers to the steamer *Crown Princess Cecelia*.

Blanquet replied when asked about the rebels' cessation of hostilities: "In the north the rebels stopped hostilities; the former Velasco army withdrew southward via San Luis Potosí. Zapata resumed hostilities and yesterday, May 3, suffered defeat at Puente de Ixtla." It appears Blanquet believes hostilities will end if his troops withdraw. The rebels will act in contradiction to all the rules of war if they are allowed the theft of victories through diplomatic negotiations. On May 2 Carden held a three-hour-long talk with Blanquet, who did not touch upon the topic of the president.

I sought out the governor of the Federal District because of Berlin's report of the murder of a Clara Beckmeyer: nothing at all that is true. In the same manner I visited the inspector general of police. Looking often into the reports of the individual officer, he declares that none of it is true. Iturbide remarked: he has available six thousand people for security service. Also, the rumor that a German had been beaten to death proved to be fiction.

Sir Lionel Carden visited. At the end he read a telegram to me that he claims to have sent to Downing Street: the Zapatistas are alleged to have defeated General Olea. (The secretary of war says the opposite.)

Olea is pulling back all his troops to Cuernavaca, and within a short time Zapatistas could be in the capital. Their goal is Huerta's resignation, but nobody dares speak about this other than in secret or privately. The educated classes are helpless. As a consequence the capital is about to be open to looting and devastation by northern rebels and the Zapatistas. In the name of humanity and civilization he asked in Washington DC to prohibit the rebels from advancing south, so that the capital remains spared from looting and massacres.

At the core of the dilemma rests: possibly, Germany wants to encourage Great Britain to, at least, help in Washington to bring about an effective end of weapons and ammunition supply to the rebels. Carden says: I want to scare London, and they will do nothing without being scared. Then I pointed out to him that in case London and Berlin would present such a position, the U.S. administration would gain perhaps a desired opportunity to step in front of Congress and public opinion and say: Europe wants intervention, we cannot help it. Carden argues that Woodrow Wilson is a model of simplicity.

I say I read his action differently: a policy, drawing the right conclusion, but whose slowing can be explained by the lack of understanding from the side of the people. Finally Carden thanks me, not for my rejection, but for the "tip" that his assumed scare in London could cause in Washington probably the opposite of what he intended. He wants to mail a second telegram that will warn against this possible action.

Carden presented the argument: if the Americans came up here they would get beaten. I asked him: by whom? From the volunteers who are currently parading in the streets? War by the demoralized, repeatedly defeated army that is streaming back from the north into the capital? He answers "by the guerrilla." I explain to him, based on the history of the war, that guerrillas will be able to slow down an opponent. But so far, they have never been able to prevent him from reaching the goal of his warfare (hampered but never hindered). I explain to him that in my opinion Huerta is in a bind: the Zapatistas are pressuring him from the southwest, mocking his attempts at reconciliation. From the north, the rebels are advancing. Perhaps the Federales might make a last stand near San Luis Potosí; from the east, the United States is threatening.

In the capital a new insurrection is emerging. Carden declared this is the most desperate situation the government has been in; one must help Huerta. I countered: the perspective that I formed during the last three years is that Mexico was passing through a period of revolution whose end cannot be predicted. Regardless, it will last longer than can be tolerated by foreign capital and the work of investment. Perhaps Mexico needs a few generations to survive revolutions. Apparently Mexico lacks the most important thing needed: a man! Carden conceded that my reasoning is well founded and left me rather depressed.

Wednesday, May 6, 1914, Mexico City

General Vinegas grants the train for the passengers of the Hamburg America Line steamer *Crown Princess Cecelia* that already had been asked for at the Foreign Ministry and Ministry of War. On the ninth of the month the general promised information about the extent of the railroad's damage. From Siemens Schuckert he purchased sixty fuses to explode mines and mercury cartridges.

Emanuel Amor one of the most outstanding Mexicans visited me. The commission of the three—Rabasa, Agustín Rodriguez, and Luís Elguero—is supposed to have received instructions, if possible, only to enter into discussions of the Tampico case and to reject all other points—rebels,

FIG. 32. Huerta's delegates to the Niagara Falls conference, F. de la Regata, Rodriguez, and José Emilio Rabasa. Courtesy of the Library of Congress.

resignation. He blamed Carden as the main culprit for Huerta's doggedness. Undeniably, Carden intends "to put obstacles into the way of U.S. policy." In addition, he represents here Cowdray's personal, material, and business interests. And finally, his outlook is how it was thirty years ago, but [is] no longer. For the time being, nobody has the courage to eliminate Huerta.

Secret agents are trying to examine the armory of the [German] community. Locked. The garrisons from Jojutla and Cuautla, Morelos, after being defeated by Zapatistas, arrived in the capital.

Interruption of telegraph connection with Tampico. Brazilian representative has news from Ambassador da Gama.

A. That Carranza has rejected the cessation of hostilities.

B. Thereupon the three ABC powers withdrew invitation to Carranza to participate in negotiations on the same level as Huerta.

C. The Tampico incident is the topic of negotiations that will begin on May 19 at Niagara Falls. Cardoso describes mediation under these circumstances as ridiculous. Japanese diplomat has news from Shinda, Washington DC: Bryan declares the occupation of Veracruz took place with the wish of the U.S. government to keep intact the railroad from Veracruz-Mexico. Unfortunately they arrived too late.

Again on May 5 Carden had a talk with Huerta. He reported: Huerta engaged in such megalomaniacal boasting that he was tempted to ask him if he—Huerta—was crazy or if you believe that he is crazy. Carden had gained the impression that Huerta was somebody who was not mentally healthy, that he was not well. Anyway, the president did not say anything about his plans. Carden added: the British government was very disturbed about the situation in Mexico City.

Thursday, May 7, 1914, Mexico City

A REGULAR DIPLOMATIC REPORT

The mediating powers have indicated to Carranza that they withdraw demand for his participation in mediation. In reference to telegram No. 65: Huerta presented to the United States the demand to stop the supply of ammunition and weapons to the rebels. If that takes place he will commit himself to putting down the revolution. Here the commissioners have been instructed to negotiate merely the Tampico incident, which would mean the purpose of the mediation of the three powers—to reestablish peace in Mexico—would be null and void. **Hintze**[19]

Thursday, May 7, 1914, Mexico City

V. Bluecher, the current commander of the German community's self-defense [unit], indicates that his company, AEG, was calling him home to Germany. I offered him a place on the train of the ninth and on the *Crown Princess Cecelia*. At the same time I referred him to the French diplomatic representative because the French steamer might be more comfortable for him.

I went with a Mr. Ruebke to General Vinegas and to the Mexican Railroad Company: the agreement reached was [to have available] two Pullman coaches for the ninth, as well as one first-class coach and a boxcar for luggage.

The Brazilian diplomat complains repeatedly that the secret police visited him and demanded Luis D'Antia, the consulting lawyer of the U.S. embassy. Upon refusal, they surrounded his house. He asked for the friendly intervention of the German Foreign Ministry. I spoke to Undersecretary of State Esteva Ruiz, who manages the Foreign Office.[20] He promised to pull back the police and to negotiate directly with the Brazilian representative: d'Austin is only a *secrétaire particulier* and not an employee of the mission that conducted Carrancista war propaganda.

Esteva Ruiz further informed me: Cuernavaca, according to his news, has *not yet* fallen. It is possible that it has been cleared. I advise him to report to the diplomatic corps in the capital about the strength of the troops.

Esteva Ruiz confirmed that the three commissioners have an order to deal only with the international question, i.e., the case of Tampico. Earlier, President Huerta *had agreed* to admit *Carranza's delegates* to the negotiations and *to negotiate with them*: it would be impossible to grant a greater concession. The president asked only that the United States [should] stop the supply of weapons and ammunition to the rebels. Then he would deal with them.

Esteva Ruiz says Obregón has driven out all Carrancistas from Sonora and Sinaloa. Three chiefs exist in the South: Zapata, Salgado, Figuiroa.

I tried today to send the two automobiles. It proved impossible. The refugees' relief service demanded constant driving, back and forth, of all the administrators and employees between the various administrative offices and institutions. Therefore, for the time being, I'd take *one back, as a minimum.*

Friday, May 8, 1914, Mexico City

I hear that the British and French legations, with the help of Secretary of Communication Lozano, are trying to get ahold of both Pullman cars whose use I had arranged for the train of May 9.[21] Once again, I visit General Vinegas because of this issue. There the promises are renewed. I ask the travel agents to do their part to hold the railroad company to their promise.

The deputy secretary of foreign affairs has addressed a note to the Brazilian representative demanding the extradition of d'Antin. Cardoso has cabled his Foreign Ministry that ordered him to refuse the extradition of d'Antin. In case of emergency d'Antin is supposed to seek refuge in the German, British, or French legation. Cardoso is supposed to ask other nations for their support. At the same time, the representatives of the ABC countries are sending by cable the note to him stating that they have directed to Mexico the "demand to leave d'Antin untouched and not to complicate situation through those steps."

Cardoso cut right through the objection: d'Antin has little diplomatic significance; and [he] informed the Foreign Ministry via diplomatic note: d'Antin is an employee (*abogado consultador y secretario*) of his legation. Foreign Ministry confirms this note and replies that the police have an oral and written order to withdraw from the Brazilian legation and not to touch d'Antin. This will probably resolve the case.

The case has been resolved, but the Mexican government has suffered damage. It could have been worse if Esteva Ruiz had not listened to my friendly suggestion.

The Brazilian legation had news that in the near future the United States will renew the embargo of weapons and ammunition export. If they have not already done so. The U.S. representatives for the mediation have not yet been named. But Cardoso assumes that one does not have to wait very long for the selection to be announced. Cardoso sees little hope for an outcome from the negotiations that will be favorable for Mexico. He asks me to give a home to his family in case of unrest in the capital during the invasion of Zapatistas.

Carden visited him and offered him his cooperation: nobody has better access to Huerta than he does. However, he mistrusts Carden and evaded his offer. [Carden] did not let him know what he thought: Huerta has to step down.

The British diplomat read me the following news provided by his consuls:

1. Villa has returned to Chihuahua with the main military force and opened his headquarters there.
2. In Parral only five hundred rebels are present.
3. In Saltillo ten thousand Federales are present with twenty-seven cannons but little ammunition.
4. The strength of the rebels moving toward Saltillo has been estimated to be forty thousand men. (When I asked Sir Lionel Carden he replied to my question: this consul is a sober and reliable man!)

5. In San Luis Potosí there are sixty-five hundred Federales with sufficient ammunition, including artillery. Twenty thousand rebels are surrounding the town and surroundings.

6. Tampico is in greatest danger of falling.

7. The railroad from Torreón to Zacatecas has been put back into service by the rebels. They are able to use a railroad connection from Ciudad Juárez to Zacatecas.

8. Pánfilo Natera did not join as he has claimed. Instead he continues to operate as a rebel.

9. Cuernavaca is about to fall.

I cannot avoid saying once again how well the British consular services inform the legation. I do not receive such news: not even following a request, because the consuls do not look after such things. They worry they will compromise themselves providing such news.

Sir Lionel Carden confided in me: all this news has convinced him "that Huerta's government is broken and that we must give him up. I had hoped to be able to tie him over the critical time until he had emerged again as elected president [as a result] of the next elections. But I see now he has no weapons. His time is up. I want your advice how to get him out. What do you think of a joint action by the entire diplomatic body?"

I replied, I consider this the least recommendable means because, instantly, it would force Huerta to assume the most pronounced defensive posture.

I am of the opinion that Huerta's departure would bring relief for three to four months, not for longer. Carden countered: practical policy cannot look further ahead than three to four months. Furthermore, I said, Huerta's path of exit should be made easier, providing all honors. That means that no outside pressure should become visible. Publicly it should appear as being motivated exclusively by personal motivation—by being a hero and martyr for the fatherland. Most certainly this would be the first condition for Huerta's acceptance of such a top secret and confidentially communicated suggestion.

Then Carden asked me: who should present this suggestion to Huerta? I say: you are the only one of the entire diplomatic corps he will listen to. But Carden wants me and one or two other representatives [to join] him, as he phrases it. So he does not have to take exclusively the "fame" for the step.

I responded, as far as I'm concerned I abstain from taking credit. First,

I don't value it, and second, because, in my opinion, the actual success depends on the fact that as few as possible are in the know and help. Still, for several years the secret would have to be kept. If I were in Carden's position I would inform nobody else but my government, and I would ask my government to agree to such a step. Carden proudly and self-confidently interjected: my government will do anything I suggest. I: so much better for you. I shouldn't fail to ask my government for a special authorization for the matter. Carden confessed: I am drafting a telegram to that effect to my government.

Furthermore, Sir Lionel told me: in the last few days he has gained the impression that Huerta is crazy. Laughingly, I said, that's nothing new to me but that is a dangerous topic.

I asked him how he imagines order [to be] after Huerta's departure; would that not be the main, central issue?

He said: an entirely neutral person as president; complete freedom of individual states to elect their governors and to determine their internal order the way they like it. Then, to deliver the northern states to the rebels; even Morelos and Guerrero to the Zapatistas. And then to see what will develop out of that.

I believe this plan means permanent revolution and if declared constitutionally legal the beginning of Mexico's dismemberment. At that moment I didn't want to reveal my old project of foreign help for Mexico's reconstruction (centralization, financial control, etc., police organization). Therefore, I only said: this plan seems to promise decreased intensity for two or three months; later new revolutions [would come].

Carden admitted the revolutions and declared: the goal of this project is to keep the United States out of the country and to keep its influence low. I believe that Carden's project of decentralization would open all the doors for U.S. influence. But I held back with this opinion. Because I don't believe that this plan has great prospects of realization, even if it is developed in theory. Carden asked me to remove the influence of Lozano and Moheno, if I didn't want to talk with Huerta.

As far as Moheno is concerned I say okay because I know his idea: only Huerta's resignation can bring the solution, perhaps salvation. I advised in regard to Lozano to drive home to him—or, better, to have somebody drive it home to him—that Huerta's game is finished: then Lozano will cave in right away.

One thing is totally clear: Carden reached his new opinion that Huerta needs to get out not through thinking and gathering of news but through a wink from London. If he had come to this opinion by himself he would not resort to such unsuitable and crass means, such as a joint démarche for resignation by the diplomatic corps. Huerta in his current state would rather have himself beaten to death serving at his post than to yield to any force. The task remains the same as before: to build him an excellent, honorable gate through which to exit. I surmise that the new and decisive direction from London is Downing Street's! I say, to advance Carden's proposal urge the United States to persuade the rebels to stop their advance toward the capital. Immediately, before Carden negotiated with Huerta about his resignation. I don't believe this to be in accord with the principle of our local policy stance: do not stand out in public and yet affect things in determined fashion.

Also, Carden created this mess for himself. It is only appropriate that he is the first to clean it up. Even if he is doing it only because he is ordered to do so. This is Carden's frequently observed method: to turn toward me when he has cornered himself into an embarrassment.

It would be easier to build golden bridges for him if, in that case, he would admit openly and honestly his pigheadedness. But he is far from this, as is shown by these pages and earlier reports. He then tries to right himself in long discussions, but he also digs deeper the hole he is in. After almost forty years in South America he has become Latino American [sic].

Carden officially ordered his countrymen to move their women and children out of the country. Today, before lunch, the train with 516 U.S. citizens that had departed here on the evening of the sixth arrived happily in Puerto México. One part of the group has embarked on to the *Crown Princess Cecelia*.

Saturday, May 9, 1914, Mexico City

At 7:00 a.m. I instruct the train with German and other refugees [assigned] for Hapag steamer *Crown Princess Cecelia*; about 120 people. English and French attempts to rip out of our hands the two sleeping cars, for which we have fought so hard, have successfully been rebuffed. In the evening, 6:00 p.m., the French train travels to Puerto México. 144 passengers, the *Espagne* is waiting for them.

Military attaché Major von Papen travels for four days to Veracruz to study [the situation].

The three peace commissioners, Rabasa, Rodriguez, and Luís Elguero, are traveling in the president's train following our train. They will travel on the *Crown Princess Cecelia* to Havana.

Following a decision by the [Mexican] Senate, the commissioners have full powers to sign any type of contract with the United States as long as the Senate has agreed to ratify it.

The Brazilian diplomat told me: he had visited the barracks of the well-known Twenty-Ninth Regiment in order to see the U.S. [citizen] Dr. Ryan who is imprisoned there. A major had accompanied him. While talking he had asked about the political situation and, as Cardoso answered evasively, the major yelled *in front of the soldiers*: "We will not have peace until we are freed of Huerta."

The Spanish diplomat reports he has information that a garrison is preparing an uprising. It will break out in about five days.

More than ever Huerta has delivered himself to drinking: yesterday, May 8, at 10:00 a.m., he was inside Café Colon; at 11:00 a.m., in Café Globo. And at 1:00 p.m. in the Cantina Madrilena. All the time drinking. No longer is anybody governing or working. His tirades about rather being dead than resigning should not be taken seriously. Recently he did transfer abroad, for no reason, four million French francs. And here, under his pseudonym, he invested great sums. What I cabled to my government on November 14, 1913, remains true: Huerta is a drunkard and he cannot be trusted.

The Spanish colony is longing for a U.S. military advance in order to avoid being exposed to Villa's ill deeds.

The rebels have established a register of sins of the Spanish colony:

A. In the Citadel in February 1913, five hundred Spaniards are supposed to have been present.
B. On February 9 news was circulated as an extra edition from the *Casino Española*: Madero is supposed to have stepped down.
C. In mid-February Cólogan allegedly had asked Huerta to resign.[22]
D. Cólogan was involved in Madero's murder. He will write a presentation of February events as a justification for himself; then, unfortunately, he did not compose a diary.

U.S. ambassador Wilson had asked him in front of Stronge and me to ask Madero to resign; Cólogan only answered: "Está bien." Because he perceived the mission as charity act. When he visited Madero, Huerta was supposed to have entered and submitted his resignation. Cólogan felt it was "too much" and had left. I recount to him the words of my diary notes and ask him about Wilson's speech. Cólogan accused Carden of trying to prolong the agony of the Huerta administration. Also, he states that Blanquet had destroyed his relationship with Huerta. The nightly executions are taking on incredible dimensions.

Cólogan repeats: the next event will be the uprising of the garrison against Huerta.

The British diplomat has news that General Solares, federal troop chief operating north of Tampico, is to have joined the rebels with his three thousand men. The president of the Senate, Camacho, approached the Japanese diplomat to intervene in developments.

Camacho, more than ninety years old, is an opponent of Huerta. But this turn has happened only recently. Adachi has asked him how he would imagine such an intervention. Camacho answered, Adachi should find out how I think about it. Adachi also mentioned the British diplomat, but Camacho protested and said, Carden, in this case, was pushing a policy in favor of his private interest and holding on to Huerta because he had granted him valuable concessions.

The Japanese delegate asked me if I was willing to do something? I answered: the local diplomatic corps could not be won over in favor of a unified action within the limits of the usual and international law. Most had no interest except curiosity; the topsy-turvy British policy has now split the ones who had been interested before. I'm not going to bank on conspiracies or support overthrows because this is against my position and my inclinations.

What might remain is a friendly counsel with a few diplomats; for example, Japan, perhaps also Spain. Unfortunately, France was not available because it is represented by a cautious chargé d'affaires who is under Mexican influence.

Then there is nobody on the Mexican side who could and should receive counsel. Thus, *for the time being*, I see no possibility but to endure current developments. Adachi pointed to the immediate threatening danger from the Zapatistas, the rebels, the mob, and the garrison of Mexico City. I answered: the way things are, one or the other of all those dangers will flood the city and, post factum, the United States will occupy the capital in order to save what has remained; that is how the usual historical path unfolds.

Tonight, at 6:00 p.m., the first train departed, organized for French refugees: to Coatzacoalcos. The French chargé was not able to secure sleeping coaches despite the fact that it would last thirty-six hours. In this tropical heat it must have been very difficult for children and women.

Sunday, May 10, 1914, Mexico City

The Brazilian representative seeks me out in order to answer a telegram from his ambassador: "looking ahead." I hand him my material and explain: his ambassador should quickly inform him about two items: In the north do the revolutionaries have sufficient ammunition and weapons in order to continue their operations? What is the explanation for the halt of their enterprise? The alleged, declared arms and ammunition prohibition by the United States against Mexico, is it imposed effectively or is it just an appearance?—The obvious, most immediate danger is that the Zapatistas, at night, rob and plunder Mexico City's rich suburbs. Next, will be the imminent uprising of the garrison in the city. The final one, one can foresee, [will be that] rebels enter the capital.

The three peace commissioners are more or less Huerta's opponents. It cannot be ruled out that they [may] accept, outside the country, Huerta's resignation since they have power of attorney to enter into any agreement with the United States. Huerta must be out of his mind to have appointed such commissioners and given them such power. Nevertheless, one must keep in mind that Huerta would not hesitate one minute to withdraw the power of attorney of the three delegates, or simply to recall them.

Carden told Cardoso that he is working toward Huerta's resignation. Cardoso, however, did not say a word about this because he mistrusts Carden deeply and suspects that Carden hands over his colleagues' confidential statements. This is not unlikely to assume, because Carden is far more Latino American [sic] than British in his way of being, thinking, and appearance. And Cardoso, he himself a Latino American, instinctively senses that.

Cardoso had news from Washington: the government has issued openings for two hundred thousand volunteers and eight hundred thousand are supposed to have applied.

The characteristic aspect of the current situation is: that it draws out without end, without noticeable progress. However, this is nothing new, but the essence of nations that are in the process of formation. And again, it is remarkable how little political knowledge our local countrymen possess. They, who have lived long in the country, they, who in overwhelming numbers married Mexican women, should possess sensibility and understanding for the political life of the Mexican. But none of it exists. They exhaust themselves complaining about the suffering due to revolution and war. And they demand of the German Reich and its local representation to make an end to the situation. In public and private I explain to them when they decry or, to the smallest part, praise U.S. policy, [which is certain to be based on] U.S. national principles, its base and goal is to reach it with as little surrender of money and blood [as possible]: the final result is to be expected, not so much from forces from without as from forces from within; and they will therefore be stable.

Probably that will stop it for a day. But soon old laments and accusations will break through to the forefront: "The German Reich is not doing anything for us!" All those interjections such as, "If one can't bite one should not bark, etc." Under such circumstances it is doubly important and necessary to help our countrymen in small measures and, in individual cases, in the most lavish, far-reaching way, wherever they can be helped. The expenses that will have to be made affect the German Reich far less than a storm of complaints resulting from "insufficient protection." Of course, I have to reject some demands because they have to be addressed by criminal law. For example, to get three boxes of oil (for the Pabst Company) to Veracruz; or a call to open a German post office in the German legation. The consuls answer such demands with the usual formulaic cover letter, instead of refusing them [while] still on location. They write, "*I seek* that the royal legation will undertake the steps to do what is necessary for the attached petition." Or something like that. With the exception of Mexico City, the majority are merchants here in the honorary consulates and do not reflect about such acts. They have their business and, in such times, it absorbs their attention primarily and in its entirety.

Many consuls are not reading their instructions or do not comprehend them. Mine are purposely dressed in the most simple way of expression. However, many instructions fail to be understood and are seldom executed correctly.

Some consuls write or cable regularly at every event, no matter what it is, "Please send instructions," even though instructions had already been given for the respective events. I have to answer them, "See my letter from, etc.," and then he is hurt and offended. By far, I am not lamenting this state of affairs, nor do I accuse anybody: honorary consuls are not state employees, they refuse to take any responsibility and refuse to make a personal decision—and rightly so. They assumed their office to function during normal times. In addition, they are paralyzed through the attacks made by their ethnic community, according to German habit.

Understandably, they prefer to refer *all* issues and complaints to the legation for decision. Including those of the troublemakers. They leave themselves an open back door, answering petitioners or the ethnic community, "Well, yes, I was willing, as you saw in my letter: I ask the *Imperial Legation, etc.*—but the legation, once again, does not want to."

Here, I repeat: I'm not complaining, nor do I accuse anybody of anything. Nevertheless, such an administrative structure does not allow greater success than is currently achieved. It lacks tight organization and the discipline of a corps of employees.

The three representatives of the three mediating powers are telegraphing the Mexican government; since the cessation of hostilities the U.S. government prohibits the export of weapons and ammunition *across the border* to Mexico. The reports state that this prohibition is strictly enforced. The phrase "across the border" apparently is supposed to hold open the back door "via sea route."

Mexican general Guasque, a reliable man, declares: rebels have ammunition and weapons *en abundancia*. Federal soldiers received no firing training. The waste of ammunition, therefore, was incredible. Each killed soldier costs, according to statistics, four thousand to five thousand shots. He had participated in a battle in Sonora that used fifty thousand cartridges. The resulting success: one dead, one wounded. The cartridge factories produce daily fifty thousand cartridges: barely enough for twelve battles. Rabago, the former private secretary of the president, told me in confidence: the three peace delegates would address the possible question of Huerta's resignation or forced removal.

In contrast, the English diplomat stated he had talked with El Guero, one of three delegates, and advised him: *to allow for negotiation about nothing, absolutely nothing, with the exception of the Tampico incident.*

On May 9 Carden attempted to explain to the president the patriotic act Porfirio Díaz had performed in May 1911 when he stepped down.

Then Limantour carried the news from New York to him that he either has to go or prepare himself for an intervention.[23] Díaz went to spare his country the intervention.

Huerta countered: Díaz did not act correctly; *if he had stuck to the presidency he would still be president.*

Carden claims that he proposed stepping down to Huerta in other ways as well. The reception has been unsatisfactory. That means, when spelled out, either Carden did not dare to say anything or Huerta rejected him. There is merit in emphasizing that Carden is living in a sudden fear of Huerta's explosive temper and is being influenced by him—even though he believes the opposite.

Carden reports a discussion with Secretary of War Blanquet in which he gained the impression that Blanquet himself would murder Huerta—if he became convinced that it was necessary.

In the near future Carden expects the advance of Villa on the capital and, before that, he intends to leave the city. He advises me to do the same. I counter with the argument that already, almost on a daily basis, I meet General Argumedo, who had created mayhem in summer 1912 as a gang leader in Durango. It was his gang that murdered the German Beel. Repeatedly I wrote diplomatic notes to the government. But it pretends not to hear. In reality, Carden fears that the rebels will pay him and his ethnic community back for his well-known blind partisanship for Huerta. If one considers the fate of Spaniards, this is likely.

In expectation of Villa's entry in the immediate future, Carden removed all British women and children from the capital. He sent them outside of the country. He trains the remaining community, which has agreed to undertake self-defense to a larger extent than the German community. For that purpose two navy officers help him here. They can be spared easier with six English ships present in Mexican waters, compared to our two small cruisers.

Monday, May 11, 1914, Mexico City

Using its Foreign Ministry, the Mexican government asked the representatives of the ABC powers whether the cessation of hostilities was limiting their operations against the rebels. A mysterious question, since Carranza refused to join such a cessation of hostilities and barely interrupts his operations. Apparently the question should be understood as *nothing* more than rhetorical in nature in order to disguise Huerta's helplessness and to present him as conscientious and honest. The government of the United States did not expose this trick but answered in a well-mannered way: the Mexican government is free to undertake its military operations against the rebels. In fact, since April 31 the Huerta government has undertaken military operations neither against the rebels nor against the United States: the situation is characterized by a complete military and administrative paralysis. It looks a little different if one counts the continuous "evacuations"—abandonment of locations—as military operations.

The consul in Tepic responded to open inquiry that General Solares has switched, with his troops, to the rebels. He himself, on his own initiative, had not considered the news important enough to report. Case in point: already on May 5 Solares's defection, near Acaponeta. Later he cabled that Tepic was about to be *cleared.*

It is close to the fulfillment of the wish he has mentioned numerous times: that the rebels take possession of Tepic. The German pastry maker and hotel owner Paglasch spread the rumor that the rebels took Pachuca; a check reveals this news to be a mistake.

The militarization of the civil service state employees continues. Daily, employees practice movements that cannot even be accomplished by military schools. Yesterday the president wanted to visit the employees of the Foreign Ministry while [they were] performing military exercises.

The state employees were present and waiting. The president did not show up. Probably he was drunk again.

The [German] Foreign Ministry asks for a description of the [current] situation for the [German embassy] in Washington. It tells me that, here, the United States is beginning to look after the fate of the foreigners that are remaining behind. From the very beginning I thought the danger for them was large. And I insisted that I do not want to burden my soul through "the forgetting of even a single German!" I propose that *all* Germans should be urged to leave the country. I was allowed to contribute only a single, well-meaning message. As a possibility, at least, I afforded the opportunity to *all Germans*—and not just once, but several times—to leave the country. Not in a manner fraught with difficulties—but entirely in comfort. Those who are still here are remaining here voluntarily. They also derive, comparatively, security for neutrals! Here nine-tenths of the population are *wild people*! There are so many reasons why so few Germans have gotten out of the country:

A. Most of them, by far the most Germans, are married to Mexican women. Those women are the master at home, and under no circumstances are [they] willing to go abroad, where customs and habits are uncomfortable for them.
B. The busy drive of accumulation of our countrymen foretells them of the coming of an economic pickup as a consequence of U.S. intervention; they don't want to miss it.
D.[24] The peculiarity of Germans, during times of comparative or complete calm, to criticize their government with utmost strength, and in times of emergency to clench onto it. Foreigners have often recognized and ridiculed it. Also, Germans themselves, even German women, [have mocked it].

The dangers that threaten rich foreigners in Mexico City are listed according to the degree of geographical proximity.

1. Zapatista raids on the rich and undefended suburbs.
2. Flooding of the capital by the beaten, demoralized federal army.
3. Unrest in the capital.
4. Entry of the Villistas.
5. Common, dangerous outbreak of the madness that obviously made Huerta ill.

The Huerta administration faces all of these dangers with complete helplessness. To counter these dangers the United States should quickly occupy Mexico City. But that does not fit into its policy: to overthrow the Mexico government with as little sacrifice of blood and money as possible, *and to realize* its policy as a moral act. The consequence of politics is that they advance toward the capitol today—twenty-one days after the occupation of Veracruz. They are not even prepared for it militarily. From a purely U.S. point of view, it is certainly correct to conduct the war through the rebels. Only the price of this method is being paid with lives and property of foreigners who have stayed behind. The Europeans have preferred to remain silent in moments that were suited for saying something *from our local perspective*: without doubt they had their reasons for their behavior. Some of them were recognizable even from here. I clearly see that now we have to say something or suffer. After we responded to the request to leave the country by doing so on our own advice. In spite of all the clamor, our suffering remains because opportunities to talk are restricted.

U.S. citizens occupied the island Lobos in front of Veracruz, just like 1847. Just like then, it appears that they let pass the season that is opportune—ahead of the rain—before they advance; if they even advance.

Tuesday, May 12, 1914, Mexico City

The Spanish representative and I agree that possibly refugees and mail will be carried on the extra trains leaving for Coatzacoalcos on Thursday or Friday: in Coatzacoalcos the Spanish steamer *Alfonso XIII* awaits them. It is routed via Havana to Spain (Coruna). I asked Carzu, Campeche, if possibly [there] exist German refugees. I again asked the [diplomatic] doyen, the Spanish representative, to talk to me about transporting mail. Also if it is possible to bring here goods landed in Veracruz via Puerto México.

Via cable Cólogan received, verbatim, Bryan's declaration stating U.S. opinion in regard to current state of affairs—if it is war or something different.

The archbishop encouraged a religious delegation to visit the president and appealed to him to avoid war.

Mexican circles close to Huerta tell me that, when he is sober, he himself is alleged to speak about resignation—when he is drunk he is stubborn again.

In Monterrey the rebels are supposed to blackmail people. But they did not kill anybody or chase them away. Pablo González took the town after five days of fighting.

Wednesday, May 13, 1914, Mexico City

The refugee train for Puerto México has been scheduled for Friday, May 15, 6:00 p.m., where the *Alfonso XIII* awaits it. I informed the consuls by telegram that *Alfonso XIII* will travel on the seventeenth of the month via Havana to Europe; also in regard to mail.

According to a Spanish officer who arrived today, a Templadores de Ferrocarriles Mexicano has been ripped up at km 3 and at Tejeria at kilometer 6. That is an exaggeration.[25]

The French mission receives a naval officer to provide aid. At the eastern coast is resting *Conde Descartes*, at the west coast *Mont Calu*. Now the communities of foreigners all have adopted our system to organize trains and steamers for refugees.

Secretary of Finance de la Lama wants to ask for Huerta's decision in regard to the transfer of goods unloaded in Veracruz and destined for the interior. De la Lama very much favors it.

Today, Cólogan discusses with the general postal inspector the transport of mail.

The Spanish diplomat gives me the copy of the exchange of notes pertaining to the cessation of hostilities. It confirms that on April 27 Huerta's government asked for cessation of hostilities through the services of Cólogan, the Spanish ambassador in Washington.

The ambassador of the United States stated: war has not been declared; Veracruz was occupied [in response] to uncounted events, as a means to satisfy a very specific demand; future U.S. action will depend entirely on Huerta's behavior. Under such circumstances a formal cease-fire is unnecessary. By himself Huerta could realize his wish to cease hostilities during the ongoing negotiations.

The note obliges neither the United States nor the Mexicans to cease hostilities. It says nothing further than: "You don't have to attack, if you don't want to fight." This voids all Mexican complaints about violating a "cease-fire"—which does not exist—the occupation of *Lobos*, changing of positions around Veracruz, and further disembarkations. The government answered this noncommittal U.S. note on April 30 and ordered a complete halt to hostilities.

The Mexican government, on April 30, ordered the cessation of hostilities across the entire line! Surely a sign that hardships must have been grave. Here it unfolds as elsewhere in the history of war: if the United States would have wanted it, they would have been able to take the railroad all the way to Mexico City with hardly any struggle.

Currently the Mexican government lives on advance payments that they blackmail from Mexican banks. They are modeled after the well-known $45 million loan from April, backed—as is known—by fifty million bonds of the sixteen-million-pound gold loan from 1913. Even though, according to contract, these bonds must not be sold. Their printed banknotes have not yet arrived. They had been ordered in New York. But the government ordered the printing of smaller one-peso notes in the capital. Until today the Banco Nacional de Mexico participated in this loan with 4.5 million pesos and raised 4.2 million pesos.

Not much of the forty-five million can exist, at least not as far as the capital's banks are concerned.

More than ever, theft is involved: recently ammunition has been ordered: price, $2.4 million in gold. The actual value of the order was only $900,000. $1.5 million in gold has been divided between Huerta and a few others. Such dirty activities [taking place] in times when the fatherland is in greatest distress. The Spanish representative reports that Huerta is supposed to have sent abroad four million francs and seeks mortgages for both of his houses and his *estancia*, both entirely new acquisitions. That is not how somebody acts who wants to die for his honor.

The budget for 1914/1915 makes visible the army's strength based on budget figures (*Imparcial*, May 9, 1914).

On May 14 the military attaché returned from Veracruz with the information that, in essence, is known and therefore confirmed. So far [the United States has] landed: Fifth Infantry Brigade (four regiments); Sixth Cavalry Regiment (880 men); Field Artillery Regiment No. Four; half [of] Engineer Battalion No. Two with lots of railroad material; four hydroplanes; sanitary and field provision formation; three marine infantry regiments: a total of nine thousand men.

The intended advance would lead to Córdoba traveling through Perote. Fourth Infantry Brigade (three regiments) is on its way. General Wood is being expected. Badger and Funston then asked to report to Berlin the serious situation of the capital because it would pressure Washington toward the offensive soon to take place.

The *Imparcial*, May 13, reports strength and organization of the United States in Veracruz. *Imparcial*, May 16, reports ships stationed along the West Coast. According to the Brazilian diplomat, the French representatives before him had suggested to the Austrian and Russian representatives the disembarkation of sailors on ships stationed along the east coast. With the exception of the United States, who should not be included. He urged they march to the capital. For political and military reasons I consider this idea ill-advised. The British representative agrees with me.

Ayguésparse does not believe in the success of mediation. But he assumes this means the United States will prohibit Villa from marching on the capital. I can't see how. Ayguésparse's words, as a rule, reflect the intentions and views of the Huerta crowd. He is inspired through his Mexican wife.

To date Carden declares: it is his goal to keep Villa away from the capital. Benton incident suggests that he and the colony would have to fear Villa in every regard.[26] Once again today, he wants to send a blood-curdling telegram to Downing Street.[27] In Huerta's environment the predominant effort is to create a good exit for him. [It should be brought about] by the declaration of the three Mexican peace mediators, suggested by the ABC powers: Huerta's resignation will pacify the country. Then he could come forward and state: pacification is his only goal, therefore he is stepping down. Huerta's family is supposed to nudge him in that direction right now. Also, Huerta seems less eager to die while on the job. Because lately he is alleged to have moved abroad several millions of his recently gained private wealth. Little by little, therefore, Huerta will make peace with this idea.

Carden read two telegrams from Downing Street to me:

1. The British ambassador had that talk with W. (Woodrow Wilson), who says: the War Department is pressuring him to land more troops, and he is resisting it with all his strength—as long as possible.
2. Also, Bryan does not wish further use of U.S. troops and expects everything from Villa.

The Brazilian representative has news from U.S. offices in Veracruz. Until May 9 the mail has been delivered, on time, to Tejeria. But there the Mexican mail administration allowed the storage of mailbags in the open air. Allegedly many [mailbags] even have been burned there—allegedly fifty. Then,—since the ninth, the United States has stopped transport of mail. After addressing the issue in person Cardoso received the answer that it has been impossible to look after mail because everyone is busy with military affairs.

Robles Gil, secretary of traffic and communication in the first Huerta cabinet, is saying that he and many other people are trying to convince Huerta that he needs to go, in his own interest and in the nation's interest. The army officers who are part of the same educated class share this point of view.

Blanquet recognizes the necessity of Huerta's resignation. Blanquet is supposed to have said: he does not want to be the first one who urges the necessity to him. But he will support anybody who will state this opinion in Huerta's presence.

The plan of this group of patriots is that the three ABC powers should issue the call for Huerta's resignation. The three peace commissioners tend to be willing to support such a suggestion. I counter, in my opinion, this would put Huerta under pressure. He would not yield. I think it would be better to appeal simultaneously to his patriotism and a sense of self-preservation. One should bring him to mention the idea of resignation out of his own initiative, "for the rescue of the fatherland." Robles Gil: "You don't know Huerta. He is incapable of an altruistic sentiment. Everything is concentrated upon himself." Only external pressure will make him yield; for example, from the three mediating powers. He will not be reached by the temptations of a dominant role.

By the way, Huerta has begun to vacillate. If this trend does not solidify, this group is also willing to use force.

I pointed out that the transition regime should prepare and present reconciliation and initiate it in order to reestablish domestic peace. Everybody needs to be determined to forgive and to forget. Robles Gil agrees in an animated way, and he says Huerta's idea is a national war, a holy war against the United States and against Protestants: in the long run both of them will not fly. In that case Huerta wants to hand over the capital and to change roles: by leading a guerrilla war in the mountains against the invaders and traitors.

Huerta is being counseled by three or four men. They declare their fates to be their own. The most dangerous is Secretary of Communication Lozano, steadily preaching: either independence or vanquished. This is neither their desire nor that of the army. The army looks at the war as a lost undertaking and a fatal adventure. Robles Gil sees as a U.S. condition of peace to cede one coaling station in the Pacific ocean.

Thursday, May 14, 1914, Mexico City

News that Tampico has been cleared of Federales, and the rebels have occupied it. After a firefight government troops have withdrawn to San Luis Potosí.

Ayguésparse learned from Mexican circles the news that Huerta is pondering ideas of resignation. I point out that that is not enough. Most of all one had to know who is going to replace him. He replied Huerta is looking for a suitable secretary of foreign affairs who would step in when he steps down.

Otherwise Ayguésparse views everything in rosy colors under the influence of his Mexican attachés.

The deputy secretary of foreign relations, Esteva Ruiz, informed me confidentially that the three peace delegates had full powers to discuss any question. They can deal with it from any angle in Niagara Falls. They have to consult the United States about points of principle. But altogether they are limited only as far as three issues are concerned:

1. integrity of the republic; no land concession;
2. the sovereignty of the state: no protectorate, no suzerainty; and
3. the nation's dignity.

Ruiz said, when gingerly probed about what dignity meant, that it is a matter of interpretation, and he hints that the points can be expanded. He contends the current state was anarchy. He blames the rebels: this is not a revolution. It is anarchy. I tell him about the annoying events pertaining to forced loans in Guaymas. He promises to pay it back in three to four days.

The national bank received news that in Niagara Falls, the United States will demand:

1. Huerta's resignation.
2. A plan to pay back the claims of U.S. and other foreigners based on United States and Mexico's consent.
3. The United States and Mexico setting the tariff of the Tehuantepec railroad according to contract.

The British representative received a telegram from Admiral Craddock, according to which the two U.S. cannon boats are tied up at the quay.

The Japanese representative reported that the last deliveries of weapons and ammunition have been held back. The Japanese government does not want to come into conflict with the United States about these deliveries, and then Blanquet failed to pay the last installment (April 15). However, a Japanese merchant ship carrying rice and national foods is expected to supply the *Izumo* crew in Manzanillo. The *Izumo* will head out to open sea to escort it [back in].

From talks with a few outstanding Mexicans [it] can be learned that they all see Huerta's resignation as the only solution for the prevailing chaos. I point out that it will not do that Huerta must be replaced. In other words: before he leaves a new government must be ready.

Yesterday the British representative sent a long telegram to London. He read it to me. He is suggesting that the European powers should strengthen the back of Mexico and the ABC powers. Then they would not feel dependent on the tender mercies of the United States. After describing the situation in the capital in darkest colors, he closes: I earnestly hope and wish that you would look for means to prevent the revolutionaries from entering the capital, otherwise bloodshed and slaughter will be unavoidable.

Carden insists that Bryan makes Villa his protégé. He sees in him a future, willing tool of Huerta's policy, while Woodrow Wilson seeks a peaceful solution.

Carden discussed the advisability of pulling in Ayguésparse. He regrets that the latter stands so entirely under the influence of his Mexican—and very foolish—relatives.

The Catholic Party is sending a delegate to me: would I be willing to receive its board for the purpose of seeking advice? I agreed to see here one or two gentlemen in a nonofficial capacity, under the condition that he appear without causing attention.

Friday, May 15, 1914, Mexico City

Today's 7:00 p.m. train to Coatzacoalcos, connecting with the *Alfonso XIII*, has been made available to the German community. Only one Schlomo from Siemen's Schuckert wants to participate. The Brazilian representative says that in answer to his question to the ABC powers—how is the situation in the capital—he received a cable with the following: "We directly asked Mexican government and informed Bryan to take measures to avoid disaster. This dispatch—according to Cardoso—has *never* arrived. He surmised it was held back because it had been passed by events. No. . . . [sic] He is on the way. Please inform us if you believe the moment has come to hand it over or what objections you have."

Cardoso suspects that this dispatch, which has not yet arrived, categorized as desirable Huerta's resignation. But in strictest confidence I hand him Esteva Ruiz's information about the instructions of the three delegates and Robles Gils's omissions without mentioning the names. He answers, he is informed that the delegates are carrying in their bag Huerta's resignation from office.

According to Mr. Ruebke, Hamburg America Co. representative Luís Elguero told him: he is aware of Huerta's word of honor. He would step down if his resignation becomes a condition. After another of my interjections: the resignation is far away from being a [condition].

Cardoso stated that the construction of a government is everything. The ABC powers were thinking to put in place a junta of three to five people who would conduct elections. He has been asked to provide names for this junta: people who are taking a rather neutral position. He thought about López Portillo, Lascuraín, and Gamboa.[28] I point out that Gamboa is a born intriguer. Cardoso asks me to think about appropriate suggestions for persons. He said that his and my information about Huerta's resignation is identical. Therefore, confidentially he will inform his government.

Yesterday General Velasco, defeated at Torreón, departed for San Luis Potosí to take on the government. Perhaps he should pick up the army—once his own army—when it—as is foreseeable—leaves Saltillo. General Moure has been sent to Cuernavaca with a small reinforcement and six mountain cannons and arrives there on the evening of the fourteenth.[29] His military position is not entirely clear.

Once again, Jimenez Castro has been named governor of Morelos. He replaces Breton, who had just replaced him a while ago. General Delgadillo has been appointed chief of Tepic territory in place of Servin at the moment when rebels occupy the territory! These never ending position changes already show the workings of a sick mind [sic].

Cardoso has news that the garrison of Guadalajara has risen against the government at eight in the evening.

I lectured about the political situation of the German house in front of the gathered community; Norwegians and Austrians were also present. While entering the hall, a certain Block talked to me, a Jewish person and French citizen: his cousin, same name, who is a citizen, is supposed to be sent from Huerta as "couchard" to listen and to see what is being said and heard in the German house. He will report to Huerta immediately after the lecture, and he will report the talk and discussion to Huerta. Therefore I have said, as usual, at the beginning of [my] talks: what is said is meant for citizens in need, not for other nationalities nor for the press. Those who cannot keep silent about this or would not, should undertake steps to relieve their conscience from a burden. Those who disagree should make the objections known. One Austrian and Norwegian asked to be admitted. After a longer time had passed, a man stepped forward, apparently of Jewish tribe,[30] demanding to speak to me alone. I declined. He asked me if his cousin told me something. I said: I'll bet. He confirmed—and asked if he could stay. I said: he and his conscience had to decide that, just as we had just agreed upon. He stayed, which was fine with me. Still, I adjusted my presentation accordingly and cut it so that Block could pass it on to Huerta without doing damage. After the end of the talk, the German-Mexican Christlieb stepped up to me and asked me to drink a glass of champagne with him in honor of Colonel Jorge Huerta, the president's son, a well-known scoundrel who was present. I declined politely and in a cold way this tasteless suggestion.

Saturday, May 16, 1914, Mexico City

Berlin informed that the United States no longer wants to undertake anything further—except [in case of] unforeseen incidents—and [wants] to wait for Huerta's fall. This, then, defines our painful situation here: between Huertista, Villista, Zapatista, and federal armies. Under these circumstances we have to be prepared daily for a catastrophe or crisis with acts of violence and outbursts. This U.S. intent leaves no room for giving up the rules of precaution put in place: house, car, food provisions, self-defense, etc.

It makes sense that Europe cannot do anything against the political intention of the United States. By all means U.S. policy can be understood, if it wants to reach the largest possible goal with the smallest amount of effort. One can also understand that it does not care much if foreigners or its own countrymen suffer under such policies. The first [policy] it needs to take into consideration only insofar as the relevant nations are willing and capable of forcing them morally or physically to do so. The United States covered its interests vis-à-vis the latter by ordering all of them out of the country or picking them up at its own financial cost.

The Foreign Ministry reported that Bryan threatened Zapata with a U.S. advance if he and dangerous foreigners enter Mexico City. Everybody living in Mexico recognizes that Zapata remains indifferent about this threat and it represents no guarantee for the lives of any foreigners. The United States cannot march into the capital even with ten thousand men—in addition to the nine thousand men currently present in Veracruz. They need forty thousand men for that, if they want to proceed methodically and according to the rules. They can realize a raid in a very short time if they want [to take] this *great risk*—but they could also make great gain. In the end, the preconditions of September 1913 remain, which, until today, have been re-created many times. The U.S. military weakness means the greatest danger for the foreigners. Therefore foreigners have to continue to look out for themselves against the Zapatistas, Federales, and, outside the capital, against Villistas. And also against the increasingly documented craziness of Huerta.

Dr. Urutia, in summer 1913 secretary of interior under Huerta and a long-time intimate friend of Huerta, introduced himself and asked for asylum. He is being persecuted by Huerta and already has been picked up once by a car filled with police. But afterward he was released. Huerta imagines that he—Urutia—is conspiring against them. I advised him, one morning at 7:00 a.m., to take the train to Veracruz. I would secure him, without mentioning his name, a passage on the *Ypiranga*. He accepted my suggestion.

General Rascon, presidential candidate and vice president of the Catholic Party, asks for my involvement in bringing about a joint intervention of the powers most interested in doing so. (It is well known that [the party's] president has fled following Huerta's threats.) Huerta's arbitrariness and cruelty are increasing daily, his dominating reign unbearable. He would *never* step down, except through the use of force. A U.S. armed intervention, going it alone, to achieve this purpose would have as consequence the collapse of the Mexican state. In comparison a landing, even only a small navy contingent, of the most interested powers—Germany, Great Britain, France, Spain—would preserve Mexico and eliminate Huerta. I countered as usual when such demands are made: that a resignation of Huerta would not suffice. But an administration capable of governing should be arranged in advance for the administration that follows it. Furthermore: that an *outside* proposal to Huerta would rather encourage him, [he] who is always suspicious of favoring stronger resistance. As far as a U.S. intervention, I considered it currently to be far less dangerous and to have less consequence than internal chaos. In no way do I believe that the suggestion of a national intervention can have a positive effect. Rather, I fear that such suggestion should move the United States to expand its intervention, i.e., to advance. I have put great hopes into mediation and suspect it will solve the internal difficulties. My advice, since they ask for it, is going in the direction of waiting to see which path the mediation negotiations will take. In response, the vice president asked if I was recommending that the Catholic Party should pass a manifesto against the U.S. occupation of Veracruz. Thus it would publicly and decisively come out against it.

I answered: time seems to prepare a transition. Such time periods are not suited for detailed, delineated pronouncements of parties. My advice is to wait. As far as my last advice is concerned: *keep the religious element out of the conflict.* It is known that Huerta wants to use the motto Fight against Protestantism! Even though Huerta himself is nothing more than an opportunistic Christian. The governing upper class is atheistic. Religion can accomplish much among the population, which is by far Native American. The *priest* Hidalgo and Morelos caused the first revolution in 1810 against Spain. A religious war would bring forth even greater horror than the current robber and highway bandit war.

Sunday, May 17, 1914, Mexico City

A REGULAR DIPLOMATIC REPORT

The recipient of the weapons and ammunition on the *Ypiranga*, represented by Martin Schroeder Hamburg, asked that both be unloaded in Puerto México for the purpose of delivering them to the Mexican government. Otherwise he would have to cover the cost of return of the freight.

The representative of the Hamburg America Line suggests, in case the United States is against unloading in Puerto México, both can be unloaded in Veracruz under assumption of temporary U.S. supervision.

Of course, the Mexican government wants the weapons to be handed over. Until now I presented this as a private matter of the purchaser. I am not in the position to learn about U.S. position. Requesting orders. [. . .] Hintze[31]

Sunday, May 17, 1914

[German] Foreign Ministry asks whether there are serious concerns if *Dresden* is sent to Santo Domingo. Taking away the only cruiser on the east coast is totally impossible. Now Tampico is a rebel port, Veracruz a U.S. one, and Puerto México a Mexican port. [Not having the cruiser] could generate larger difficulties and conflicts: unloading of goods, contraband for different addresses. A warship is a must-have in this situation: to provide assistance to convoys and probably [to avoid] illegal interference with unpredictable consequences. Furthermore, the capital is constantly being threatened by the five known dangers. Finally, the community *demands* in times like today at least one ship as a potential backup cover.

Shipping representative von Rhode, Hamburg, who was supposed to have received the weapons of the *Ypiranga*, demands to unload them in Puerto México for the benefit of the current government. I had not been informed about the terms of this shipment—my only instruction had been, *Ypiranga* solved. Neither can I learn here the position of the United States in regard to unloading. Therefore I ask the Foreign Ministry for specifics.

The Germans of Puebla can communicate freely with Veracruz, as the clipping proves; i.e., they can travel there if they want to. As the Brazilian emissary's statement shows, the representation of U.S. interests is being realized through consulates in a rather colorful fashion: initially French, then British, and lastly German. Huerta has given some agents three hundred thousand pesos so that they organize bandit groups in Texas: with *such* guerrilla small-scale warfare he hopes to bring about a turn in his favor. A childish idea that Carden shares. Also, Generals Argumedo and Rojas, both "generals" of Huerta's creation and formerly criminals, are moving north with similar orders. They failed to create a guerrilla in the capital. "General " Rincon Gallardo has been sent to Zacatecas to hire such bands.

Monday, May 18, 1914, Washington DC

A REGULAR DIPLOMATIC REPORT

While talking in Niagara, Canada, on eighteenth of month when the mediation negotiations began, the Brazilian ambassador told me he had no hope for an essential success of mediation due to Carranza's nonparticipation. One will talk until the end of the month and, in the meantime, Carranza or another one will have gotten rid of Huerta.

Accordingly, the mediators are in the partisan group of the U.S. governmental policy that is based on reaching its goal with the least possible unfolding of power. The mediators hope, as the Brazilian ambassador hinted, to save intact at least a reasonably independent Mexico, whereas a U.S. advance in the end would lead to a war of conquest. **Bernstorff**[32]

Monday, May 18, 1914, Mexico City

From different sides I receive the news that the expected *cuartelazo* will break out during these days. I have warned some Germans who can be trusted. I cannot warn the others because, based on experience, they cannot keep quiet in spite of solemn promises. The government keeps the troops in the garrison.

The Brazilian diplomat officially complained on May 4 to the Brazilian ambassador in Washington that Sir Lionel Carden attempted to counter his efforts to balance opposite positions and to seek reconciliation. Thereafter, on May 15 or 16, he received a telegram that the British government instructed Carden to support the efforts aimed at Huerta's resignation. In fact, this order was issued in a strict and harsh way.

Carden visited Cardoso and offered him help. Cardoso has behaved with reservation. He says he will be happy if Carden lets him proceed. He does not want to count on Carden's aid. The British diplomat regrets that he does not see Huerta anymore: "He seems to have an inkling that I can't support him any longer and tries to avoid me. When I ask him why he does not travel behind him by car, as he usually does in order to catch him, [he answers], 'To tell you the truth: I'm afraid it is of no use. He will not listen.'" Also, he has news about the coming *cuartelazo*. [Ambassador to Washington] Spring-Rice cabled to him today that he has visited Bryan with the Dutch diplomat to protest against the forced loans of the rebels levied upon the oil company in Tampico. *Dresden* reports nothing about such loans.

The Japanese representative today received from his consul in Guadalajara a telegram that, there, events of concern are going on with grave consequences. The German consul has reported and cabled, following renewed request: all is quiet.

Tuesday, May 19, 1914, Mexico City

A REGULAR DIPLOMATIC REPORT

Brazilian diplomat who represents U.S. interests here has complained about the work of British diplomat that counters [his work]. Thereupon British diplomat received strict order to work toward Huerta's resignation. Secret.

President [Huerta] has empowered delegates to enter into an issue declaration without concern to his person. **Hintze**[33]

Tuesday, May 19, 1914, Mexico City

D'Antin (Brazilian legation) has news from Guadalajara that Chapala and other locations in the surrounding area have been taken by rebels. The German consul does not communicate at all. I urge him telegraphically to follow his instructions in case of danger. From confidential side I hear that the Carrancistas are ready to start with the revolt in the capital. They are one thousand men strong, organized and equipped with weapons. In order to unleash their attack they are waiting for the rebels to get closer.

Secretary of Infrastructure and Communication Lozano, this most wretched creature of Huerta's, is stepping down. Moheno's resignation can be expected. This might be an early sign of Huerta's own resignation. Because after Lozano's resignation the entire cabinet is composed [of men] in favor of Huerta's resignation. Many Mexican and other families are leaving the city as the bloody uprising in the city is about to take place.

General Velasco reports that in the battles near Torreón actually he never had more than six thousand men. He lost two thousand. Then he vacated the city with four thousand men; each of them still with sixty cartridges. Near San Pedro he encountered the relief column led by Maas, Moure, and Garcia Hidalgo. The battle of San Pedro was supposed to have been bloodier than the one near Torreón. General Moure, Maas, etc., instead of fighting sat down, drinking in San Pedro's railway restaurant: carrying his revolver in his hand, Velasco chased them out to the frontline.

Natera is approaching Aguascalientes. The governor, General Ruelas, is sending his family to Mexico City. Certainly the mission of General Rincon Gallardo is rather a means to save himself by leaving the capital, where the pending catastrophe can be expected. Rincon's cousin is the French chargé d'affaires, who entirely identifies with Huerta. Of course, he is rather far away from wanting to die with him.

Consul Weber reports from El Paso, *after being asked*, pushed from the outside instead of out of his own initiative.

The secretary of foreign relations regrets having lacked the time to deal with the forced loans of Guaymas. He is overloaded with work because, just recently, he fired his *official mayor* due to lack of discipline.[34] But, since [then] he promised he will fix the issue immediately (?!) [*sic*].

The Brazilian diplomat read me a telegram that he had written tonight (eighteenth to nineteenth of the month) to the Brazilian ambassador in

Washington. The content: "Carden tells me he cannot get ahold of Huerta." He was avoiding him, "therefore, he also cannot advise him to resign!"

It is being suggested that Huerta's resignation is a necessity and the only way to avoid the revolt threatening the capital and the atrocities that will accompany it. Huerta's resignation is being suggested either by three Mexican delegates or the three ABC powers in the first session of the conference. And this suggestion needs to receive the largest possible publicity in order to avoid a bloodbath in the city as well as damage to property and lives of foreigners. Cardoso added, if he does not receive an answer until tonight he, again, will cable his ambassador. Such approach from outside is necessary and urgent and needs the support of the majority of the cabinet. Cardoso's perception is identical with that of Esteva Ruiz. I note that this equanimity is not based on exchange of ideas, because both do not see each other. In accordance with the abnormality of this continent [Mexico], both of those diplomats conduct political negotiations only via Washington—instead of talking here confidentially and thereby building paths. Cardoso thanks me in a somewhat overboard way for my cooperation. I emphasize that Huerta's curious way of thinking makes a "stimulus" from outside unavoidable. That his resignation is the condition to preserve life and property in the capital against great danger. But this reason justifies our actions, because we do not have other means available.

In my circles of influence, I work toward postponement or moving of the barracks revolt. The news that such an attempt has already been made is becoming more solid. On Sunday, May 18, that revolt is supposed to have taken place in the barracks of the Twenty-Ninth Regiment. Nevertheless, it has been repressed. The shipping agency Hamburg America Co. has news that the *Dresden* arrived in Veracruz on May 19. I do not have any news about that.

Wednesday, May 20, 1914, Mexico City

Yesterday Huerta, on May 19, late evening, after a long advisory meeting with his confidant de la Lama and with foreign secretary Esteva Ruiz sent a telegram to the Mexican delegates. In it he empowers them expressly and again to declare at the beginning of negotiations "that his person should not be a hindrance to an understanding."

News about the alleged arrival of *Dresden* in Veracruz is again missing last night and this morning. It should have sent a signal when it would be in Veracruz. The British diplomat had repeated the official announcement, in a decisive manner, to move all British women and children outside the country.

One Austrian in the Mexican service, Colonel Schega, informed me about the apparent uprising on May 18 in the barracks of the Twenty-Ninth Regiment: one officer supposedly was being taken to the Santiago military prison when his girlfriend secretly passed him a revolver, which he used to shoot the commanding officer of the escort. Other officers rushed to the scene and killed this arrested officer with several shots. All of that unfolded at the entry of the barracks, i.e., the southern side at the Palacio Nacional. Then the populace on the street and in the neighboring plaza began to scream, Huerta! Huerta!, assuming a *cuartelazo* was unfolding. Whatever was left of the Twenty-Ninth Regiment and was still there, about three hundred men, came out of the building and cleared the place.

General Juvencio Robles visited me and stated his view that Zapatistas and Villistas are close to marching into the city. General Moure would not be able to hold Cuernavaca, since his soldiers are recruited from the prisons. Besides, Zapatistas would let the city remain quiet and move past it toward the capital. Tlaxcala is supposed to be stripped of troops. Villa moves via Zacatecas-Aguascalientes. It is known that in 1912 Robles led the most successful campaign against Zapata. He claims that Zapata can reach the capital in two day-long marches. The detachment of Rurales, guarding the entry to the valley, cannot do more than mark their arrival: to delay their advance even temporarily would be impossible because they are too weak.

Mr. Bernal (a Mexican) reports that Tlaxcalan troops have moved to Córdoba. There Garcia Hernández is commanding. Garcia Peña was supposed to have led the Córdoba and the Perote divisions. The Austrian diplomat says Rincon Gallardo was sent to Villa near Zacatecas with a direct order from Huerta to negotiate with him. Rincon has accepted this mission with joy, because it allowed him to leave the hot ground of the capital.

The Japanese diplomat sent a telegram from the chair of the Japanese Society of San Luis Potosí, according to which San Luis was attacked. But the rebels have been beaten back. Two hundred deaths. I asked the German consul. He has not heard a word from him.

During the afternoon I learned that Huerta, after a long talk with Sir Lionel Carden, withdrew the stipulation that his person is not supposed to be an impediment to an understanding.

Together with Carden he wrote the following directive to be cabled to the delegates: "My remaining in power I offer to the nation solemnly and exclusively as a guarantee for peace and order. And, in order to realize this goal, I wish that my remaining in office not be taken into account."[35] The difference is obvious: the sentence "realizando este proposito" gives Huerta a completely free hand to decide *when* he is supposed to step down.

Thursday, May 21, Mexico City

Sir Lionel Carden visited me to tell me the details of the change in instructions, but he missed me. I visited him, and after some back and forth, I learned the following version:

Some time ago, Spring-Rice had informed him of the wish of the mediation powers—rather, their representatives in Washington—that Carden would like to participate in the effort toward Huerta's resignation.

Later the London government cabled him in the same spirit and added, "You need not take any action you may deem inexpedient." Then Spring-Rice cabled to him that the three mediators considered Cardoso—the Brazilian diplomat—to be pretty weak to stand up against Huerta. They said they would be grateful if Carden could make his influence felt. As I deemed it expedient, I went to see Cardoso and we arranged the instructions. But Huerta had remarked negatively, after holding long counsel, about the decisive point—[point] 3—the exclusion of his person, and finally he accepted only the changed formula. Huerta himself remarked about this, he is very wily. This instruction to the delegates was followed by the message: "It should be taken for granted that his—Huerta's—decisions will not be influenced by any foreign power. Please explain the earlier said [ideas] as introduction."

Cardoso's presentation and Carden's differ significantly.

"My remaining in power I offer to the nation solemnly and exclusively as a guarantee for peace and order. And, in order to realize this goal, I wish that my remaining in office not be taken into account" decidedly depends on each other. The countervailing clearing consists of Spring-Rice and Downing Street sugar-coating the pill to Carden as much as possible with the exception of the one order from Downing Street. That states strictly and firmly: Carden should work toward Huerta's resignation.[36]

But, as previously, I found occasion to remark: Carden loves to present as his own corrections of policy stances and orders that he has received.[37]

The British legation received news from Guadalajara that attacks have been made against the city, the surroundings of the city, and inside the city itself. Everything is quiet.

The German consul does not answer. From San Luis [Potosí], Carden heard—communicated through his consul—that yesterday, on the twentieth, at noon, an attack again took place. To the north and the south of San Luis [Potosí] the railroad has been interrupted. In Tampico, everything is quiet: customshouses open; traffic without any hindrance and normal customs rate. Tepic has fallen.

Carden's large and lasting fear is: the rebels could move into the city. He also fears for himself and expects for the British colony the same treatment Villa dished out to the Spaniards. He has these fears because of his close relations with Huerta.

I talked to him about replacing Huerta with a junta. He brushed it aside. His idea is "another Huerta," based on his descriptions, with a front against the United States. Furthermore, complete decentralization: every state should be free and handle itself independently.

Quick word from the peace conference is necessary to prevent atrocities. Most of all it is necessary that Huerta's declaration of resignation should receive the widest possible publicity so that plans that aim at his violent removal come to a stop. Today he wants to repeat the same with urgency.

Consul Weber wires that Saltillo [is] cleared and occupied by rebels. The *Nürnberg* [has use of] wireless for the first time since May 8: Tepic was taken on May 15, rebels lost five hundred men; Federales less; but two hundred prisoners have been murdered. The boss, General Servin, the one who had sworn to die [fighting there], rescued himself. No wonder Guadalajara is being attacked. The consul there is quiet as far as my last dispatch is concerned.

The U.S. consul for Saltillo, Silliman, left Saltillo on May 15. With him arrived here Degner, a German American. He is being accused of spying. He reports that the stretch between Saltillo and San Luis Potosí is in the worst possible state. His train traveled accompanied on both sides by cavalry and the train of repair workers. First they were attacked on the seventeenth and later, once again, near Moctezuma. From Bocan four military trains full of troops have been dispatched to aid them. They arrived in San Luis Potosí on the twentieth. Rebels penetrated once on the twentieth to the plaza in front of the Palacio de Gobierno, but they were driven back. In Saltillo at the time of withdrawal, the army had ten thousand Federales, with twenty-seven field artillery pieces and eighty-five mitrailleuse, poorly dressed, poorly fed, and unpaid. Even among officers a bad mood is supposed to dominate against commanding general Maas, who, in the end, showed himself without courage and unwilling to act. Even officers emphasized the necessity to vacate Saltillo. In the city are supposed to be three to four thousand Federales, the rest in suburbs and along the line. The railroad line to San Luis Potosí is well occupied. It is unknown which rebel general operates against Saltillo. It is not supposed to be Villa. Against San Luis Potosí are operating Gutierrez and Torres. From San Luis to Mexico City the line is supposed to be in working order. Mrs. Schnuck traveled to San Luis with child and cousin Remy and remained there. I ordered the consul in San Luis Potosí to send them here.

The attached request for resignation of Secretary of Communication Lozano and Huerta's answer prove again either his disloyalty or his disturbed mind. He cited the decline of imports and exports during the last months.

Alberto García Granados, previously secretary of interior in Huerta's first cabinet, has learned from General Fredorigo Gonzalez [sic], son of a previous president of the republic, that Huerta is supposed to have said to him that on Tuesday he wired the Mexican delegates to offer his resignation. González did not believe Huerta because Huerta is such a terrible liar, and therefore he went to Blanquet. Blanquet assured González that, this time, he could believe Huerta. Blanquet had read the dispatch himself. Blanquet was supposed to have been very discontent with Huerta and thinks his resignation is unavoidable; a *cuartelazo* could break out any day.

News from the British legation that Oaxaca's governor, Bolaños Cacho, has declared himself, including his troops, in favor of the revolution,. When asked, a royal consul replied, "All is quiet," an answer that, based on experience (see Torreón), can be understood in two ways.

At the French legation yesterday at 7:00 p.m. a telegram arrived from Ambassador Jusserand. It was transmitted on the spot to Huerta by the chargé d'affaires. They are of the opinion that, for the time being, Huerta is not thinking about resigning. Rather, he will let himself be hassled by the circumstances. His removal cannot be expected for about a month.

The attached article by Borzini, the well-known war correspondent in Tripoli and the Balkans, summarizes in a short manner what my reports have elaborated for three years now. In banking circles outrage reigns about Huerta's business activities and their dirty side. At least they do allow somebody to make money who so desires, in whatever fashion, but not while *dying*.

Confidentially the [Mexican] foreign secretary told me: the goal of U.S. policy was, in some form, the annexation of Mexico. For a long time this goal has existed. The predecessor, Porfirio Díaz, recognized this goal and focused everything on gaining time. In the meantime he strengthened the country so that it was becoming too big and too rich to gobble up. Examples of successful playing for time: Transvaal, Canada. As part of this endeavor Porfirio Díaz committed a big mistake.

He did deliver the country into their [U.S.] hands instead of pulling in Europeans and attracting European capital. This mistake was joined by a second one in the last years of Porfirismo: Díaz's engagement on behalf of Zelaya (Nicaragua case); and one additional one: when he said no to the U.S. suggestion to join in taking over the guarantee for Central American nations. Now, for these mistakes Mexico has to pay the bill. Instead of winning time they have created an open conflict with the United States.

Now the issue is to find the possibly cheapest price and, by the way, to resume a policy of winning time.

The first issue—the price—has been initiated in a way that suggests hopefulness. Huerta's resignation has been prepared. He and others are in the process of convincing him that it is he who needs to declare the resignation in a spontaneous way. It would damage his country's dignity and his own if he waits until even the least, harshest hint from the outside. He—Esteva Ruiz—hopes that the next days would bring about the decision.

I elaborate: that is desirable. Otherwise, here, Villistas and Zapatistas would grab our throat. Esteva Ruiz hopes, before then, to hand in his resignation: both parties have submitted their "propositions" to the mediating powers. The representatives are in the process of studying them. Because they are smart they did not share with any of them the suggestions of the other. Gently, I advise Carrancista participation. Esteva Ruiz: I'm working toward it. It could not come about in a direct way. He has submitted the idea to the mediators and he hopes that Carranza, González, and most of the others would be open to it and, therefore, a true truce would become reality. Villa, however, is what gives him true fear. He cannot be held back from invading the capital. Perhaps the United States could prevent him from advancing by applying, in a strict manner, the weapons export prohibitions.

Esteva Ruiz repeats that Huerta's stepping down "is well on the way"; Secretary of Finance de la Lama is joining him. As Huerta's confidant he is the main tool in the undertaking to move Huerta to resign.

In spite of his solemn promises, Esteva Ruiz still has not brought about the repayment of the forced loan of Guaymas. He promised it once again.

It is delightful to find for once a Mexican statesman who appraises the country's outlook in cold blood. Esteva Ruiz, at one time, was a member of Mariscal's office when Díaz moved into the scene against his adventurers at Zelaya. Later followed the cancellation of the Magdalena Bay Treaty and the cuddling up to Japan. A correct action by Díaz was to grant Great Britain concessions of the Tehuantepec railroad and Tampico's and Minatitlán's oil fields. In addition, the railroad concessions went to the United States and the admission of U.S. capital in real estate and mines was continued. The economic penetration by the United States was directly supported under Díaz: this was placating the United States, facing her political desires. Until he lost the role because he was ill advised and became old and had to move aside. But Huerta was well liked among Americans as long as he followed their ideas. As soon as he became independent, the U.S. ambassador began to organize revolutions and made them come true all the way to Madero's murder. Huerta was Ambassador Wilson's weapon: I know—because I was there—Huerta would not have dared a coup d'état without Wilson's encouragement and promises. Because Huerta discovered himself only later. Immediately after the coup, and for quite some time, Huerta was still the willing tool of Ambassador Wilson, who truly governed Mexico. Only the *personal* experience, precisely, that Wilson could not push through Huerta's diplomatic recognition—drove Huerta to position himself in opposition to and gain the enmity of the United States. Purely personal reasons are also the reason for Huerta to hold on to his post.

Saturday, May 23, 1914, Mexico City

Cardoso visited me and read a dispatch to me that he received this morning, 2:00 a.m., from the delegates of the ABC powers: Dispatch No. 31 (with description of situation) has disquieted us greatly. We work day and night but are held back because no answer is coming from the White House. This morning, May 23, we will approve the question of Huerta's succession so that when he resigns a government is in existence. Please continue to inform us by wire about the situation; *bon courage.*

My impression that I passed on to Cardoso—after all the manyfold talks I have had with outstanding Mexicans, whose names I don't know—is the version that Huerta will resign in the next few days, and I told him that I reported the situation to the German Foreign Ministry as threatening without providing details. He asked me if and what he should do here to accelerate Huerta's resignation. I counsel against action, with the exception of a prevention or stopping of a *cuartelazo:* or an uprising intended in the capital. This in order not to reach ahead of the conference's work, or perhaps even to disturb it. As I do, Cardoso has the impression that, besides some fanatics like Carden, *every man* drives toward Huerta's resignation. Once again, as long before, I pointed out that Huerta's stepping down will not suffice. That we have to have organize a government that *follows* him. He wanted to wire this position to the conference.

As I, he rejected the idea of—once again—[putting in office] a provisional president, because such a [president], in this country of personalities, would only lead again to the formation of a new personalist party and would take into consideration a commission that could better take into account the wishes of different parties. Cardoso confirmed Esteva Ruiz's statement that the Mexican government is making the effort, once again, to move the Carrancistas to participate in the negotiations, using ABC mediation.

Cardoso says that Carden (too!) explained to him his project to "calm" the country through complete independence of the states. For example, to hand Morelos to Zapata; Chihuahua to Villa; election of governors in each state [to be] completely free. And, he adds, Carden has asked him to present this plan as *his*—Cardoso's—invention and to recommend it to the ABC powers! Cardoso says he thought this suggestion to be highly strange, and it perplexed him. Therefore he did not mention to the ABC powers a word about Carden's projects. I state my concerns that this plan *perhaps* will create calm for one month, but afterward it will lead to the disintegration, decay, dismemberment, and fall of the Mexican Republic. Cardoso agrees. The Banco Nacional de Mexico moved its main assets to safety: to Veracruz, on May 25. The Japanese delegate had news (certain, as he calls it) that Zacatecas has fallen. Villa stands between Zacatecas and Aguascalientes. On a daily basis the Brazilian diplomat receives news from the French consul about the situation. Our consuls remain silent. Also, Cardoso had knowledge of news from Morelos that is attached and intended to cable it to the ABC powers.

The Japanese delegate reported on the Japanese steamer *Seyo Maru* as far as boarding is concerned.

This morning the Hapag steamer *Bavaria* arrived in Puerto México with weapons and ammunition for the Mexican government and is unloading them. The *Ypiranga*, most likely, also will unload its weapons and ammunition in Puerto México, according to the representative of the Hamburg America Co., describing his directions as coming from Hamburg. I believe this satisfies the intentions of the M. Schroeder Company and the weapons suppliers. But probably not those of the Hamburg America Co. or the local Germans, because it prolongs the agony of the Huerta government. It is possible that the rebels are making progress that is too fast for the United States. Of course, it is not in the U.S. interest to have in Mexico a strong Carranza instead of a Huerta. Therefore, probably the invitation to Carranza to participate in the negotiations will be repeated, and therefore the embargo of weapons and ammunition exports [will be repeated as well]; and finally also, from *Bavaria* in Puerto México, the shipping of weapons—for the federal government.

Obregón,[38] the former vice president of the Senate, General Juvencio Robles, and the former secretary of foreign relations, López Portillo, are asking for asylum. I grant it to them in case of emergency. Also General Chellar asks for it.

In the evening, 7:50, I see a squadron of the Ninth Cavalry Regiment, carbines around their shoulder, moving toward the National Palace gates. Normally the regiment is located in Tacubaya. News that an uprising took place in the garrison. It was repressed right away. Five died, thirty are hurt. Even though these small military revolts have not had large consequences, they are at least symptomatic of the unease governing the military.

Sunday, May 24, 1914, Mexico City

The commander of the *Dresden* replied to my repeated invitation to come here in order to inform himself about the situation: he considered the situation not yet clear enough to accept the invitation. But already in Veracruz the commander had and does have the opportunity to correct the opinion that the *Dresden* was not needed here, which he had cabled from Tampico a few days ago. H. Heynen, the representative of the Hamburg America Co., traveled yesterday evening—May 23—with H. Holste, representative of the M. Schroeder Company, to Veracruz in order to take charge of the cargo of the *Ypiranga*, to gain access to weapons and ammunition.[39]

In order to learn about yesterday's military revolt, I visited the barracks of the Ninth Cavalry Regiment and the First Artillery in Tacubaya: nothing took place there. After searching for a long time I find a cavalry detachment where previously there had been Rurales—where nothing is known in regard to a mutiny; but they point me to Santa Julia.

After a long search I find a farm location where, until yesterday, a command of twenty men, led by a lieutenant, had resided. The owner animatedly complains that the government has not paid her for this mandatory stationing of troops and that soldiers have lived there with disrespect. Yesterday some became drunk. A cavalry captain joined them and set up an outpost in front of the house and courtyard. Thereupon the rebel soldiers were enraged and reached for their carbines and yelled, "Beat them to death." The cavalry captain escaped into a nearby house and called for help from there, by telephone. It arrived after a short while. The rebel troops were overwhelmed after some exchange of fire. The loyal troops led the commanding lieutenant and sergeant to the neighboring agricultural school and shot them, on the spot, as responsible for the uprising.

[Carden] read me a telegram from Ambassador Spring-Rice: He had called to Bryan's attention that the advance of the Villistas to the capital was imminent and that Europe considered the United States as being morally responsible for the excesses that can be expected to be imposed upon life and property of foreigners. Bryan is supposed to have replied: Villa, more so every day, accommodates himself toward civilized war leadership. And, besides, he will not soon enter the capital. Then Spring-Rice pointed out that, before Huerta leaves, one needs to take care of his replacement (this Carden initiated at Spring-Rice's response to my steady encouragement); also Cardoso's, at the ABC powers. Bryan answered: the representatives of the ABC powers already have taken that into their hands. The second telegram was from Carden to Sir Edward Grey and demanded allowing delivery of the weapon and ammunition supply to Huerta "as the only organized government, so that he can keep the rebels from the capital."

This request is based on Carden's fear of Villa. He asked for instructions in case Villa entered the capital. He received the reply, "You better ignore him." An enraged Carden protested about this "wisdom of the foreign service." That is not only likely, but certain, and means, in concert with the U.S. threat coming from Veracruz, ongoing and increasing damage of German interests. Also, it is a steady and growing, serious endangerment of German life and property because it will renew itself for an undetermined time. I announced to the [German] Foreign Ministry the change in situation and outlook. The British representative Sir Lionel Carden described to me his outlook for Mexico's future: the aristocratic classes and the rich will all be massacred. They demonstrated themselves as unworthy of the name México. He expects the well-being and salvation of the nation to continue to come from the Indians! There one sees that Carden, who maintains that Huerta is in his pocket, is under Huerta's complete influence. With enjoyment he prefers to say that a Native American of Zacatecas is governing Mexico.

May 25, 1914, Tokyo, Japan

A REGULAR DIPLOMATIC REPORT

First of all I should remark that the Japanese as well as the U.S. governments are making great efforts to conduct their relations [in] as friendly [a manner] as possible. The new (Japanese) cabinet, in contrast to the previous one, assumes a determined, friendly attitude vis-à-vis the United States. An indication of this is the rejection of Huerta's request to represent Mexico's interest in the United States; furthermore, the decisive endorsement of the cabinet for the Panama exposition and the official statements of Minister President Okuma about his position on the Mexican question. [. . .] Part of the Japanese press does not agree with the behavior of the government. For example, "Nichi Nichi" describes this as cozying up to the United States that goes too far vis-à-vis the United

States. In light of the outlook, what Japan offers Mexico—the decline of protection—the paper states, should not have happened.[40]

Monday, May 25, 1914, Mexico City

Today's *Imparcial* publishes the distribution of U.S. ships along the Mexican coasts. In confidence the secretary of war tells me: contrary to expectations, only 2.1 million cartridges for guns had been unloaded from the *Bavaria*. They also had expected weapons but, according to the *jefe de las armas* telegraphic report, they were not present in Puerto México. On the *Ypiranga* are five million cartridges and artillery ammunition, as well as supply for a mitrailleuse, which he was very much counting on.

Again I point out that the cargo was addressed to here, the local representative of M. Schroeder Co., and therefore needs to be dealt with as legal private business. Blanquet says he was in the process of having the *Ypiranga* unload in Puerto México. In addition, he says all he demands from the U.S. side is curtailment of weapons and ammunition supply to the rebels. Once this is realized to the strictest degree and his war matériel supplied without hindrance, then he would be willing to deal with the revolutionaries. The later ones are now suffering from lack of ammunition and, consequently, are condemned to inactivity.

Confidentially Blanquet answered my question: Huerta is not at all considering resigning. He again received supplies of weapons and ammunition. This changed his decision to stay and to tough it out. Yes, perhaps he would step down if the peace conference would give peace to the country, but not before then. My news (received from the *Nürnberg*): in Salina Cruz the president was supposed to have made preparations to embark—turns out to be entirely baseless.

In light of the lack of ammunition on both sides, the de facto circumstances have created an armistice. Once again the import from the *Bavaria* and the expected one from the *Ypiranga* have changed the situation: Huerta again turned very stiff-necked and is again mulling over the idea of perhaps being able to put down the revolutionaries. It will not be difficult for him to disown his own peace delegates. Also because their instructions can be interpreted and stretched—that is proven by experiences with his decisions.

The Brazilian diplomat received a telegram from Niagara Falls: the Mexican delegates should make Huerta's resignation the foundation for future negotiations, under the condition that Huerta is succeeded by a Mexican government capable of governing Mexico. That sounds very determined, and Cardoso is very optimistic. He has said before: if it suits him, Huerta will not trouble himself with thoughts of contradicting his delegates.

Regarding the revolt of the guard commander in St. Julia, I learn that Blanquet has hurried to the location. The following day—May 24—students of the neighborhood military agricultural school were supposed to have been shot to death without much ado because they refused to act against the soldiers in mutiny.

Tuesday, May 26, 1914, Mexico City

Today's *Imparcial* publishes the present graphic presentation of the distribution of U.S. ships in Mexican waters. Next to them the newspaper displays their names. This display of sea power is not necessary from a military point of view. Perhaps it can be explained by the slight mobilization of U.S. naval forces and a wish, at least, to be part of the action.

The Japanese diplomat told me that the visit of the *Azama* and *Azuma* to Mexican waters has been given up for good. Also, the *Izumo* wants to return to Japan; the commander is suffering from homesickness (nostalgia), but he—Adachi—had resisted these moves.[41] Now Capt. Moriyama was citing the example of the *Nürnberg*, which is also leaving its station despite apparent dangers.

I learn from the ministry of foreign affairs that the Constitutionalists have decided to participate at the peace conference and Carranza has sent former deputy Cabrera to Niagara Falls as his representative. This information contradicts Consul Weber's telegram from today, who had answered my inquiry with, "Carranza is determined to continue operations until the capture of the capital." Furthermore, I hear from the Foreign Ministry that the cabinet works in favor of Huerta's resignation; that the entire world is tired of the struggle, with the exception of the army. The secretary of finance, de la Lama, represents the soul of factions aiming at an understanding.

. . . Today I talked to him [de la Lama] and asked him about the progress of the conference: he told me that the mediators are in the process of establishing the principal conditions for negotiations, with both parties meeting in separate sessions. And therefore they have not yet come to conclusive agreements. I continued asking about the dispatch of Cabrera. He claimed not to have any knowledge about that. In his opinion, Vasconcelos is Carranza's representative in Niagara Falls. He esteems him as a conciliatory spirit and fears Cabrera as intransigent and a socialist. Now only one frame of mind must dominate: that of reconciliation.

The secretary of finance assured me that the forced loan of Guaymas was about to be repaid. This morning the president has given his nod of approval. I replied that I have dozens of presidential promises but they hold no market value. De la Lama laughed and promised to give me [assurance of] repayment in writing.

Tuesday, May 26, 1914, Mexico City

Mexican commissioners have offered Huerta's resignation as foundation for future negotiations, under the condition that he would be followed by a government capable of governing Mexico. The United States has accepted, expressing its satisfaction.

Today, however, the president is in no way disposed to step down. Rather, he hopes to beat the rebels because their weapons supply has been cut off, and he has received some from the *Bavaria* and the *Ypiranga*. He expects them [to arrive]. In light of this, battle is prolonged and, therefore, great danger for German property for undetermined time. **Hintze**[42]

On the afternoon of May 27 some arms were successfully unloaded from the *Ypiranga*.

Wednesday, May 27, 1914, Washington DC

NAVAL REPORT NO. 83

1. Talk with Agent Sommerfeld

By coincidence I made the acquaintance of Mr. F. A. Sommerfeld, known as a secret agent of murdered president Madero. Sommerfeld is working on behalf of the Constitutionalists, and his main headquarter is at El Paso, Texas, at the Mexican border. There he works with the well-known consul Carothers, who represents the United States. He described himself as a friend of Villa. His relationship with the current local official representative of the Constitutionalists, Mr. R. Zubarán, is somewhat tense.

Sommerfeld stays for a limited time in New York and Washington and, in recent days, he has held several discussions with the [U.S.] secretary of war and his assistants.

FIG. 33. Felix Sommerfeld (*left*), with President Madero and other visitors.
Courtesy of the El Paso Public Library.

Yesterday Sommerfeld visited me without me asking him to do so. On this occasion the essential part of the discussion, which is about to be reproduced here, went beyond regular news of military political character.

2. [Political] Development of Mexico

The Constitutionalists must and will enter Mexico City in order to drive out Huerta and his entire regime (*científicos*). Then an interim president (dictator) will be announced by the Constitutionalists, who, due to his power of dictatorship, will undertake a few changes in the constitution. Then, under this provisional president, elections to Congress and the presidency should take place. This Congress will be presented with the constitutional changes ordered by the dictator president. Among others, accepted for consideration as provisional president are General Villar, right now in Mexico City, sixty-six years old, a friend of the deceased Madero; as well as General Ángeles, right now serving the Constitutionalists in the field. Carranza cannot become provisional president for constitutional reasons, because he is supposed to be elected as president.

3. The Position of the United States

The United States knows this plan and supports it. The United States communicates with the Constitutionalists through John Lind; here using U.S. lawyers Douglas and Perkins, who themselves are in touch with the above-named Zubarán and Sommerfeld. Until now, Secretary of State Bryan refused to deal directly with Zubarán. Sommerfeld told me in strictest confidence, whispering, that the U.S. government let the Constitutionalists know they should not let themselves be hindered by the mediation but should operate as fast as possible against Mexico City. Urgently they recommend sending representatives of the Constitutionalists to the mediation in Niagara Falls, in order to win time to realize the operations against Mexico City.

4. The Plan of Attack against Mexico City

The Constitutionalists' plan is to attack the capital from three sides. For one year Zapata has belonged to the Constitutionalists and receives his orders from them. He signs orders, reports, etc. as "General of the Southern Division."

He is not supposed to enter into Mexico City but to remain in Cuernavaca. Because of their lack of an artillery, Zapata's forces are not coming into play for an attack. Zapata's only task is to make the capital nervous. In case Zapata does not follow the Constitutionalists' orders, two Carrancista generals are in his vicinity with about ten thousand men, in order to make him come to his senses.

Foreigners, including U.S. citizens, will have nothing to fear from a Constitutionalist entry into Mexico City. Especially Germans can remain completely calm, because their representative is held in highest esteem among the Constitutionalists, as the one-time friend of Madero. But it cannot be denied that some Germans are almost as disliked as the Spaniards because of their Díaz-Huerta friendships. Sommerfeld named German consul Kueck in Chihuahua as one such German.

5. Constitutionalists for an Independent Mexico

The Constitutionalists desire an inpedendent Mexico. A U.S. entry from the north, crossing the Rio Grande, as well as its entry into Mexico City, would unleash a war against the United States. In order to rule this out, the Constitutionalists are moving between the U.S. troops in Veracruz and the Federales located between Veracruz and the capital. (This [information] too is highly confidential, Mr. Sommerfeld states.)

6. Villa and Carranza

It is supposed to be incorrect that Villa and Carranza can't stand each other. By all means, the first recognizes Carranza as leader of the revolution and sees himself only as a soldier. He does not interfere in political steps being taken.

He is not the brutal person he is so often described as being. The death of General Orozco and several officers, which has been reported lately, was a consequence of literal street and house combat.[43] The officers shot in the course of the campaign, following his order, had been previously, almost without exception, prisoners who had broken their prior assurances not to fight against the Constitutionalists.

Villa is a daredevil and upon that nature rests his successes. The other Mexicans only know defensive warfare. Villa is anti-alcohol. When entering into a city, one of his first steps almost always is to close all cantinas and pulque sales outlets. After capturing Torreón he punished six hundred of his soldiers who had gotten drunk. Villa's weakness is the female gender. He has one wife he married in church and one married in a civil ceremony.[44]

7. The Weapons Supply

U.S. secretary of war Garrison's weapons supply prohibition is still valid. Currently Constitutionalists are denied weapons and ammunition that could come via crossing the Rio Grande or via Tampico. An attempt failed to take a load of weapons in Havana ([on the] *Crown Princess Cecilia*), destined for Huerta, due to a refusal of the involved companies.

Right now Villa still has five hundred to six hundred cartridges per soldier. From the U.S. side, the Constitutionalists have been promised that no difficulties will be put in the way of a weapons supply from the United States that is intended [to be made] in the near future.

The reinstatement of the weapons supply prohibition, as is known, was a consequence of the protest telegram to the United States [sent] by Carranza following the news that Veracruz had been occupied. This telegram turned out to be a great stupidity, and Sommerfeld explained to Carranza that the United States, following Huerta's refusal, had no other choice but to either declare war against Mexico or to occupy Veracruz. Sommerfeld, together with Carothers (see above), fixed matters by telegraphing right away that Carranza's protest had been B.S. (bullshit [*sic*]) and [asking] the Washington government quickly to send a telegram that would afford Carranza an honorable withdrawal. Then Carranza received an official message from President Wilson emphasizing that only Huerta is an enemy of the United States, etc., after he had been neglected by U.S. diplomacy for a long period (according to Sommerfeld).

8. Nervousness in Regard to Veracruz's Security

Of interest in connection with Sommerfeld's statement is State Department publication Marine Bulletin No. 380, published May 24:

"The Spanish ambassador communicated to the State Department a message just received from the Mexican Foreign Office to the effect that a Constitutionalist force of three thousand men has entered the state of Veracruz, and the Foreign Office explained that the movement of federal troops in the neighborhood is against the Constitutionalists and not against the Americans. The explanation was made by the Mexican government in order that its activities in that direction may not be misunderstood."

According to the *Washington Post*, May 24 and 25, certain circles are, indeed, becoming nervous about the gathering of troops in the state of Veracruz. One [counts] a total of seventeen thousand men (troops in support of Huerta, Villa, and Zapata). According to what Sommerfeld said, I consider it impossible that these diverse parties could, suddenly, join and turn against the United States in Veracruz. I do not believe the relatively high number of troops stated in the newspaper. The newspapers, in regard to the capture of Saltillo by the rebels, seem to be incorrect. Lately, again, news by General Joaquin Maas has been published, according to which he still occupies Saltillo with about ten thousand men.

9. About the U.S. Fleet

About the U.S. fleet lying off Mexico's coast, it is reported that this week the cruiser *Birmingham* and ten destroyers have departed to their home ports. And that the First and Second Division of the fleet have practiced troop movements in front of Veracruz.

In Veracruz, on May 26 of this month, there was great humidity and a temperature of 103 degrees (40 Celsius). A large part of the U.S. press demanded more and more energetically the relocation of the Veracruz garrison to the highlands (Jalapa or Esperanza) because of health reasons. **Signed, Boy-Ed**[45]

Wednesday, May 27, 1914, Mexico City

Secretary of Agriculture Tamariz is stepping down from office because on Sunday, May 24, ten students from the agricultural school were shot dead. They refused to move against revolting soldiers in Santa Julia. He is one of the few decent people in Huerta's cabinet.

The Brazilian diplomat claims to know that Huerta has ordered the murder of Lozano, the current secretary of transportation.

Cardoso inquired about participation of Carrancistas at the negotiations and received the answer, "Uncertain news, today we are going to a fiesta in Toronto."

Rightfully he complains about the nonparticipation of revolutionaries; rightfully so, because this way, the pacification of the country becomes more difficult and is postponed.

I point out to him that it is in the interest of the United States to keep the revolutionaries from getting too strong. Therefore, perhaps, [they will give] the approval to unload weapons and ammunition from the *Ypiranga* and *Bavaria* as well as from a Spanish ship. Cardoso does not understand these deliveries, as far as two points are concerned:

(1) That the United States [would] allow them. I explain to him that, in the end, the United States sees the revolutionaries as difficult and independent; apparently the United States uses Huerta to calm them down a bit and let some steam out. (2) That Europe [would] agree to such weapon deliveries, even though here Europeans suffer under the extension of agony. I reply that apparently Europe views Mexico as a purely U.S. affair on the American continents and, as far as possible, wants to stay out of it. In sum, I explain to him: the United States is conducting this war through the help of the rebels or through the Huertistas, depending on what suits her— and the other interested nations here are paying the bill. From the perspective of the United States, a policy by all means clear and understandable.

From the *Nürnberg* a telegram reports the fall of Mazatlán without great fight; I believe this to be a mistake of the cipher clerk.

Parents of students talk about the recent executions in the agricultural school. These boys had hit the lieutenant and the sergeant so poorly that after the salvo, both had remained alive. These boys were shooting even worse than the soldiers. Thereafter somebody detonated an explosive cartridge underneath the head of the lieutenant. They literally butchered him. When revolutionaries or bandits do the same, then the press, paid by the Federales, raises a terrible clamor, shouting "Barbarians" and "The Wild Ones." Here such atrocities occur in the midst of "civilization" of these people, because of an order and in the presence of the lawful and recognized government. Even though this event matters so little, it is new support for the thesis: the Mexicans are incapable of governing themselves.

Thursday, May 28, 1914, Mexico City

Secretary of Finance de la Lama is sending a confidant to me with the request to influence the president to step down. On May 21 suddenly Huerta was supposed to have sent a telegram to the delegates at Niagara Falls. The content said he did not want his person to be an obstacle to peace. But this does not mean that he will give in to foreign influences. The delegates answered, how they should understand this telegram? De la Lama, with effort, moved Huerta to declare that he meant to say with the telegram that he was stepping down.

However, again, Huerta reversed his decision and yesterday, May 27, the president declared he was not thinking about stepping down (the explanation is simple: since May 26 the *Ypiranga* unloaded its large weapons cargo in Puerto México).

Huerta trusts me greatly and was supposed to have said several times: when I go, I will give all my affairs to Admiral Hintze.

De la Lama asked me to influence the president so that he steps down. So far he has made four conditions. They are:

1. peace;
2. the rebels must not advance farther;
3. the United States has to withdraw from Veracruz;
4. and a personal security assurance.

I limit my assurance, based on the condition of discretion, to talking with the president about the question of stepping down.

Lozano has more influence than ever on Huerta and urges him to continue in office. The representative of Schneider Creuzot y Hersent—the group that has undertaken the construction of port facilities in Túxpam—as well as the Belgian banker Lemmens are alleged to have turned to Lozano. Finance Secretary de la Lama had criticized the contract as fraudulent and disadvantageous for the government. Simon, the director of the National Bank who evaluated the contract, declared he is entirely in agreement with the secretary of finance. Nevertheless, Lozano has pushed through the immediate approval of the contract by Huerta with the justification: *he too could earn a small sum doing so*. As a matter of fact, Lozano was supposed to have received from Lemmens ten thousand pesos. In comparison to the giant size of the business that we are dealing with, it is a surprising pittance.

Cardoso has received a telegram from da Gama, the Brazilian ambassador in Washington. It says that the representatives of the ABC powers assume that the United States intentionally allowed the supply of weapons, because it had been irritated by the revolutionaries' minimal willingness to acquiesce. In the same telegram da Gama says that the ABC powers are working to move the United States to prevent the supply of weapons to the rebels via Tampico, but the White House does not reply. Da Gama explains the approval of unloading of ammunition, etc. from the *Bavaria* and *Ypiranga* with the fact that since the offer of Huerta's resignation by the Mexican delegates on May 24 the United States has counted on Huerta's resignation as an established fact. It did not want either the rebels or the Zapatistas to occupy the capital. Da Gama closes by declaring the negotiations have a bit better prospects every day. Following a State Department suggestion, Cardoso requested that [for] the goods that are to be moved from Veracruz inside the country to Puerto México *should not pay customs dues in Veracruz* so that they don't have to pay customs twice. An answer to the telegram left on May 26 is still outstanding.

Cardoso showed me the telegram from May 24, from the ABC powers pertaining to Huerta's offer to step down. The formula has the stipulation: under the condition that a government capable of maintaining internal order is established—therefore not, as remarked on May 25, capable of governing Mexico.

News from Zacatecas, El Paso, San Luis [Potosí] allowed the conclusion that the revolutionaries momentarily have interrupted their advance.

Sir Lionel Carden reports a new plan to me: he is about to move Huerta to assume the command of the army against the rebels: "I shall work him up to it" [*sic*]. It is likely that a few victories, or at least advantages, will win the army for Huerta. The chances are favorable, since Huerta has ammunition and weapons whereas the rebels are short of it.

May 30, 1914, Washington DC

A REGULAR DIPLOMATIC REPORT

The *Dresden* telegraphed May 29 from Veracruz. The *Ypiranga* and *Bavaria* have landed ammunition after being asked to do so by the Mexican government; U.S. officer in Veracruz imposed financial fine. Ship has launched protest. **Bernstorff**[46]

Friday, May 29, 1914, Mexico City

The president, whom I met yesterday, invited me after he had hinted that I had not talked to him for a long time. And I agreed to visit him today, this morning around eight o'clock.

And I just had a one-hour talk with him. To begin with he showed me the first instruction to the three delegates. Then a second one in which he instructs the delegates in a stern tone to reject any exploration of governmental change, i.e., his resignation. Finally, the third and final one. It was sent late yesterday evening, May 28. In this last one he repeats that his only goal is the pacification of the country. They should accept everything that has to do with the decorum, sovereignty, and integrity of the nation and, therefore, work toward creating specifics. However, without change of government or what comes after that: the task is to end the international conflict with the United States but not to deal with the internal affairs of the republic.

That conflict should be solved on the following basis: the U.S. troops march out of Veracruz and, if the SALUTE is raised again, ask for simultaneous salute.[47] Delegates should remember that elections have been set for president, vice president, deputies, and half of the Senate, as well as some members of the high court: Huerta guarantees absolute freedom of voting in the places where he is in power and [that he] will abide strictly by the outcome. The negotiators should limit themselves to listening and waiting for U.S. proposals.

In addition, they should steadily keep in mind that they are dealing with the three mediating powers, not just directly with the United States.

Huerta elaborates with the words: England initially behaved very well toward him but then abandoned him; France, he found out, is a nation of a great people, but [it] has done nothing for him. He puts his confidence in Germany and Japan. "Germany is suffocating in its borders; it must consume Austria and Denmark; Germany's most natural enemies are Great Britain and Russia. Germany wants to be a colonial [power] and needs oil." He offers Germany 150,000 km² of land and Tampico's oil fields, which would be taken from U.S. companies through legal measures. He had been forced to a standstill due to lack of ammunition. Now, thanks to the *Ypiranga* and *Bavaria* shipments, he is supplied for a long time. He has promised a fortune to the agent [Holste] of the German firm that will deliver the weapons. Once he hands over to him the unloaded war matériel in Puerto México—he will keep his word. From now on, Mr. Holste will be a rich man.

Although [Huerta] lacks the twenty-five thousand men that he ordered to be raised, he still has seventeen thousand, and he calls an adjutant and orders the report of [troop] strength for today. The adjutant delivers the one from yesterday, and Huerta barks at him. Then the adjutant begins to tremble. The deathlike fear that dominates him becomes visible. Finally the report comes. Huerta points at thirty thousand men stationed at San Luis Potosí, and [says that] within a few days forty-five thousand men will be concentrated there. Once again Huerta points out the changed situation: that due to the supply of war matériel that he now has and due to the rebels' lack of ammunition, they will suffer. Without reservation I have to agree with him; he answers my thoughts: whether the elections will be held, he does not know. At least they are his government's goal.

After Huerta apparently considers his remarks finished, I begin to speak. I begin by saying that I will answer his frankness with similar frankness, based on confidentiality. It is in the German interest, as in that of many other European great powers, to have a happy, prospering Mexico. Because with such a Mexico, European trade and traffic interests would prosper. However, the representation of these economic interests has been blocked by the present political thinking, which could be expressed well in diplomatic action and friendly services, but it has had to stop short of more active measures.

The reason for this is the extreme political tinder in some parts of Europe. There are the opposing political positions and escalated armament efforts—this is a situation for a great and mighty war that would decide the existence of nations. Rightfully, every European nation has concerns about committing itself and its men and weapons across long distances. For any European nation—regardless of which one it might be— doing so would signal for the others to attack. Not due to hostility against Mexico, but because it offers the opportunity to exploit the temporary weakness of an opponent. As far as I could judge, and speaking not as a German diplomat but as one old military hand to another one, Huerta has nothing to expect from Europe, with the exception of discrete diplomatic help in one or another case. Such is the international situation.

Inside the country, after four years of steady fighting and confusing upheavals, Mexico is exhausted. Not only the country, not only its resources, but also the entire nation's people and even the army. I have observed the land and people for three years now and can tell Huerta honestly and without bias: almost everyone wants peace. Peace no matter what the price. Almost nobody wants war, neither war against the United States nor the continuation of domestic war. Huerta has made heroic efforts to pacify the country but now violence has created such a fiasco. Huerta admits this fact.

Now, since nothing can be gained with violence, there remain as other means skilled diplomacy and reconciliation and concession measures of one to the other. For a long time I have remained baffled why Huerta denies himself the use of diplomacy even though his race—the Latin one—has such undeniable superiority over the Teutonic peoples: in skill of maneuver, in bending, in the use of the spoken word, planning, and suggestion. I imagine that with skilled diplomacy—but none conducted in bad faith—one can and will soon come to an understanding with the United States. But such settlement would leave open, following my last instructions, the great question that would form the goal of his life: the calming of the country. Could Huerta not admit once more that here he has created a fiasco with violence? He admits this—well, why should he not try reconciliation?

Huerta repeatedly gave assurances that he is not hanging onto power and not to his office—Huerta says: the ideal of his life is to live as a ranchero. As soon as there is peace in the country he would abdicate and withdraw from any politics. Well, then he should seek agreement with the revolutionaries without regard as to who they are. Such agreement would come about easily and simply under the current conditions. Because the Constitutionalists are also Mexicans. Such agreement should take place before the elections, not afterward. It presupposes from Huerta a spirit of reconciliation and willingness to sacrifice. This role is larger and more full of honor than the one in which he remains unyielding as [the one] who sacrifices his nation for his personal goals—no matter how lofty they might be. The nation should not be sacrificed and it is in his hands to prevent its demise.

Huerta listened with great attention, several times voicing agreement, and replied that the establishment of peace through settlement with the revolutionaries is an idea that has slept inside of him for quite some time; also, some beginnings in this direction have been made. In Sonora, the rebels joined the federalists. Following my look, full of complaint, Huerta corrected himself—only part of the rebels, and anyway, just a small number. He has maintained agents in Chihuahua. He could reach an understanding with Carranza, not with Villa.

He was grateful to me that I revived the sleeping idea of a settlement and that I encouraged him. Right away he will take it and pursue it in the most energetic way. I interjected that such negotiations must not be disturbed by military operations. Goodwill for reconciliation must be proven also, [through the] standstill of military activities.

Huerta reflected and then said: the forty-five thousand men near San Luis Potosí should maintain a wait-and-see attitude. Triumphantly, he added, he had already interrupted the connection of the rebels between Chihuahua and Ciudad Juárez.—Thus the discussion ended.

Looking at the instructions that have been sent to the delegates tonight, I see immediately that Huerta has pushed away any thought of resigning. This is possible thanks to the supply of weapons and ammunition that has come to him and the lack of them to the rebels. His instruction's goal was to win time. Huerta wants to use this time to defeat the rebels or, at least, to have them experience a few embarrassments. Probably he assumes, rightly so, that a few successes will allow him to win back the army. I recognize, looking at his speeches and instructions, that the request for his resignation has no possibility of success through the path of a conference and encouragement of the mediating powers. Based on the conviction that has guided me so far, when I proposed—in the name of reconciliation with the rebels and acceptance of personal sacrifice—

that Huerta is no longer the man who can give Mexico peace, he openly considered it. I doubt that he is very serious about it and surmise that, for now, he will try once again to be lucky with the use of weapons. If he hurries, that means if he moves earlier then the rebels, he can supply himself with ammunition and weapons. Then, probably, he might be right to pursue his plan.

The assumed influence on the political situation resulting from the unloading of the *Ypiranga* and *Bavaria* once again emerges in this discussion. It completely toppled Huerta's resolutions. Germans in the country and German interests see themselves anew in serious danger, with the resumption of hostilities between both parties. They had rested quite soundly for a while, due to lack of war matériel on both sides.

Yesterday the Austrian and British diplomats received telegrams from their respective ambassadors in Washington, stating that the U.S. government is furious about the unloading of the *Ypiranga* and *Bavaria*. The Brazilian diplomat showed me a dispatch from da Gama, from [the] Niagara Falls [conference], in which he surmised the unloading had taken place with U.S. support because the United States had counted on Huerta's resignation, based on the first introductory remarks of the Mexican delegates—"don't take into consideration me as a person"—as a firmly rooted fact. And they wanted him to have the means to prevent the entry of rebels and Zapatistas into the capital.

Based on the instruction that I received following my inquiry, I left the question of unloading to the shipping agency Hamburg America Line and the company of Mr. Schroeder. I cannot take a position about the possible eternal conflict of opinions or, rather, news, because both representatives of [the two companies] have acted independently and left me without news. I am attaching a list of ammunition and weapons.

De la Lama's confidant—the secretary of finance—who, right now, is the soul of foreign policy, visited me and asked me about the result of my talk with Huerta. De la Lama knew that it took place because he saw me in the president's house. The confidant is the president of the National Bank, Joséphe [*sic*] Simon. I made him swear on his word of honor to keep it secret and authorized him to tell de la Lama nothing more than that I was "consterne" [frustrated], recognizing the president's determination to keep his resignation out of the negotiations at Niagara Falls. And that everything that I could describe as a result of the conversation was that

Huerta wants to continue negotiations that included his resignation. It is not possible to share more with de la Lama about the confidential negotiations. That de la Lama does not come to me personally with his request can be explained by the surveillance of his and my steps and [by the fact] that, if he visited me at my house, Huerta would deduce without any problem the connection between my ideas and those of de la Lama.

The attached exchange of notes between Bryan and Carranza is perhaps meant to gain in importance, if Huerta should succeed and reach an understanding with the Carrancistas.

Saturday, May 30, 1914, Mexico City

Consul Gertz cables from Veracruz that the U.S. Customs Office has imposed a punative tariff against the steamer *Bavaria*. This is because it unloaded in Puerto México goods destined for Veracruz, contrary to manifest and loading documents. The representative stated that they are protected by customs law, No. 2 and No. 4, stating that the federal government does have the power to approve it. I don't know yet if they had such approval for the *Bavaria*. Neither can I learn about it here because (commercial) representative Heynen has traveled to Veracruz.

I report the incident to the Foreign Ministry because it represents a claim against the U.S. administration.

The British diplomat [Carden] visited me: he claimed to have news that Huerta's refusal to give in to demands to resign will cause an uprising in the capital in the next days. Secretary of Finance de la Lama visited Carden this morning and pointed out to him, pleading with him at the same time, that he should point out this very danger to Huerta and try to move him toward resignation. Otherwise the uprising is certain; also that the mediating powers would withdraw.

I told Carden some news from my discussion with Huerta yesterday. Apparently that is the reason for Carden's visit. After listening to me he believes that he wants to propose to Huerta to put himself at the head of his troops. He wants to do this, asking Congress for permission to step away from his office for the time being.[48] Now that the rebels are out of ammunition, Huerta will win a few victories with ease and win back his popularity and his influence over the army.

I countered, telling Carden that Huerta, I, and many others knew that as soon as such permission has been requested and he has removed himself from the capital, the Congress and representatives would declare him and his deputy insane and strip him of his presidency—a step for which the constitution does provide the means; and several predecessors have presented this as lawful and successful.

Furthermore, I countered Carden's explanations, saying Huerta knew this better than anybody else and that this is the reason why he is sticking to his post. Carden replies: then they will murder him. I doubt that and rather suspect that Huerta—in homage to the cynicism that dominates this country in spite of all beautiful phrases—at that very moment [of an attempted coup] will seek shelter with him—or at my place.

The British diplomat agreed after some arguing against it. This evening he will visit Huerta to talk him into putting himself at the head of the army. He is less hopeful than when he came to see me. Now that he actually plans to do it he is at least aware of the enormity of his mission. I wish him luck.

Yesterday evening I felt that the only certain way to make Huerta walk away would be violence. He would yield to violence—and seek asylum. A coincidence or a mishap could bring about his murder in this process. I just do not find it convincing that as a way out Huerta will chose to put himself at the head of his own troops. I mentioned several reasons to Carden, one of which is that Huerta knows that he is not a battlefield commander. Finally, to me the solution appears to be incomplete, because the United States has repeatedly explained it would not be content with Huerta temporarily stepping aside and heading his troops.

Through personal inspection on May 28 and 29, I determined that the true strength of the Twenty-Ninth and Fifth Infantry Regiments—i.e., the infantry garrison [garnison] of the city has apparently been doubled.

The Brazilian diplomat is absolutely optimistic as I directly inform him of my opinion of the strengthening in recent days of Huerta's intransigence in regard to his resignation. This is based on "talks and feedback with outstanding and interested Mexicans in official positions." Continuously he emphasizes that the declaration of the three delegates in regard to Huerta's willingness to step down at that opportunity is supposed to have occurred during the plenary session—irrevocably so.

I ask him, what type of violence would force Huerta to do this? When did he change his opinion? He did not reply. He only repeated, "This declaration has been made officially and all participants [are] abiding by it."

I ask him if he had heard something about a new instruction to the three delegates. He says no but sticks to the opinion that even new instructions would not change anything. The official declaration has been made and its existence is justified.

I explained this optimism for the time being only in the following way: Cardoso has news that the United States wants to advance with sufficient troops—which I consider as likely—or that Velasco or some other general in command of the main fighting force wants to rise up against Huerta. Otherwise I cannot name any positive base for Cardoso's certainty of victory.

Today I learned (through the Foreign Ministry) that the *Nürnberg* traveled to Panama merely to exchange the crew. Then she will return to the Mexican west coast. Until today all the news I had had from the *Nürnberg* was that it would leave the west coast to return to East Asia. Thereafter my three times repeated plea to leave the *Nürnberg* here became unnecessary. It had been based on wrong information about the *Nürnberg*'s travel plans.

Sunday, May 31, 1914, Mexico City

The consul in Veracruz demands instructions about the U.S. Customs administration's demand pertaining to some manifested goods on the steamer *Bavaria*, scheduled for unloading in Veracruz, upon which has been levied a penalty in Puerto México. The substitute representative of the Hamburg America Line—as it is well known, the regular one departed on May 23 for Veracruz—responded to a phone call saying that the relevant federal government permit had been issued for the ammunition only. Exactly in the form of a telegram from the president of the republic.

Aside from that, without permission, the *Bavaria* has unloaded iron wire and carbonic acid. At the [offices of the] secretary of finance there is nobody at the moment who can provide information: it is Ascension Day. I wired the facts to Berlin so that, from there, the U.S. Customs organization in Veracruz can be influenced via Washington, without holding up the *Bavaria* too long.

The *Dresden*'s commander—who, earlier, had cabled me that he thought the cruiser was expendable on the Mexican coast—writes today (May 25), "Of course, I'm sorry that I did not recognize the task ahead in Santo Domingo. However, I agree completely with Your Honor that the ship still remains indispensable."

In Tampico, the Austrian consul who replaced the German consul during his absence—he traveled to Veracruz—cabled that the rebels have passed [to him] a customs order that shipments to Tampico approved by Huerta's consul would have to undergo retroactive legalization: "This order puts a complete brake on foreign ship traffic and I ask for *instructions*."

The Hamburg America Line explained, after being asked, that retroactive legalization costs one or two pesos. I cannot see complete stoppage of foreign ship traffic. The British diplomat has not received a complaint from Tampico about the decree. If we bark at the Constitutionalists because of every small matter, we will pay later once they have pushed themselves into power. I wired the consul with a request for additional facts and justification of his claim.

Sir Lionel Carden visited and showed me a written suggestion that he had made to President Huerta yesterday, May 30, in the evening. It started with the headline: memorandum. It stated: at the moment presidential elections are impossible; they certainly cannot be free elections right now; also, regardless of the outcome they would satisfy nobody. Then followed:

Agreement Proposal

1. The mediators will propose to the rebels and, at the same time, to the federal government that it will verify elections for state governor as soon as a time is fixed.
2. Once verified, the president will announce the results through Congress. Because he puts himself at the head of the campaign to pacify the country—he will present his resignation.
3. The revolutionary states will have representation in the new administration; until then the government cannot proceed to verify new presidential elections.

Carden told me that last evening Huerta was not drunk. During the day he constantly had himself reminded that he had to see the British representative in the evening.

Carden described to him the advantages of the stated rules: every state will govern its own territory; the power of the federal government would be free of this responsibility; and each of the revolutionary chiefs could come to power within a state. For example, rebels would come to power in

Morelos and Queretaro and, for a while, each of the governor's demands would find satisfaction. What would come afterward, nobody knows.

Huerta showed himself entirely delighted with this magnificent project. It may be that Zapata would even be handed two states.

Carden's major motive became completely visible, and I did not keep that from him: he wants to legalize the existing anarchy through complete decentralization. Even to strengthen it in order to show the world how foolish the United States had acted as it pushed for his [Huerta's] removal.

Huerta urges approval. Carden's justification for the project is transparent and he [Huerta] sees—entirely like Carden—in advance the anarchy that will result from this arrangement. He counts on anarchy allowing him to remain in office, which would be wished by all powers, or at least his return to office.

An accompanying factor of this devilish plan is the permanent and growing endangerment of everybody who lives in Mexico. And permanent and increasing damage to every interest in Mexico. And Carden, after my admonishment, can see all that. But [he] brushes aside my strong objections with the remark that [it allows] breathing space, [and] more could not be advised. I don't share that opinion, but it does no good to talk with Carden about this further. For Carden, in pursuit of his own goals, acts with a healthy native Mexican recklessness.

Yesterday Huerta asked Carden to come this morning with his project one more time: he wants to compose the respective instruction to the delegates. This *morning* Carden went and reported: Huerta was drunk. He swore, wanting to cable his choice of words without changes. Previous experience has smartened Carden, causing him to doubt Huerta's promises. Then Huerta promised to come to the legation this afternoon at 5:00 p.m. with the text of his new instructions for the delegates.

Naturally Huerta did not come. Carden is very beaten-down about this fact. He calculates the necessary time to elect governors to be twenty days. I consider this to be far too little.

From excellently informed Mexican circles I learn that the Mexican delegates [at the] Niagara Falls [conference] have made the following propositions:

1. Huerta's diplomatic recognition by the United States and the ABC powers.
2. Following this moral satisfaction, Huerta's resignation.

3. He will be succeeded as interim president either by Carlos Castillo (a decent man) or Flores Magón (a political corsair) or Zamacona (a measly financier).

General Guasque, who is the president's confidant for congressional matters, suddenly has been asked by Huerta to work toward extension of the session. By law it expires in May. Earlier and until recently Huerta's orders have been that Congress will not meet one day longer than the law prescribes! This indicates that Huerta still wants to use Congress for the possible recognition of decisions of the Niagara Falls conference.

Monday, June 1, 1914, Mexico City

The situation is as follows: the three delegates, perhaps backed by the majority of the cabinet, are working toward Huerta's resignation.

Huerta wants to stay in office and works accordingly. He will not long avoid withdrawing the authority given to the three delegates or declaring it as invalid. These contradictions, over [the] short or long [term], will lead to a violent clash in the capital; therefore, the continuation and increase of endangerment of life and property here.

Consul Gertz wires that Heynen bases [his action] in regard to the unloading of weapons, ammunition, and other goods from the *Ypiranga* and *Bavaria* on the oral permission of the secretary of finance and the decree of the federal government of May 13. I point out that the consul should object against penalties at the U.S. Customs administration, referring to Heynen's specifics.

French diplomat reports that he sent the *Espagna* to Coatzacoalcos after the *Ypiranga* incident of April 21, out of fear of a potential load of weapons: but the ship did not have any. After being asked, I describe the penalties to him as an act of a lower-ranking employee and the unloading as a private matter between the Hamburg America Line and the companies that unload.

Japanese diplomat Adachi is traveling for five days to Manzanillo and provides me with the following telegram from Ambassador Shinda: the conference of Niagara will determine the basis for Mexico's participation and will affirm an agreement whose points are the following:

1. The formation of an executive junta composed of a president and four secretaries, to which General Huerta will relinquish authority.

2. The junta's five members will be ones who have been recognized by all political parties and by the government of the United States. They will have equal responsibilities and will proceed, according to the agreements of the Niagara [Falls] conference, to hold elections for president and vice president of the republic and the deputies of Congress.
3. This protocol will establish the principle that will address agrarian reforms and public instruction.
4. The U.S. government will immediately recognize the new junta, evacuate the port of Veracruz, and recognize the legality of measures taken by Congress in the area of finances.[49]

He says he showed this telegram to the Brazilian ambassador, who characterized it, all in all, as correct. The *Dresden*'s commander cabled that today, June 1, he proceeds to Tampico in order to protect German shipping.

Tuesday, June 2, 1914, Mexico City

Secretary of Finance de la Lama asked me to influence Huerta on an ongoing basis; to make him stick to the deal, i.e., in clear language: to move him to resign.

Results of the recent work in this direction were sent the night of June 1 and 2 as the following instructions to the Mexican delegates:

1. Huerta and the revolutionaries will present to the national Senate popular governors, each of them for the state he is currently controlling; the Senate will name them and they will be given control of the states without restrictions.
2. President Huerta will resign.
3. Huerta and the rebels will each name two cabinet secretaries; i.e., Huerta and the rebels will reach an understanding between themselves, selecting one neutral person as president ad interim.
4. The United States loans to this new government her unconditional moral and material support.
5. In four to five months elections will take place for the presidency and Congress.

My part in this plan consisted [of suggesting] the creation of the junta with a president ad interim as head; this approach—[using a] title in order to respect the constitution—and my work went toward strengthening the central power: through money (loans) and the federal army creating usable troops that can be deployed by eliminating "waiters" and "lawyers."

The Mexican participants in this plan are attempting, as far as they are opponents of the Huerta government, the removal of Huerta. They do not look beyond that. And as far as they are participants in the Huerta government, they are seeking to secure through these plans their own skin and the wealth they amass through theft.

The other foreign participant, Sir Lionel Carden, threw into the discussion the idea of handing the states to autonomous governors. His effort aims to create anarchy, which proves U.S. policy as a failure in front of the entire world and will cause the entire world to call for Huerta as the strong man. His determined stubbornness and the passion with which this man confirms his hatred against the United States as he nears the end of his life—even to the detriment of his country and his countrymen— is remarkable. This chaos would cause the destruction of many lives of unknown people and property.

Repeatedly I analyzed these consequences for Carden. Regularly, after some resistance, he admits my scenario's validity but brushes it aside with cold-blooded cynicism with the words: for 1 to 1.5 months this plan will create calm and he does not need more to be able to leave. And away he desires to go. I do understand this. But in my opinion it does not justify a plan with the consequence of Mexico falling apart and, at the same time, in overwhelming fashion, the lack of central power for Mexico. All one has to do is to consider that Carden wants to hand to Zapata the responsibility for the states of Morelos and Guerrero! I explain to Carden that this part of the plan can receive neither my approval nor my cooperation—to which he reacted as more than piqued.

Huerta favors handing the states to the old popular governors. Popular means here: the largest criminal gangs and gang leaders. He is "delighted," in his words, to see Zapata among these governors. His motivation is clear: he sees his own game coming to an end, and "after him the deluge." The age-old drama of the desperate. Furthermore, he counts on something being won for him out of the state of anarchy that is to be expected.

The salient point is: will the Carrancistas agree to the plan? Today the chances for that are slim.

The Mexican delegates are playing a pitiful role. They are entirely out of touch [with the situation] here, and power is located here. Their private cables mirror this mood.

Wednesday, June 3, 1914, Mexico City

On May 30 the consul at Veracruz reported that the former División del Bravo and that of Nazas—in all only five thousand men—are expected to arrive there under Maas's leadership, returning from Saltillo. The railroad from Saltillo to Tampico, as well as from there to Aguascalientes, is in rebel possession. Therefore San Luis Potosí has only one rail line open: that to Mexico City. Secretary of Finance de la Lama has asked for asylum at the [German] imperial legation—in case an uprising breaks out in the capital. As far as unloading the *Ypiranga* and *Bavaria* is concerned, the attachment presents the event in its context.[50]

Thursday, June 4, 1914, Mexico City

The undersecretary of foreign affairs informs me that he has pulled from the general treasury the amount to repay the forced loan levied against Germans in Guyamas—27,400 pesos. I replied that I have received nothing. He shows me the payment order and promises to send the money to me. He told me confidentially about the development of the peace negotiations: the ABC powers have not yet answered the last suggestions—i.e., the instructions to Huerta's delegates. I asked if names have been given to the mediators for future president ad interim. He answered: no. They could not do so before the Carrancistas had not accepted this plan in principle. I explore the advisability of negotiating directly with the Carrancistas. He answered: until now they had talked with them only via a detour using the ABC powers. That is incorrect. Huerta himself confessed to me that he negotiates directly with the revolutionaries. Furthermore, I emphasize the necessity of moving the Carrancistas to a cease-fire. And finally: the unavoidable necessity to strengthen the future central power. Esteva Ruiz seems to comprehend all of this and wants to use it.

The Brazilian diplomat does not know the final instructions from June 1 and 2 but has heard that state governors should be made independent as part of the plan included in the instructions and, as is well known, speaks against it. Our reasons are the same. We look at the project as an intentional attempt by Huerta and Carden to introduce anarchy using the law, with the purpose of reopening Huerta's path to the presidency. Or, as far as Carden is concerned, to lead into absurdity the U.S. policy of getting rid of Huerta.

Cardoso mentions that the United States is beginning to make difficulties in regard to clearing Veracruz. According to this news, the Carrancistas have not yet accepted the plan. Huerta has not yet named his candidates for the two secretaries he is supposed to name and the interim president. Indeed, the president ad interim and the four secretaries are supposed to form the junta as presented in the compromise, but the name junta is supposed to be avoided in order to stay within the language of the constitution.

On June 1 Cardoso received news in the evening from a *New York Times* reporter: that a Foreign Office employee was issuing [the news] that, once and for all, Huerta has given up any intention of resigning. Thereupon he rushed to Esteva Ruiz, who questioned its correctness; as is known, in the night from June 1 to June 2 instructions were mailed stating the opposite.

On June 2 Esteva Ruiz wrote Cardoso another note that counsels more caution in regard to accusations of Foreign Ministry employees. Cardoso sent this note back unanswered and complained to the president. The president promises a verbal remedy—apparently Esteva Ruiz has been reprimanded, but only gently. At least now the latter felt sufficiently motivated to retrieve and to answer some of Cardoso's questions that have remained neglected until now.

Friday, June 5, 1914, Mexico City

Gen. Velasco has been relieved of the command of the army of S.L.P. [San Luis Potosí] and General Maas, the president's nephew, has been put in charge. Velasco's son told me that his father has been selected as the next secretary of war. Huerta will resign on June 8. He also reported that Generals Orosco [*sic*] and Argumedo, in Satillo, have been captured and hanged.

It is reported in plenary session that the Mexican delegates have repeated with explicit power given by Huerta vis-à-vis the United States the first explanation: that Huerta does not want to be an obstacle to peace;

and they have published that they made the statement. The government, with all its might, represses this news. The press circulates no word about it out of fear of trouble.

The Brazilian diplomat confirmed the above-mentioned news and added, after being asked: thereupon the United States will be willing to leave Veracruz. He does not know yet what position the Carrancistas will take facing this new situation. According to his knowledge they have not yet expressed an opinion about it: they will not be as silly as they appear to be.

From a Mexican source I learned that Huerta had wanted to put López Portillo in charge of direct negotiations with Carranza. This followed my urging him to seek agreement with the rebels. But then he moved away from López Portillo because he does not trust him.

Furthermore: movement toward San Luis Potosí comes from Villa via Aguascalientes and Ángeles from the north, along the national railroad. Velasco's recall from command can partially be explained as jealousies between him and Maas.

Besides, Luis Mendes has rejected [an offer] to serve as interim president. A strong party in the capital wants to appoint Garcia Peña [to this position]. Finally: Huerta, for the entire day, had decided to resign and, on the following day, denied any [such] intent. It is necessary that the conference finish its work before the seventeenth; otherwise, due to the president's voluntary abstention from office, an extraordinary session would have to be called; Congress would have to participate because of the constitution. This would cause long delays.

However, the decision is located not in Niagara Falls, but here. Mexican friends are telling me that Bryan has reached an agreement with Zapata using Mr. Hall, the U.S. owner of the Morelos Hotel in Cuernavaca. Allegedly he promises to follow Bryan's directions in exchange for money, weapons, and ammunition.

Secretary of Finance de la Lama visits and tells me the text, the instructions, which have been given to the delegates in the night from June 3 to 4.

They are the answer to the delegates' interjections to the instructions of June 1 and 2. They had objected to the naming of governors of individual states as proposed because they would encounter objections and, as a consequence, long drawn-out deliberations.

Better to drop this part of the program and say: the delegates will be empowered to agree, with presidential accord, on the following basis:

1. U.S. withdrawal from Veracruz and the withdraw of the U.S. squadron.
2. The rebels put down their weapons and ammunition.
3. As secretaries of administration the president will designate a Huertista and a moderate. The revolutionaries will designate a partisan of their own: and a northern moderate.—Furthermore—Huerta, naming a neutral person as president ad interim, will use the constitutional process of naming him secretary of foreign affairs in order to build a transitional government.
4. The president will step down.
5. The transitional government will schedule elections for Congress, president, and vice president and will assure the unequivocal freedom of elections. The president will leave all details to the delegates: for the purpose that the transitional government will be honored and complied with by *all* Mexicans and, furthermore, that it will be assured international recognition and respect.

A second, *highly confidential* dispatch states that the president clarified the June 3 declaration using the sentence "realizada la paz" [created the peace]. He ordered the delegates to deliver it in such a way that it means in harmony with the revolution in the north (with Carranza!), not just the destruction of all rebel bands or suppression of all revolts.

A third dispatch from the president, this one also highly confidential, adds that Huerta is willing to name his three candidates for the transitional government as soon as the government delegates report to him that the above stipulations have been accepted.

Lama asks for my opinion and advice. First I answer that I congratulate him and his country because he dropped the unfortunate and fateful plan to hand individual states to yet-to-be-named governors. Because this would have been the legal introduction of anarchy, as I had described several times. Furthermore: now everything depended on whether the president would completely commit himself, really for good, to these final *instructions*. As de la Lama claims is fact. After many turns Huerta came to this decision and will keep it.

Now, then, two points remain:

a. To win the revolutionaries to this project.

b. If this could not be accomplished, or not fast enough, then to force them by cutting off their supply of U.S. money, weapons, and ammunition, and by the withdrawal of U.S. moral support.

Using long explanations I present my old plan to enter into indirect negotiations with the Carrancistas. De la Lama describes this as impossible: because Luis Cabrera, the guiding spirit and secretary of exterior under Carranza, has published a program according to which all Porfiristas and Huertistas should and would be killed in order to give birth to a new, cleansed Mexico. All that my well-meant prodding succeeds in achieving is that the Mexican delegates should enter into direct negotiations with Carranza's delegates, Zubarán, Vasconcelos, and Cabrera.

No mediation by the mediators or the United States, de la Lama declares, arranged anything; the Huerta government has done its part. Now everything depends on the Carrancistas and the United States: if the former don't want to do it, then the latter would have to force them.

The secretary of finance also reported: Senator Owens, head of the U.S. Senate committee for foreign relations, has told Luís Elguero: Huerta's remaining in office is impossible; his departure is a sine qua non. This explanation influenced Huerta strongly. Because [in Mexico] people assume that this committee is the actual leader of U.S. foreign policy.

The Huerta government has begun to consider the Carrancistas as unrelenting and seeks to use the United States to tame them. When I share this with de la Lama—in a flowery, Spanish way—he raises such a vivid objection that it proves the correctness of my conclusion. He only concedes that the United States should withdraw its moral and material support if they do not accept the new plan.

De la Lama cites the example of "the *Antilla*," on the way to Tampico with weapons and ammunition, and of U.S. officers and enlisted men who serve in the rebel army: I counter that both are rather exaggerated, according to my information.

De la Lama expects tomorrow, June 6, the answer to the latest instructions. Carden has learned that his Machiavellian plan has collapsed and tells me, "It is time that I go and I will leave in July." He is right.

Saturday, June 6, 1914, Mexico City

Secretary of Finance de la Lama today has an answer from the delegates in Niagara Falls: entirely satisfied with the last instructions. The U.S. government is supposed to have entered into negotiations with the rebels. [They are discussing] truce and participation at the peace conference. If the negotiations have a satisfactory result, they would step forward with suggestions according to their instructions. I use the opportunity to talk to the finance secretary anew about the outstanding payback of the forced loan in Guaymas. He asks me to come to his ministry on Monday morning to receive the money.

When I touch on Ketelsen and Degetau's claims, de la Lama says he has already paid the checks of about thirty-seven thousand pesos. Also, the payment of the reclamation is in the works. The military attaché learned from H. Garcia Pimental, a large hacendado in Morelos, that Cuernavaca has fallen and the federal garrison has withdrawn to Mexico City.

I test the news with Mexican friends and I learn: June 3 Cuernavaca was attacked by Zapatistas. In the morning of June 4, reinforcements had been sent from the capital to [Cuernavaca]. However, they only reached a bit south beyond Tres Marias. There they found the railroad reinforced and they encountered Zapata. The reinforcements stopped there. They must have had firefights there as well. Because on June 5, in the afternoon, wounded men arrived here in sixty cars, and they have been moved to the San Juan de Dios hospital.

Telegraph and railroad connection with Cuernavaca is interrupted. This development moves toward greater likelihood of a Zapatista raid on the capital. Because of Bryan's assertion that he told Zapata that his advance onto the city would be followed immediately by a U.S. intervention into the capital. One can only comment on this strategy with laughter. Because Zapata can be in Mexico City within one- or two-day marches. According to Bryan's own statements, the U.S. Army would need at least a month.

Today the danger for German life and property is greater than it ever has been. The military attaché received from local commander General Bravo the strength report of the garrison: Twenty-Ninth and parts of the infantry regiment (the last one is known as auxiliary); Second and Ninth Cavalry (this information is incorrect); parts of First Artillery Regiments and five in its entirety: three thousand men; add to that three thousand

Rurales. Altogether six thousand men. Of course, governor statements have to be greatly reduced. I assume that a total of about two thousand men are garrisoned in Mexico City, including the suburbs. That is not many. Politically the policy is unreliable.

Sunday, June 7, 1914, Mexico City

The attached order from Bryan limits government-paid return of U.S. citizens to the homeland to those who need it. This causes bitter accusations against the U.S. government inside the U.S. community.

From General Guasque I learned about the fall of Cuernavaca and that General Romero has been shot. His troops—about two thousand—have been dispersed. That the secretary of war tells him already on Friday afternoon that the situation is *horripilante* [sic], because the reinforcements— about two thousand men—have been cut off near Tres Marias and are without connection with Mexico City.

Sunday night further reinforcements were dispatched. No news until today about how far they were able to go.

If an agreement has not been found at the conference by June 15, the extension of Congress expires automatically. If the forging of the agreements takes longer than [extends past] July 5, the current Congress goes out of existence and then the elections would not have a quorum. Even if they could be held—because more than half of the country is in rebel hands; thus from July 5 on, under these disruptive circumstances, no government exists.

The commander of the *Dresden* arrived here after my repeated invitations. It was motivated because I learned from his reports how much he was lacking the correct insight into the general situation. Since his arrival in January 1914, when I briefed him about our and his tasks, he has stayed in Tampico almost the entire time. There he was occupied with the protection of Germans and, temporarily, cut off from the rest of the world. It is only natural and understandable that he developed into a *tampiqueno* without recognizing it himself. While he is here, I will brief him in depth about developments since January 1914.

Monday, June 8, 1914, Mexico City

I recognized that the last cabinet instructions to the Mexican delegates are known only to the secretaries of finance, war, and foreign affairs. The rest of the secretaries are informed only superficially but, without exception, [are] in favor of Huerta's resignation.

Again I point out that it is important to enter into direct negotiations with the rebels. Because the conference probably can make decisions but cannot execute them against the revolutionaries. In case the decisions have to be accomplished there, U.S. intervention would mean the end of the Mexican Republic.

Once again Secretary of Finance de la Lama asks me to influence the president. I tried to reach him but gave up when I learned that he already had visited this morning (11:00 a.m.) Cafe Chapultepec and Cafe Globo. At another moment I mention that the rebels would hesitate to accept the theoretical suggestions of the delegates until Huerta named his two candidates for secretaries and his successor. Because, as true Mexicans, theories, principles, and systems mean nothing to them but people mean everything. This is accepted, but one answers me that up to this morning the president has refused to name names. All over again this nurtures doubt about his good faith.

De la Lama says that the United States raised objections against lifting the Tampico blockade. The *Antilla* (with weapons and ammunition for the rebels) was prevented from reaching shore.

Mr. Wunderlich demands through telegraph that I obtain a presidential order that his beer will be transported from the brewery in Toluca to Veracruz. But General Garcia Peña refuses.

Mr. Huber desires that I free from military service twelve of his workers who have been drafted. These are examples of the demands that I am presented with. Mr. von Reisbach, owner of a local company, appears as a third person demanding to know what the country's situation will be in four weeks. Because he wants to send a ship here from Holland.

Tuesday, June 9, 1914, Mexico City

This morning I held a 1.5-hour-long discussion with Huerta, with the goal of moving him toward naming his candidates for the provisional government. So that the increasingly unbearable pressure will be lifted. . . .

The president wanted to deflect me with platitudes. However, I told him, appropriately drawing him in, that this game was over and it is about finding a way out that keeps open a future for him or the nation. He interjected, "The U.S. colossus has sent ships here and threatens me with its army. I am sitting here quietly and conversing with you. What can they do to me? I don't have 250,000 men but I have Guadalajara, Zacatecas, San Luis: 70,000 men against the rebels and here 30,000 men against the United States."

I counter, "The nation and the army are exhausted and don't want war. I am astonished that a man of your intelligence does not recognize this. You have to provide the nation with time to catch her breath. The use of force has failed. What remains are other means that are at least as strong. You may be worried about not showing weakness, but to put honor above everything else no longer works. This is not about weakness, nor self-love, nor honor. This is about the existence of the Mexican nation and your own. What you have to do in this moment is: *recoiler pour mieux sauter*," which I translate as "one has to pull back a little bit in order to jump ahead better at a later time." The rebels, like the mediators, are all members of the Latin American race [*sic*], i.e., as far as this sentiment is concerned: they believe neither in a few reasonable promises nor [in] suggestions. They believe in facts and people; your suggestions are not believed by the rebels nor by the ABC powers. But if they would have to name the candidates today, they would be facing all creditors. Huerta fears that this will be interpreted as weakness. He prefers to die while serving at his post rather than to dishonor himself and the country.

I express my disbelief at seeing such an important man dominated by such an opinion. His death will not heal Mexico's destruction as a nation. What needs to be achieved is to find a path that preserves him and the best future for Mexico.

Huerta interrupts and says to me,

As a friend, I want to tell you the secret of my policy: the conference will end and its decision will introduce chaos and everybody will want me back in my post. I won't share this with my secretaries of administration but with you I do: total anarchy will break out and people will scream for me to return. Therefore my suggestion for a precondition is: a rebel cease-fire.

As soon as they (i.e., the delegates) cable me that the truce has been accepted by the rebels and the United States, I will cable them the names of my candidates. Not before, because earlier would be a sign of weakness.

I doubt that and, I repeat, nobody in Niagara Falls will believe in the ethics of his intentions, unfortunately, until he has divulged the names of his candidates. This he attributes to mutual distrust. Huerta interjects, "As soon as the delegates report to me acceptance of a truce, I will step in front of Congress and say: my work has been done; the country's pacification has begun; hostilities have stopped; I will depart. But if the rebels do not accept the truce, I will allow elections to go forward regardless of the outcome" and, he says, he would submit to the results of elections.

I admonish him, because, right now, the outcome of the election would remain without results because no quorum could come together, since two-thirds of the country has been removed from his control. He does not deny this and remarks, "Well, then everything stays as it was."

Once again he trusts me with his conviction that only anarchy will result from the conference and, before the end of this year, the entire world would call for him: that remains the foundation of his policy. When I urge him again to give, as proof of his goodwill, at least the names of his delegates, he says, "Just be a little bit patient. Soon I will show you that I remember well your advice: one has to pull back in order to advance better later."

He calls the end of Tampico's blockade a sign of his weakness: the U.S. officials are not honest people but bandits. All I was able to gain was the promise that he will name names as soon as the rebels accept the ceasefire. Anyway, that is something: somehow the mediators and the United States have to move the rebels toward that step.

Once again this conversation shows that Huerta is not thinking about stepping down unless the force of circumstances becomes overwhelming. He will not leave office of his own free will. Also, he wants to arrange his departure in such a way that, soon, he can again take the reins. Literally, he says, "I am not leaving but am going to reserve for myself a decisive role in the government," and further, "I will not leave the city; I will stay here because they will call me."

He offers me copies of all his instructions to [the delegates at the] Niagara Falls [conference] and urges me to visit him again after reading them.

At the end of his talk, the president says to me that the negotiations at Niagara Falls are moving forward too slowly. He will not wait more than ten days.

The Brazilian emissary cabled to his ambassador the following suggestions.

1. To end negotiations before June 15, because Congress expires.
2. To demand a truce from the rebels.

The British diplomat [Carden] has news from his consul according to which the central railroad, from Torreón southward, is in the hands of the revolutionaries. Any day Villistas could move into the capital. He thinks of them with the very greatest worries and [expresses], in a very lively fashion, that he wishes to leave.

Mr. Heynen brings the attached exact list of weapons, i.e., the cargo of the *Ypiranga* and *Bavaria*. I hand to him to read my report about the incident. He states that the report he wrote about the incident is identical with mine, in all parts.

Wednesday, June 10, 1914, Mexico City

Secretary of Finance de la Lama visits me, saying: in twenty days, money will be gone, what to do then? He shows me a telegram from the delegates, dated June 9, that arrived today:

The mediators made suggestions to the United States that deviated little from ours. The U.S. delegates declared themselves in agreement, except in regard to the person who would become the president. He would have to be a Constitutionalist, not a neutral person. In the same telegram is repeated [information that] I learned from an absolutely secure source, that, privately, Bryan expressed himself, saying: their policy was aiming to create a Constitutionalist regime in Mexico. Only with this intention in mind has the United States accepted mediation. Therefore it will agree only to a Constitutionalist as president.

At the very least, it is not skillful to admit to have accepted mediation with the intention of bringing the Constitutionalists to power. In the spirit of friendship, I have counseled reacting to this admission with the confidential naming of the president's three candidates: this, then, would establish a fact to which the others would have to take a position. De la Lama says the president already has talked about a successor who would be unacceptable for the rebels as well as the United States (most likely that is Blanquet). I say this should be avoided. He has to appoint an entirely neutral person. De la Lama asks if Germany could influence the United States in favor of accepting a *neutral* person? I say: the great obstacle for direct and purely amicable support is Huerta's unreliability and constantly changing state of mind. After some reluctance de la Lama admits this. I promise to think about his request.

De la Lama visited the British diplomat regarding the same issue. Sir Lionel Carden tells me: I would leave no stone unturned. The phrase: the president to be named *by mutual accord* from the Constitutionalists is nothing but that: a phrase. I add: mediation was aiming only at establishing a transitional government and would leave the raising of the final one to a government expressing the will of the nation—as far as possible; later new elections [would be held in] which it would be unethical to grant *one* of the two parties a decisive weight because of mediations.

Sir Lionel [Carden] critiques bitterly an addendum to the delegates' telegram, calling it proof of the United States' bad faith. [It says:] the U.S. government accepted mediation only as a means of bringing the Constitutionalists to power. I counter that I considered it proof to explore terrain. Carden says, right away, he will cable a translation of the telegram of Mexican delegates to Downing Street [London] and add to it: Great Britain must not allow Huerta to be driven into a corner. He is a desperate man and is being pushed into a situation where he does not shy away from any violent act. In addition, the U.S. demand is extremely inappropriate.

It shows the bad faith of Carden's usual style as soon as the United States is dealt with.

I cable the [German] Foreign Ministry that the U.S. suggestion is to select a Constitutionalist as president. I add friendly advice to counter [the move] by having Huerta name three candidates; as well as Carden favoring British support. This way the Foreign Ministry will not be surprised by [a] potential British proposal. If the [German] Foreign Ministry wants to participate in a possible support of the British position my approval is not needed, and I can save the money for the words that would have been necessary to do so.

Carden picks up my idea to move the president to name his candidates.

De la Lama asks me to influence the president to announce his three men. I commit to it. I intend in this way to achieve, indirectly, a truce so that the endangerment of German life is reduced.

The British mission has news that in Saltillo rebels are keeping strict discipline. The Federales are supposed to have murdered, burned, and looted by setting fire, etc.

General Morelos Zaragosa arrives here with the remaining defenders of Tampico.[51] Along the way he lost one thousand men. I am trying to see the troops in their barracks; no success.

One of Colonel Schega's letters to the military attaché mentions that few troops are facing the United States at Cordoba. He complains bitterly that the government has not built any of the divisions (?) against the United States that he promised and announced publicly to the diplomats.

One lament from an officer in the field strongly criticized Huerta's statement of June 9. He has raised thirty thousand men against Veracruz. A visit to the barracks shows that parts of the Fifth Infantry Regiment are still in the capital (San Ildefonso barracks) and that the large remnants of the regiment have been sent to Cuernavaca. Furthermore, all barrack guards and the guards of the Belém prison and the *penitenciaria* are supplied by the Twenty-Ninth Regiment—a sign of how much other troops can be counted on.

Also, Consul Weber reports from El Paso the rebel attack against Zacatecas. The connection with Zacatecas has been cut off. Also the cable connection. Guadalajara reports attacks from near Juanacatlan that have been beaten back.

Since yesterday the president rests in bed with fever. Since yesterday he does not receive anybody. Also, news from [the] Niagara Falls [conference] is being kept from him (see June 10).

Machine guns from the Citadel and ammunition from the cargo of the *Ypiranga* and *Bavaria* are being brought to the train station. Today the questions circle around the following points:

1. Will the Carrancistas hold up reasonably well under Natera after insubordination of Villa; or, better stated: do they hold together in a sufficient way?
2. Are they able to organize sufficient ammunition?

Consul Weber cables from El Paso that they have been supplied via Tampico with ammunition. A U.S. newspaper states that this has come from the steamer *Sunshine* from Galveston [with] allegedly three million cartridges.

The attached excerpt communicates the treatment of mail from and to Veracruz.

The attached excerpt from the *Mexican Herald* of June 6 illuminates the, until now, unknown Blythe-Wilson interview. This article posts a rather unknown declaration of the Carranza representative.

According to private news, the troops of General Rubio Navarrete are near Santa Fé on the interoceanic railway. They are *not* under the order of Garcia Penia; a curious situation. On June 9 the United States demanded from the mediators a revolutionary interim president, instead of a neutral person. Then the [mediators] declared to the United States that they considered negotiations as broken off. Thereupon the United States, for the time being, gave in. The Brazilian diplomat in Mexico proposed via cable to da Gama to involve the Carrancistas under all circumstances; regardless of whether they maintain a cease-fire or not.

General Ruelas, an industrious man, governor of Aguascalientes, has been asked to resign and also, some time ago, General Moure from Morelos; the latter has been replaced by General Romero. The constant changes in the position of army commander and governors point toward the activity of a sick mind.

Thursday, June 11, 1914, Washington DC

NAVAL REPORT NO. 87

Armed intervention of the United States in Mexico. VII. *Ypiranga* case—weapons supply via Tampico—Annapolis speech—Fletcher report—regarding the fleet in Veracruz

As far as the naval political report is concerned, dealing with the Mexico situation the [following] events stand out during the last fourteen days:

1. The *Ypiranga* case.
2. Weapons supply via Tampico.
3. President Wilson's speech in Annapolis.
4. Admiral Fletcher's official report about the fighting in Veracruz.

Anybody in Niagara Falls trying to evaluate the behavior of the local administration and in regard to the weapons supply question has to gain the impression, in my opinion, that the U.S. government sees in the entry of the Constitutionalists to Mexico City the only solution to the Mexican question.

If one makes this assumption the basis [of consideration], then one can explain all other curious measures and often-illogical-appearing measures and administration statements.

It is identical with what the Constitutionalist agent Sommerfeld states. [...]⁵² The Constitutionalists are hoping to be able to march into Mexico City at the beginning of August.

1. The *Ypiranga* Case

The Hapag steamer *Ypiranga* unloaded significant amounts of ammunition and weapons for Huerta in Puerto México.

Because Puerto México is an open port and no state of war exists between Huerta and the United States, there existed no doubt that it was legal to deliver the weapons to the person who had ordered them.

But whether this measure can be recommended, from the point of view of German interests, has to be doubted seriously.

Not only local government circles but also public opinion interpret this action of the German steamship line as shameful.⁵³

Especially inside the [U.S.] army and navy there is an angry opinion. Letters from U.S. ships stationed in front of Veracruz contain bitter statements about this. Naturally they are directed against their own government and hysterically argue that due to the *Ypiranga* case the sacrifice of nineteen soldiers who have fallen in Veracruz has been in vain.⁵⁴

I include a copy of a letter that reached me via a *confidential* path, [written] by a passenger of the fleet's flagship *Wyoming* because it is typical of the mood that is dominant among the U.S. troops in Veracruz. [It is] addressed to the Republican senator Lodge. [...]

The letter gives the Navy Department responsibility for the ship withdrawal from Tampico, which has been commented on in many places. It accuses the secretary of the navy of acting against better judgment, because in the official statement he shifted responsibility away from himself to the commander of the navy.

Admiral Mayo is being described as a "broken man," a consequence of this injustice.

Moving on to discuss the *Ypiranga* case, the letter writer—a close friend of fleet commander Badger—asks, Are those in [positions of] responsibility not guilty of murder and should they not be sued, having committed such a crime? When Badger inquired at the Navy Department what he should do in case the *Ypiranga* tries to unload the ammunition at a different location on the coast, he only received the answer "Give *Ypiranga* the clearance papers."

The Constitutionalists' mood, in addition to that of the United States, has been soured. If one may believe their secret agent, Sommerfeld, the Hamburg America Line, under a Constitutionalist regime, will have to do serious penance for her actions, [in the form of] trade and shipping difficulties.

Local representatives of the Constitutionalists explain the measure with the allegedly notorious greed of the Hapag representative in Mexico City, and they spread the news—which, in my opinion, is highly unlikely—that the captain of the *Ypiranga* has received ninety thousand pesos from Huerta's people for unloading the weapons.

Compared to such bad opinions, Huerta's feelings of gratitude cannot have high value because, in a few weeks, perhaps even in a few days, this man will no longer be able to do much thanking. [He] is a man hunted like wild game, for whom, in my opinion, because of his personal courage one cannot suppress a certain sympathy.

2. Weapons Supply of the Constitutionalists

In general one considers as proof that Huerta is beginning to admit the weakness of his position that he withdrew the order to blockade Tampico. The steamer *Antilla* of the Ward Line therefore has been able to unload without any harassment a load of ammunition consisting of 1.8 million cartridges for the Constitutionalists. The delivery had been organized by Sommerfeld and, as he states, with the expressed intention to force the present administration to take a clear stance. This should make clear whether the United States truly and sincerely is willing to support the Constitutionalists or not. (It is supposed to be impossible to gain a clear understanding of Bryan. One day he talks like this, the next he'll say the opposite. [Sommerfeld]).

This proof never materialized. [In] preventing a Mexican blockade of goods from the United States, it would be very difficult, with the world watching, to justify an action with the wish "to keep Tampico open."

Especially in view of the truce negotiated in Niagara [and] mediation between the United States and Huerta, using violence to prevent such a blockade would have constituted a partisan act of war.

The U.S. support of the Constitutionalists' weapons supply took place when the schooner *Sunshine* from Galveston, with the alleged destination of Havana, unloaded one million cartridges of U.S. origin in Tampico on June 5. The unloading was under the leadership of a Mr. Brown (a newspaperman from Washington and agent of the local lawyer Douglas, the representative of the Constitutionalists). The U.S. ships did not interfere.

3. The Annapolis Speech of the President

On June 5 President Wilson, at the graduation of 154 naval cadets to the rank of petty officers, gave a speech in which he said, relating to Mexico, "I ask God that our boys will not have to use more violence down there." He has, just as during the occasion of the funeral in New York,[55] then declared again that the U.S was not pursuing conquests in Mexico but only was trying to serve mankind.

Signed, Boy-Ed[56]

LIST OF THE UNLOADED WEAPONS AND AMMUNITION

from the Hamburg America Line steamers Ypiranga and Bavaria[57]

Boxes	Pieces
Ypiranga	
Cartridges (2,000 each)	15,750
Machine guns, approx.	40
Shells (59 tons)	717
Caissons(500 kg each)	78
Guns, about	10,000
Bavaria	
Mauser cartridges (2,000 each)	1,400

Friday, June 12, 1914, Mexico City

The Foreign Office reports that Bryan holds on to the idea that the conference is making little progress, because Carranza does not want to accept the required cease-fire—the precondition for admission to the negotiations—and without Carranza no progress can be possible.

When Bryan does make this thesis the basis for his policy, then the conference will certainly dissolve. According to their actions, the Carrancistas are under the impression that Huerta has reached the end of his strength, and he holds on only through the *vis inertiae* that is germane to the Mexican race [*sic*].

Therefore they might be convinced that they do not need the conference in order to reach their goal: to claim power and to loot. This is proof that they advance again on the central [railroad] line.

General Velasco demanded to be relieved from the command of the army of San Luis [Potosí]. Due to his wounded arm he cannot dress himself nor mount a horse without aid.

On the left one can see the exchange of notes between Carranza and the ABC powers. On the back of the lose clippings and on the *right* next to it are *chispazos* that show the mood of the U.S. troops in Veracruz.[58]

Saturday, June 13, 1914, Mexico City

One "bando" consisting of:

Twenty-Ninth Infantry Regiment—456 men in one battalion
First Infantry Regiment Supremos Poderes—in two battalions, one of 200, the other 180 men
Three squadrons Ninth Cavalry Regiment, each about fifty horses
Guardia Presidencial: 48 men
Guardia Bosques: 50 men

Headlines at the main street corners announce the latest constitutional change: the appointment of the members of the highest court by the president with the participation of the Senate.

General Velasco visits me. He reports: at Torreón he had commanded only six thousand men. All his requests for troops, ammunition, and money had remained unanswered. He had not received money since November 1913. When he reconquered Torreón, after eight victories in the field, he wired: now it is time to advance toward Chihuahua. No answer. Finally, after a long wait, he received the order: remain put in Torreón.

Once he left Torreón he had fifty cartridges per man and not a single shot more per cannon. He had intended to withdraw to Zacatecas, because there the troops were under his command. No news from Mexico, no money, no bullets. Finally he began to believe someone *intentionally* wanted him to die there. In San Pedro de las Colonias he encountered the generals Moure, Garcia Hidalgo, Romero, and Maas. He had hoped that they would have cartridges. They told him they had used up their bullets while advancing! Velasco had to dig them out with the remainder of his troops; fifteen hundred of his six thousand men have been wounded or killed. The enemy had taken three times the number of losses. He had come to Mexico City in order to heal his wounds. Until now he had been an optimist.

But he became a pessimist once he had seen the government officials' unique corruption and mismanagement, as well as their lack of patriotism and use [of resources] for their own purposes.

The government sent him again to San Luis [Potosí] as troop commander and governor, stating he would find an army there. He found two thousand recruits, in addition to an armed gang and an officer corps that acted with abandon and in a dirty way. Among them was General Maas, capable, but inexperienced and money hungry. At this point he told himself: the demise has been sealed, and he asked to be called back due to his wounds.

Once he arrived here, at first he intended to complain, but—due to the enemy in Veracruz—he remained silent. The army is no longer in existence, only gangs in uniforms. General Huerta has caused the demise of the army with his waiters, barbers, lawyers acting as officers and generals.

Velasco possesses no political ambition. He will not accept a political post. Huerta allows himself to be lead, by the wrong advisers, to the nation's demise. Because peace and order also will not be brought by the triumph of revolutionaries, *outside influence is the only salvation.* (The general begins to cry.) He sees no hope, only desperation. I always preach: unification and reconciliation—because force has failed.

Sir Lionel Carden pays me a visit and declares: his telegram requesting influence on the United States to select a *neutral* person as interim president received the answer: England could not do anything like this. It would have to limit its actions to take care of its local subjects. Now he recognizes that the situation is hopeless. His goal had been to maintain an independent Mexico so that the British interests in the country were protected against a takeover by the United States. He has convinced himself that it would be impossible to hold the United States back: Mexicans themselves were opening the path.

He remembered that I have always held that opinion and, now, he has to say I was right. The British government has given Mexico away. Now he is supposed to introduce press propaganda through capable, local British [citizens], so that the British people would recognize the sacrifice taking place here, not merely of Mexico, but in all of South America.

Carden shows to me a telegram written by [ambassador to the United States] Spring-Rice from June 11. Bryan told me three suggestions have been made and are currently being negotiated:

a. Huerta announces the appointment of a Carrancista as secretary of foreign affairs, who automatically would take his place as soon as Huerta has resigned.

b. Huerta appoints Lascuraín as minister of foreign affairs and steps down, so as to reestablish the status quo ante from February 18, 1913.

Mexican delegates protested against (a) and (b) because they (a) are impossible and (b) would make the entire Huerta government look nonexistent.

c. The three mediators select a provisional president as Huerta's successor, who would quickly call for new elections.

Proposal (c), according to Bryan, has the most promising outlook. Spring-Rice adds that his impression is that the U.S. policy intends merely the enthroning of the Carrancistas.

The private secretary of the secretary of finance visited me. The secretary of finance is in dire straits. He [de la Lama] would have come himself but does not dare to do so because his visit to me and to other diplomats immediately would have been reported to Huerta, and it would make Huerta suspicious of him. I want to visit him.

Secretary of Finance de la Lama says that my advice—to move from theoretical proposals to the naming of candidates for the presidency—has yielded excellent fruit.

Huerta has considered General José Maria Mier and wants to name him as soon as the rebels have stopped hostilities, but not before. The Mexican delegates, on their own initiative, have suggested the naming by emphasizing the lack of authority. In confidential talks [they suggested] Lic. Liceaga or General José Maria Mier or General Lojero.

The United States countered with Pánfilo Natera, Felipe Riveros, General Ángeles—all three Carrancistas. [Other possibilities would be:]

Carbajál (member and president of the Supreme Court)
De la Lama—
Lascuraín (previously secretary of foreign affairs under Madero)
General Lauro Villar

De la Lama would be, of course, impossible. The president would soon view him as his most bitter enemy. But Carbajál's [candidacy] proves how correct my advice has been to move on to the selection of names, instead of theoretical disputations about whether a Carrancista or a neutral person should be selected.

The difficulty remains: in the president's [court] is the objection to Carbajál because he is not military. A general would be better. With enthusiasm I endorse Carbajál because I know him and consider him to be a civilized man. Urgently Lama asks me to keep talking to Huerta, nudging him to see Carbajál as the man for his selection. With that they would avoid the terror that the capital is being threatened with. Huerta's government will simply collapse in the next week or two due to lack of funds. I declare: Huerta's waffling makes any discussion with him almost impossible. But I wanted to try one more time to talk to him, urging him in the spirit of friendship.

Sanchez Navarro, rebel and refugee, states: in one or two weeks the revolutionaries will strike inside the capital; the acts of horror will, by far, surpass the Decena Tragica of 1913.

Sunday, June 14, 1914, Mexico City

Today I visited the president. I was motivated less by the request of de la Lama, who represents the government in foreign affairs, but rather with concern for local Germans and German interests, to avoid a catastrophe during the transition of power. One has to seek, if only just temporarily,—an adjustment in the only way that one can control, a peaceful one.

Doing this I am not using any means available to the German Reich, nor do I oblige the imperial government to anything. I am merely working with my *personal* influence. I am merely speaking and acting as a person, not as a German diplomat, an emphasis I repeat each time.

My behavior's justification and the reason I act is that the Germans residing here, and the German interests represented here, demand pacification of the country. And a transition to it without a forceful push. German policy here does not want to stand out or step forward. Nevertheless, it wants to encourage favorably the above-defined goal.

For 1.5 hours I conversed with Huerta. My goal was to talk him into sending a cable to Niagara Falls, [naming] Supreme Court president Carbajál as his successor. The United States would be entirely content with such a completely neutral personality. Through the U.S. influence, the Carrancistas would have to declare their agreement or—namely through U.S. force—would have to agree. Because without the material aid—money, ammunition, weapons—of the United States the revolution would continue but could not win.

Huerta began, as usual, expounding on the strength of his position. At least today he claimed that near San Luis Potosí there were now more than twenty-five thousand men. I, on the other hand, with clarity and openness, present to him the true situation of the country: desperate, no army, no money, no trust, no courage. Only exhaustion and disgust facing the continuation of the present regime. Anew I am preaching the wise counsel, saying: in order to jump forward better, one has to pull back first. His answers are the usual tirades: for him, his life counts nothing, but his honor counts for everything. I reply that his life has value and, perhaps before year's end, could mean the rescue of his fatherland.

In all likelihood, the transitional government seems to be condemned to end in anarchy. He should keep this possibility in mind and consider that, in a short time, the entire world—including the United States—would beg for the return of the "strong man" to the government; i.e., Huerta's return to the presidency.

In earlier talks Huerta had experienced this part of the talk as moving; now, again, the argument has its effect. He confessed that during the next elections he will run for office. In the meantime, after stepping down from office he will position himself at the head of his troops and, on the battlefield, move against the United States.

He can do so with great security, because after his resignation, the United States will be happy to clear the entire country.

He wanted to give me a proof of his trust: yesterday he had cabled to a delegate that he is ready to name his successor—as soon as the rebels stop their hostilities. I point out to him that he is voluntarily giving his opponents an advantage by letting the rebels determine the timing of events. In military life the offensive means everything. The defensive means slow demoralization. In diplomacy it is similar. Having the initiative assures him everything; waiting for the action of the opponent turns him into a slave of their strength to make a decision. It is necessary to cut off this mess of elaborations and theoretical suggestions—their authenticity and truth, furthermore, are not being believed with certainty by any of the parties—and, now, to move ahead of one's adversaries by being the one who names his successor.

Huerta now showed his cards and named Blanquet. Immediately I cut off this proposal: Blanquet would be impossible. Right away Huerta admitted: he is a man without culture und no intelligence. Then he proposed General José Maria Mier. Referring to historical precedent, I pointed out that a general, once raised to the chair of the president, in the long run had always founded his own party, even if he had been appointed there with the best of intentions.

Huerta would only create Blanquetistas and Mieristas and only complicate the already-hexed situation. Next, Huerta should consider that a general as president would exercise his influence on the army in a way that would be dangerous and prevent Huerta's reentry into the presidency. Huerta could see that.

Thereupon I proposed Carbajál. Huerta interjected: he is young. Whereupon I answered: exactly. Because of this Carbajál had a greater chance of surviving the time of his provisional presidency.

Then Huerta named de la Lama: he is his friend. I followed along with his suggestion because I knew that de la Lama had been categorized as acceptable candidate. Therefore, I counseled him to name both: Carbajál and de la Lama. Huerta agreed.

He shared with me in confidence that today he had cabled the delegates: they would have to hurry, because on the seventeenth of the month Congress's session would expire. Huerta should resign and justify it with illness; and, indeed, in about five days his left eye has to have cataract surgery. (At the beginning of 1913 the right one had been operated on.) He requested telegram forms and, in my presence, wrote the following telegram:

A Sres Rabasa, Rodriguez, Elguero

Niagara Falls. Confidential. To be communicated to the mediators.

The citizens whom this government proposes for the provisional presidency are de la Lama or Carbajál, president of the current Supreme Court. The government reserves the right to name two secretaries.

FIG. 34. Huerta's delegate Rodriguez on his way. Courtesy of the Library of Congress.

I assured Huerta that, as he mails this order, he is taking the first posi-tive step during the negotiations. Huerta reassured me: I will immedi-ately put this telegram into cipher and ask for it to be sent. It will be sent about 1:00 p.m.. Using tricks repeatedly, I make him repeat this prom-ise. Huerta declared, furthermore, as a sign of his regard for me, he em-powers me to inform immediately the imperial ambassador in Wash-ington DC.

This authority I used indirectly. I drew up a telegram to the German Foreign Ministry that I will send when I receive the news that, indeed, Huerta's new order has been sent. If he does it perhaps then the catas-trophe in the capital can be avoided, as long as the United States will deal with it positively. Huerta shared with me the news that he ordered his army in San Luis Potosí to act defensively. A sign of how weak he feels, together with his demoralized army.

The [German] imperial consul in El Paso responded to my cable, stat-ing that Villa is now obeying Carranza's orders. He is now withdrawing from Torreón with all his troops, going south; for the time being to support Natera and Contreras, trying to take Zacatecas. Federal general Medina Barron, who is commander there, has been partially paralyzed by being swiped with a shot near his spine. General Garcia Hidalgo has been sent with reinforcements from San Luis.

Frigatte Captain Koehler, the commander of the *Dresden*, has returned to Veracruz after an eight-day stay here. As well as I could, I have informed him about the situation, the outlook, and the tasks laying ahead. And I presented him with my evidence. I will make an effort to have personal contact more often with Captain Koehler so that I can brief him about the situation. Written reports must not be used due to the existing "black cabinets" [decoding devices]. Telegraphing is too expensive.

Monday, June 15, 1914, Mexico City

The Japanese diplomat has been held in Sayula. It was known that he had traveled for three days to Manzanillo to welcome the cruiser *Izumo* and to discuss the situation. During this time, rebels or Federales dynamited bridges and tunnels. The escort offered to bring him to Guadalajara using swords. Adachi declined. Thereupon the escort tried to fight its way through alone —and was thrown back with a loss of ten dead and eight hurt. Adachi tells us he had been treated by the rebels with all signs of appreciation. They had been absolutely certain of their victory. The leadership of the rebel forces and of the Federales, it is stated, is absolutely identical, turning to robbery, burning, and murder. Also the rebels offered to help him, but he rejected this too.

On June 8 a small Japanese expedition—twenty officers and eleven men—from the *Izumo* reached him. Together they used horses to start a journey to Guadalajara. But before [they reached] Guadalajara his legation secretary, Minre, reached him with three automobiles and the legation guard. Three thousand men are stationed in Guadalajara; General Zozaya recaptured Zacoalco for a few hours but then withdrew to Guadalajara. Everybody in Guadalajara, even the Germans who have visited him, wished the rebels would capture the city. The governor, General Mier, receives faulty reports from the government about the situation. Mier has repressed all newspapers and thrown the reporters into prison. The federal troops are not paid and are demoralized. The rebels did not want to know anything about the peace conference because they are not certain if they will succeed. Obregón, the rebel general, is still 200 km away from Guadalajara. Adachi states that Guadalajara will fall shortly.

Secretary of Finance de la Lama tells me that, indeed, the president has sent yesterday's telegram—see the fourteenth. De la Lama immediately explained to him that under no circumstances did he want to accept an interim presidency. Because he knew that, in spite of prior friendship with Huerta, he would be in danger and loose his influence, because from that moment on Huerta would see him as his presumed successor.

Thereupon Huerta called Carbajál on the telephone and negotiated with him for a longer period of time. Carbajál has accepted. Then today he—de la Lama—cabled the delegates: Carbajál has accepted! Support him.

Yesterday evening the following cable arrived from the delegates in Niagara: "In private session with the negotiators and the U.S. delegates the latter suggested as interim president Iglesias Calderón, or Cabrera, or Villareal—all three of them Carrancistas." Thereupon he [de la Lama] answered: the United States itself has suggested de la Lama and Carbajál. It would be absolutely impossible to step back from that proposal and name one of the new persons. Because of the pending end of Congress, the delegates were in a hurry. Preparations have been made, communicated as confidential information, to call together Congress to an extraordinary meeting after June 17 and to keep it in session.

De la Lama considers the game lost and believes the United States simply wanted to draw out negotiations with its new proposals. I comfort him by saying I heard Carranza's voice coming from the newest proposals of the United States. The United States is pursuing the negotiations like a business negotiation and negotiates in a cagy way for what it intended to extract.

De la Lama desperately wondered how he should carry the news to the president. Since yesterday it has ruined how he felt. I say that I consider it unnecessary to inform the president about it, since the latest suggestions of the United States represent not proposals but only presentations in private session.

De la Lama does pick this up and tells me the French diplomat brought him the telegram from Jusserand. It states: according to Bryan's utterances the United States is determined to allow only a constitutional government. I reply that this is the old business of haggling over words. The United States should stick to the naming of individual people, a principle that has been accepted as advantageous.

The Mexican government cabled today to its candidates: six thousand rebels have been driven to flight near Zacatecas. The army at San Luis

Potosí has received the order to start an offensive against Saltillo and Tampico—because the revolutionaries never stopped war activities even for a single day. The delegates were now urged to hurry. The telegram closed with the question of concern: Would an insistence on Carbajál's presidency mean that the conference would be shut down prematurely? Probably tomorrow the U.S. answer will arrive as far as Carbajál is concerned. De la Lama thanks me for exercising my influence in favor of positive proposals on the president.

According to rebel statements the delegates support the ABC representatives and their proposal: to make a *neutral person* and *not* a Constitutionalist interim president. Furthermore, they report that U.S. public opinion is turning in their [the rebels'] favor.

Tuesday, June 16, 1914, Mexico City

Pedro Lascuraín, the memorable president of the republic [on] February 18, 1913, paid me a visit. He presented a describtion of the situation in the city that is called: flexible. The masses do not show a reaction and are in a stupor; the middle class—as far as it exists—partially is involved in conspiracies that are being acted against in a bloody way every night with little investigation.

Segments of the higher classes have fled. Or some segments are being terrorized. Only a strong leader is missing for a powerful unleashing of these activities. We are sitting on top of a volcano. Huerta no longer has any followers. Everyone is yearning for him to disappear. He asks me about my opinion. I answer: even after Huerta's departure I cannot foresee any lasting calm until Mexicans agree to accept conversion to the concept: unification and reconciliation.

Under running tears he states that I am correct, saying that the solution will take on a form identical to that of the Decena Tragica.

Once again I have prepared for violence in the capital and wire all consular offices, "I empower you, in cases of emergency, if you cannot reach me, to wire your requests directly to the Foreign Office in Berlin."

The Mexican delegates report (see under June 15), "The United States has rejected Carbajál as candidate in a meeting of the U.S. representatives and the mediators. They request that the provisional presidency be entrusted to a revolutionary." The Mexican delegates rejected this with determination. Furthermore: the question of admitting insurrectionists to the conference finally has been decided by rejection.

The Mexican government has asked why the U.S. government rejected a candidate that it had put on the list.

Wednesday, June 17, 1914, Mexico City
Ambassador da Gama cabled Cardoso:

> In light of both parties' intransigence—as far as the person to be named provisional president is concerned—further deliberations will not yield any new results. The conference will convene again on Friday the nineteenth. No meeting will take place the seventeenth and eighteenth because of the absence of the Argentine delegate, who has to travel to New York on official matters. I have to conclude, as far as the discussions are concerned, one should declare the talks are finished and move toward making decisions. Saturday, the twentieth, or Monday, or rather Tuesday next week, the conference will dissolve: regardless of whether an agreement can be reached or not. We believe because public opinion stands so favorably in support of the three mediating powers the U.S. government will step back from its claim to put into place a revolutionary as provisional president in favor of a neutral person.

The Mexican government received an answer from its delegates to the question of yesterday, why Carbajál was rejected all of a sudden. Washington now insists on seating a Constitutionalist as interim president—however, Washington no longer mentions a name.

Furthermore, the delegates cable: that on Friday the nineteenth at the deliberations proposals will be made and on the following day, the end of the conference, regardless whether it ends as a failure or anything else. A failure would be highly detrimental[59] for the U.S. government in light of public opinion favoring mediation and paying respect to its many domestic difficult issues. The delegates urgently discuss energetic resumption of military action against the rebels. It is clear:

1. The United States, forced by its pact with the insurrectionists, has committed itself in favor of a revolutionary to succeed Huerta.
2. The Mexican delegates insist on a neutral person. The mediators share this opinion but do not reveal whom their neu-

tral person would be. The mistake is the method of negotiations: immediately the real situation would become obvious if all three or at least the *mediadores* would name the candidates that they would accept.

The delegates advise energetic military action and they put their finger on a sore point: the federal army is incapable of moving on to the offensive; it remains in a defensive position, in spite of all orders.

The Brazilian diplomat bitterly complains about how the United States interprets the mediation. It is obvious that the United States had assumed that the ABC powers would prostrate themselves and would play its game with Mexico; however, it is mistaken.

The ABC powers would prefer the failure of mediation. I ask Cardoso why he does not advise the mediators to name their own interim presidential candidate or candidates. Actually, that would remain entirely within the boundaries of their task, even their direct task.

Hesitantly, Cardoso says he is cautious about showing his cards and abandoning his reserve. The U.S. government has heaped up mistake upon mistake. But he hopes that between today and Friday an understanding may be reached.

The Mexican government cabled to its delegates, saying, "Try to find out who the mediators see as their candidate and, right away, cable the name here, so that we can telegraph you if he is acceptable." I ask de la Lama if Lascuraín is considered to be acceptable. He answers, "For me, certainly, and I believe I can talk the president into accepting him."

I meet Lascuraín and jokingly ask him if he wants to be president again. He counters in a serious manner, "The suffering is not so urgent that every man must pick up his part to save the fatherland."

Also, Cardoso mentions Lascuraín. I believe that he does not want to receive public attention here and [he wants] to avoid taking the wind out of the sails of the representatives of the ABC powers in Niagara Falls. However, because he himself urgently desires the mediation to be successful, and he fears its failure, I talk to him in a friendly tone. I ask him to do his part so that the mediators and the Mexican government can agree and select one person who is also acceptable to the United States

[I do so] because I believe I can feel more instinctively that, based on information, the United States will try to avoid the failure of the conference, because of the approaching elections and in the interest of the Democratic Party. Its rejection of Carbajál falls under the category of a "bluff."

At the very least I want to know what the United States intends to do once the conference has failed.

According to private Mexican telegrams, (Hernández) Natera's loss near Zacatecas has been a complete one; Argumedo is supposed to have fallen onto his back coming from Guadalupe.

Yesterday—June 16—in the afternoon, the Chamber [of Deputies] and Senate elected a committee of fourteen people, each of whom will serve on a permanent commission during the end of the conference. In case the conference does reach a conclusion, then the Congress will need to come together—stating the reason—in a new, extraordinary session.

The British diplomat received a telegram from London: "The negotiations at the conference have reached a deadlock." All around him he sees chaos. His information says Carranza refuses to accept a successor for Huerta named by the conference. He wants to avoid the appearance that he receives it under U.S. guidance. Furthermore, he has information that Villa has withdrawn into the United States. He claims: federal troops are preparing to recapture Tampico and are in the process of repairing the railroad coming from San Luis Potosí [to Tampico]. Huerta will place himself at the head of the army of San Luis Potosí. In short: Carden's old utilitarian optimism.

Consul Weber cables from El Paso: "Villa has severed his connection with Carranza and operates alone up to Torreón. His followers have arrested many of Carranza's sympathizers and have taken control of the railroad and the telegraph. The connection has been interrupted."

This open split in the Carrancista camp provides Huerta with new possibilities. The president has given governors the task of immediately raising three thousand soldiers. Once again prisons are being emptied. Huerta has still not recognized, in spite of numerous and tough experiences, that prisoners cannot be turned into soldiers just like that.

Thursday, June 18, 1914, Mexico City

Huerta proposes to call Congress to an extraordinary session, using a letter from June 17. He envisions an extraordinary session "for the time necessary after the international mediation with the object that the executive will submit to the Chamber . . . the result of the conference approval and seek actions for any further direct or indirect questions related to the agreements of said conference and in respect to questions of international order or in relation to domestic affairs of the land."

This general version allows dealing with all possible questions. Before, the version stated, "Besides, it is very likely to come to some agreement between the interim constitutional government of the United States of Mexico and the revolutionary Carrancistas. This will come about thanks to the good wishes of the mediating powers and their active involvement, and it will result in the political calming of the country."

Secretary of Finance de la Lama visited and informed me: Cardoso, the Brazilian diplomat, told him yesterday, June 17, that the mediators looked at Lascuraín as a feasible candidate and one that the United States would accept. Cardoso was fearing very much that the negotiations would proceed without result, and he would like to do something to prevent such an outcome. Did the Mexican government not want to enlarge the list of its candidates for president, adding Lascuraín?

Cardoso expressed the wish to be received by the president to propose this [idea] to him. For today, de la Lama has held him back from doing so because, as he says, he backs Lascuraín's candidacy without reservation. He sees it as a "last way out" and fears that an endorsement by *Cardoso* would have the opposite effect, namely Huerta's rejection. Lama asks me to talk with the president about Lascuraín. I am tired of [exercising] such influence on the president and, furthermore, do not want to step further out of the necessary reserve than has happened until now.

However, de la Lama says that Lascuraín as a candidate is the final means for coming to an understanding domestically and achieving temporary calm. I counter that the successful beating back of the rebels' attack against Zacatecas and the news of Villa's retreat will put the president again in a victorious mood. And he will not want to hear anything about an end of the war against the revolution and reconciliation.

Now the split in the Carrancista camp is apparent. But de la Lama declared with conviction and without much ado, "No one talks anymore about a continuation of the war."

He has presented the news to the president without restraint and in full clarity that finances would come to an end within a few days. Not a penny will be available to pay troops. The entire machine of the government will have to come to a standstill—due to lack of money. I declare myself willing to talk with Huerta to avoid anarchy or a catastrophe, perhaps both. It would put Germans in unpredictable danger.

I used the following arguments with Huerta:

1. The United States has committed an unlawful act by rejecting Carbajál after it had proposed him.
2. The United States also nominated Lascuraín. Its injustice will become even more apparent when the United States also rejects him, once Huerta makes him his candidate.
3. As I learned yesterday, the mediators had looked at Lascuraín based on U.S. statements in favor of his run for office.
4. The United States has the same interest in a *successful* conference as all other parties, according to my feeling. Huerta should build for the United States a golden bridge by selecting Lascuraín.
5. If he does not want to do that, he would have at least an opportunity to move toward the mediators' [position] by naming Lascuraín. He has emphasized repeatedly that he owes gratitude to the mediators.

Huerta countered in my presence:

1. Lascuraín is a member of the Catholic Party and will carry the religious question into the quarrel. I reject this based on my knowledge of his personality.
2. Lascuraín is incompetent. I counter, therefore, that the succession in the form of a competent man would not be in Huerta's interest. With laughter, Huerta agrees. He says he tends to like the idea.

This afternoon he awaits a cable from Niagara Falls, will check it, and afterward, 6:00 p.m., will come to me to discuss the question further.

I repeatedly declare that I am talking with him about this matter not as a German diplomat but out of pure friendship and as an old military man. Huerta emphatically accepts this.

Huerta tells me: From today on the revolution has been exterminated!! Yesterday he sent two thousand men as reinforcements to Zacatecas; this afternoon an additional four thousand will relocate there; near Perote and Esperanza are thirty thousand to forty thousand men. His agents have informed him that the United States has selectively loaded its artillery onto its ships. That is supposed to be wrong. Thus he would also have to be prepared against the United States.

In one month he will have reconquered Sonora and Sinaloa. In two months the border states. He shows Taft's speech in which he condemns Wilson's policy as that of the "Professor of Princeton." And he praises his own policy of nonintervention.

I recognize this as a sign of change taking place in U.S. public opinion. Furthermore, I see [in it] one more reason to build the U.S. administration a golden bridge by accepting Lascuraín's candidacy or to embarrass it in front of the entire world.

Secretary of Finance de la Lama visits and declares he has certain news that, Saturday the twentieth, the conference will conclude its work. It will continue if a successor in the person of Lascuraín is named for the resigning Huerta and if the revolutionaries as well as the United States will accept him. The president deceives himself, assuming that he could continue to hold presidential power. The entire world is against him. Huerta is supposed to have ordered the governors each to raise five hundred men within three days—impossible! And what will they do with these soldiers? They could not be paid nor fed. Therefore they would soon revolt. *"Within one week, at the most at month's end"* all financial means would be entirely exhausted.

I interject that Huerta might and most likely will attack the cash reserves of the capital's banks under the heading of "forced loan"—which he already is supposed to have threatened. De la Lama: "That would be theft." At that moment he and the other members of cabinet would hand in their resignation. I state: Huerta will find others. Lama replies, "Possibly, but anarchy and revolt would be the answer." He repeats, "The only possible path remaining is the naming of Lascuraín as candidate for a transitional government." Urgently he asks me to move Huerta to that point. I explain to him: my steps, until now, had been dictated by the effort to prevent a catastrophe. It would have endangered an ungodly amount of lives and much property. Besides, they had taken place in a context of friendship and not an official way.

The president told me that he wanted to come today at 6:00 p.m. for a visit, after receiving a cable he was expecting from his delegates. [Thereafter] he wanted to talk more about Lascuraín. I was having my doubts

FIG. 35. Group picture of diplomatic negotiators at the Niagara Falls conference. Courtesy of the Library of Congress.

[about] whether the president would come because he is known to be unreliable. De la Lama says he did not know which telegram Huerta was expecting. His last telegram to the delegates asked who the candidate of the mediators was. Or, rather, charged the delegates to find out who the candidate of the mediators would be. Until now, no answer. Lama predicts it at 6:30 p.m. He suspects that immediately after the talk with me, Huerta will need him.

The Brazilian diplomat visits and shows me a telegram to his ambassador, da Gama, dated June 17. It says, "Since two days ago I have been working with prudence in mind, but energetically, to convince the Mexican government that the conference will end in a dramatic failure unless it succeeds in naming as Huerta's successor a person who is acceptable to the revolutionaries and the United States." He continues, "Today such a person could be only Lascuraín."

He predicted the failure of the conference, unless Lascuraín was named. Today at 5:00 p.m. Cardoso will talk to the president about that. Following negotiations he has already had with Esteva Ruiz and de la Lama, he found both quite willing. Following a question, I inform him about the result of today's conversation with Huerta and emphasize that he, as representative of one of the mediating powers, [was operating from] an entirely different basis than I. I had spoken only, and could only speak, without the weight of my government behind me, in a purely personal way and in friendship. *If in case* I present to Huerta my opinion about the situation and the means necessary to adopt, following requests of the Mexican government, then I would be doing so in order to prevent a violent turn of government power. The interest of German citizens living here requires it.

Cardoso does not state directly that Lascuraín has been identified to him as a candidate whom people would accept. But he lets me know that he has talked with Lascuraín twice already, and he found him willing to serve under certain conditions; in particular, that he would also be accepted by the revolutionaries. Knowing Cardoso as I do, he would not have stuck out his neck that far *without an order*. He mentions that, as far as he knew, differences of opinion also existed: not only about the person but also about the way the government should be handed over.

The revolutionaries and the United States did not want to let it take place with Huerta doing [the handing over of government]. For example, if he would name as his successor the secretary of foreign affairs. Because doing so would mean for them a recognition of Huerta's government and the validation of his acts of government. I interject that the mediators should take care of that and the United States and the revolutionaries would make concessions in regard to form—after which Huerta would find himself willing to name Lascuraín as successor.

Cardoso agrees to that and calls the United States' intent "nonsensical" because, already, they have signed a protocol with Huerta' s delegates— the one that governs the conference's business proceedings. In doing so they recognized Huerta indirectly. Following his request, I told him how I usually tend to speak to Huerta while emphasizing again that he has a much better basis [on which to talk with him]. He replies that he considered my action complementary but insufficient and therefore he has to go to the president.

I return the courtesy, asking him not to pay attention to my vanity because I do not have any: "I would be the first one to applaud and celebrate your success."

Lascuraín's candidacy is satisfactory as far as two aspects are concerned. First, Huerta is willing to accept it because Lascuraín is neutral and not dangerous. And indirectly he can name him successor by making him secretary of the exterior. And on the other hand, the revolutionaries and the United States will accept him because it would allow the interpretation that the status quo ante February 18, 1913, has been reestablished: namely, Lascuraín as legal successor of the then-president and vice president Madero and Pino Suárez.

Late in the evening Secretary of Finance de la Lama visits me [and is] greatly excited: everything seems to be lost. This evening the Brazilian diplomat has talked to Huerta about Lascuraín as a candidate and probably committed a mistake [as far as] respect and tact [are concerned]. Because Huerta became excited and yelled that he would not allow foreign countries to force a candidate upon him. And Lascuraín would mean an "imposition." What right does Cardoso have to interfere in the domestic politics of Mexico? Cardoso, shocked, then sought to achieve a face-saving exit. Huerta offered it to him by, on the one hand, refusing Lascuraín but agreeing to Augustín Rodriguez as candidate. De la Lama got this description of events from Esteva Ruiz, who had been an eyewitness. Now he was asking me to go again to the president and move him once more to accept Lascuraín. Lascuraín is still the only possible rescue. In a few days money will be gone; inside the capital and among the military a revolt will break out; the catastrophe is approaching us, unless Lascuraín, as a last way out, is pursued.

In a friendly tone I decline and advise him to bring it about instead as an initiative by the mediators. Their silence pertaining to the candidates could not be explained with the material that was known to me. Nor why the Mexican delegates have not motivated the mediators. In spite of the harmony [between them] that they always talk about: to adopt as their own the Mexican candidate (Carbajál) or to recommend a different candidate to the Mexicans. Lama is taken aback, thinks for a moment, and says: that is wrong. The delegates most certainly did not answer his telegraphed question about the candidate and his order to recommend Carbajál to them. I advise him to underline this right away, sending a cable to demand that the delegates execute his order. As far as Rodriguez is concerned the president has talked about him for weeks. Always in the sense that Rodriguez would be impossible for all parties, because

1. He is an outspoken member of the Catholic Church and would push the religious question still further into discord.

2. He is fundamentally conservative and therefore impossible for the revolutionaries.
3. Rodriguez has refused, through formal means and with great determination, ever to accept the presidency.

Therefore, I consider the president's sudden change of mind about the presidency to be subterfuge. In a lively way de la Lama expresses agreement with me and adds that the conference will see the suggestion of Rodriguez as a new sign of Huerta's bad faith. With great emphasis he asks me to instruct Cardoso to propose, via cable, Rodriguez as candidate for office. I counter, because Cardoso is sickly it is not good to visit him in the evening. De la Lama asks me to at least telephone him. Right now I want him to cable at least the delegates—once again—either to win [over] the mediators to vote in favor of their candidate or to move them to name one of their own. I consider the urgency appropriate and counsel in favor of it. It might be that the mediators have their reasons not to show their cards. But here their holding back is driving us toward the catastrophe we want to avoid.

When I call Cardoso he asks me in great excitement to visit him. He tells me he had visited Huerta between 5:00 and 6:00 p.m. and gained the impression that Huerta was drunk. He considered it to be an inopportune moment but, in light of the urgency of the situation, he decided to mention Lascuraín.

Huerta cut him off and shouted that this was an imposition and an interference in Mexico's domestic politics that he would not tolerate! Why would Cardoso feel like posing such a concern to him? Does Cardoso not know that he will have thrown the United States back into the ocean within fourteen days? Already the revolution is no longer in existence, etc.

Cardoso's apprehensions about the president's rage intensified and, openly, he said that it appeared to him that he came at the wrong moment and wished to withdraw. Whereupon Huerta padded him on the shoulder and told him he wanted to give him proof that he meant well: i.e., to name not Lascuraín but Rodriguez as his candidate.

Immediately Cardoso sent a disheartened telegram. Mediation appears to him to have failed, because Rodriguez as a candidate is apparently unacceptable for the revolutionaries; they will refuse to realize the transition to the new and provisional government within the forms of the

Mexican constitution—so that Huerta would not be recognized. Practically speaking, as Mexican and U.S. delegates signed protocols at the conference, the recognition has already taken place.

[With] the little bit of confidence that he still possesses, he was betting on da Gama's dispatches wherein he was talking about the "plan of the mediators," saying, "Now the Mexican mediators are expecting the order from the [ABC] mediators."

Cardoso has no explanation for the fact that, until now, the mediators have not named a candidate of their own. They have not even named one on a confidential basis.

Since Cardoso has already cabled Rodriguez, I give up on moving him toward an additional explanation. Besides, I feel the spontaneous one he gave suffices. Now I am putting my hope on de la Lama's telegram to the Mexican delegates. He informed me *about the content of the protocol that has been signed in Niagara Falls on June 12* (apparently Protocol No. 3, which later became famous, note from July 6, 1914):

1. A transitional government will be formed in Mexico.
2. This transitional government will be recognized immediately by the ABC powers and the United States.
3. The transitional government will quickly call for presidential and congressional elections. The Tampico incident has not been a topic of discussion at all. In contrast, there was discussion of the general principles pertaining to the questions of landownership and school education in Mexico.

Friday, June 19, 1914, Mexico City

De la Lama shows me the cable that he sent last night to the Mexican delegates: "It is of utmost importance that you find out the name of the presidential candidate of the mediators and transmit it so that the president can be prepared before the negotiations."

Mr. Holste, the agent of M. Schroeder Hamburg Co., tells me that he has even more weapons and ammunition for the Mexican government in Europe, which have been partially paid for.

De la Lama shows me a dispatch from his agent, Simondetti, former editor of the *Diario*, not an individual with good reputation: "The break between Villa and Carranza is now complete. Villa is favored by Washington. Villa is moving toward Zacatecas. Ángeles is in command of his artillery. Probably Villa will attack during the night, as usual."

Undersecretary of War General Salas says that his brother—major, not general, Medina Barron—has been hurt near Zacatecas.

The permanent commission accepts the law pertaining to the extraordinary meeting of [the Mexican] Congress: for the purpose of dealing with the following questions: The agreement and treaty with the United States and the mediating ABC powers and all topics that deal with them directly or indirectly. The internal affairs that are connected with the pacification of the country. The extraordinary session will last the time necessary to solve the above-mentioned points and, to come to a conclusion about them, a law will be conceptualized very broadly that prepares for the continuation of this Congress beyond its legal time limit.

General Ruelas, the governor of Aguascalientes who had stepped down, tells me that the rebels are advancing from Tepic toward Encarnación; in the south they are coming from Aguascalientes. From there, probably, they would reach the national railroad via San Felipe and, therefore, cut off Zacatecas and San Luis Potosí from the south. The connection [between] Mexico [and] Guadalajara is interrupted near La Barca due to floods. Rebels have surrounded Guadalajara. Near Túxpam and Zapotlán the Guadalajara-Colima railroad is in the hands of the rebels. Hacendados have risen up in the states of Guanajuato, Aguascalientes, Jalisco, and also [on] the smaller rancheros because they considered Federales, plundering and requisitioning themselves, to be worse than the rebels. The government is supposed to have sent[60] reinforcements to Zacatecas, but they could not stop the advance of the rebels to Encarnación. The greatest danger is coming from the federal troops themselves and their subordinate officers: armed hoards without discipline and individuals who yesterday would have been homeless on the streets. Any leadership of the military operations is not exercised; the only motto issued: help each other!

The general staff is supposed to concern itself with questions of uniforms and with far-reaching reforms that now, of course, could no longer be realized. But it never deals with military operations. Blanquet deals with the administration but not with the leadership of the army. This way everybody is doing what he wants to do.

All that General Rincon Gallardo, up in Zacatecas, supposedly has protected is merely his own hacienda. Ruelas once directed him toward

Pinos; instead of marching north he marched south, but he did send his lieutenant, Gomez, with sixty men to the northeast. Not encountering anything, Gomez marched toward Pinos and there was attacked by rebels. He is supposed to have been wounded there. His people ran away. Rincon Gallardo never entered the fight. He is one of Huerta's favorite generals. He, who until now has only been a bouncer, had been promoted, without much ado, from this position to the position of general.

Saturday, June 20, 1914, Mexico City

Secretary of Finance de la Lama visits me, saying the delegates have sent an official dispatch: the United States answered the last note in " a moderate style" and emphasized that, in its opinion, differences about the person of the candidate are not reason enough to break off negotiations. Orally they added that the victorious advance of the revolutionaries proves that the majority of the people wish the triumph of the revolutionaries. Therefore, it is advisable to name a revolutionary as interim president.

De la Lama shows to me an official, nonconfidential dispatch from the delegates that states: the mediator's candidate is supposed to be Luis Mendez. De la Lama had just talked to the president, who ordered him to increase the list of candidates that he would approve by adding Gorostieta[61]—presently secretary of justice—and Blanquet. No talk anymore about Rodriguez, who, at the conference, is not being named as a candidate.

De la Lama is aghast and asks me for advice: the naming of two such impossible candidates as Gorostieta and Blanquet would be interpreted as subterfuge and bad faith. I suggest making it Huerta's decision to increase the list by adding Luis Mendez. De la Lama states that is not enough. He has reason to believe that the rebels might be happy only with Lascuraín. Huerta should name Mendez *and* Lascuraín and he should move him [to do so].

I remind him that a day ago Huerta had already agreed with me to support that. De la Lama interjects, "But the unhappy intervention of the Brazilian diplomat has ruined everything!" I suggest—because I don't want to engage myself twice in the same issue—that he share confidential knowledge with the British diplomat as well.

Happily, Lama picks up the idea and suggests that Carden and I together go to Huerta. I have my concerns and am against that step. Carden's interests and his methods are not the same as mine. However, I bring de la Lama along to a visit with Carden. De la Lama explains to him the neutral facts and his request. At first Carden replies: Spring-Rice has cabled him about a talk with Bryan that took place on June 11, during which Bryan stated that the United States has proposed Lascuraín as interim president, but Huerta rejected him. De la Lama contests this version, explaining the version of the obviously true unfolding of the story [of the naming] of candidates—whereupon Carden stated with well-meaning nodding of the head: then the secretary of state has given the ambassador incorrect dates. I add to de la Lama's presentation: regardless of later decisions, it appears to me as practical that first Carden and then I would talk with Huerta about Mendez-Lascuraín. Carden accepts, with the explanation that Huerta could read the concurrent appearance of two diplomats as an attempt to force candidates onto him. I help him, stating, Huerta should look at our *parallel* visit also as a matter of official formality and, also, he has his special way of talking with everybody. Usually when two or more are with him he becomes a poser.

De la Lama openly explains to us: the economic situation is desperate. He has no more money to pay troops nor anybody else. Lascuraín is [the candidate] with the greatest chance because the rebels like him. It is agreed that Carden should visit Huerta at 12:30 lunch. I will wait until I know the outcome of the mission.

Via "bando" a change in constitution is being announced. It downgraded Morelos to the level of a territory and separated Chihuahua into two territories and one state. A more than unnecessary and damaging measure because it provokes those affected and makes them bitter and, on the other hand, the federal government has no means at its disposition to realize the change in constitution because Chihuahua is in Villa's and Morelos in Zapata's [hands].

At 4:00 p.m. Sir Lionel Carden visits me. He declares his attempt to move Huerta to name Mendez and Lascuraín as his candidates has failed. Huerta talked with him from 12:50 p.m. until 2:00 p.m., but he could not be moved and insisted: he does want war with the United States.

He will force the United States into war. As before, there can be no talk about concessions. He would not think about naming Mendez or Lascuraín. Carden should keep in mind that he—the president—has reached his decision and it cannot be changed. He will get money, even if he has to

steal it. At the most extreme, what he might do would be to name Carbajál, Gorostieta—i.e., the secretary of justice—and Agustin Rodriguez.

To some degree Carden's vanity was hurt that Huerta did not allow
him to say much and that his mission has failed. But in essence Huerta's
decision to force war upon the United States is identical to his passion-
ate desire to tie the United States down here in a long-drawn-out war.
Carden categorizes the landing of weapons in Tampico from the *Antilla*, against the mediator's assurances to the State Department, as being
in accordance with the reported course of events of U.S. policy, and he
adds, "And think that this is the damned country we've paid an indemnity to for the *Alabama!*"[62]

Sunday, June 21, 1914, Mexico City

I take into account that now it is Huerta who refused to appear on Carden's
dance card. And, in particular, because Carden did not advocate a peaceful solution with great zeal, my attempt to change Huerta's mind will
most likely have no success.

Nevertheless, I will make this last attempt in view of the endangered
German interests and lives. I am hoping to depend [on the fact] that, until now, Huerta has always extended his graces to me.

Our discussion lasted from 11:00 to 12:30. Once again I presented all
my old arguments: the principle "to pull back first in order to jump ahead
better at a later time." I illustrated it and reinforced it with the reproach
that he was not exploiting the [fact that] U.S. public opinion was turning
in his favor and, therefore, that the failures that have occurred until now
have boxed in the Wilson administration. He replied: anyway, Wilson's
period to govern would last only another 2.5 years and he—Huerta—will
personally dig his grave.

I pointed out that the Republican government that likely would follow
would extend an even less favorable attitude toward him. He admitted
that the Republicans are imperialists and expansionists but [added that] it
would not be fruitful to make policy today looking ahead to 2.5 years from
now. He has done all that is humanly possible to make concessions, but
now he is done with *that*. Today he called to the *attention of* the Mexican
delegates by cable that it is their charge to come to an arrangement with
the United States about the Tampico and Veracruz cases. And they have
not yet said a single word about either of them. They should not agree to

engage in discussions of *internal* questions of Mexico and should not tolerate any foreign imposition. At the same time, he has sent thirty telegrams to the governors and commanders with the order to send into the field so and so many rank and file. Within the shortest time he will have forty-five thousand men around Veracruz and will attack. *The danger is located over there!* (El peligro esta por aca!), Huerta repeated several times fiercely. And if possibilities for great battles no longer exist then he will engage in guerrilla warfare. Mexican mountain ranges are unwelcoming to U.S. troops, which is not a popular army but an army of mercenaries (at that moment I heard Carden [through Huerta's words], and I was surprised by this underestimation of a professional army by a professional soldier). He will be able to hold on five years and longer. The U.S. popular spirit will shatter as it encounters fortress "Mexico." A people who do not know patriotism but who are led only by greed for money (I am hearing Carden's words again). He himself knows how to organize money. Better an open war with the United States than the current secret one: near Zacatecas 180 U.S. citizens have been killed or wounded as members of the rebels.

Altogether he will raise two hundred thousand men. I dispute such numbers based on my knowledge of the Mexican army and tell him openly, *he* might think such offensive ideas, but the nation wants peace, almost peace at any cost, and the army is tired. He falls into a rage and says that public opinion is a prostitute and, anyway, dares to come to the forefront only if one is not in command of it (he is right about that), and the army will listen. He insists as he has said before: the young Mexican nation, almost still wild, in the process of formation, could withstand a devastating war longer than the United States.

He makes reference to the example of the Philippines. Queen Christina had not wanted to surrender the Philippines. Sagasta had counseled her to take the twenty-five million and to let the Philippines go. In fifteen years the United States would want to be rid of it again. Then he moves on to Germany and paints the picture of an expansive policy as an unavoidable necessity of the German empire.

At the same time, excitedly, he expresses his surprise that such policy is not being followed by Germany. I respond that he should see, in Germany's example, that even the strongest is being forced by circumstances to pursue a prudent policy. And it allows bringing into the game not only strength but also diplomatic means. Finally I ask him why he was moving to the position of a desperate [man]. By no means is his situation desperate. He should demonstrate the flexibility of his race, to take one step back in order to jump ahead later.

He replied, "My will cannot be shaken (with the customary Spanish formulaic forms addressed at me); already I have given the orders. I want to reveal to you the secret of my policy. I will let elections take place. *I will emerge as president from the elections.* In the same moment I will resign, move to the head of the troops, and kick the U.S. citizens out of the country." Again, I point out to him that he will find few followers. Nation and army are tired and exhausted. He repeated, "That they rob, that they enter with blood and fire, that they insult women—that is the way war is."

Huerta's most recent decisions have to be seen in light of two important points:

A. he considers the U.S. demands a bluff and counters them with
   a bluff, surely so that he can extract the most for himself; or
B. they are the outgrowth of a sick mind.

For us the result is the same: continuation, yes, increase of the serious dangers for German life and property in Mexico. And, in the capital, the growing possibility of an uprising or a military revolt, or rather both.

Today the Zapatistas attacked near Xochimilco, one hour away from the capital. The military attaché was a witness. According to the *Mexican Herald* of June 18, the Zapatistas had attacked Texcoco on June 14, about 25 km away from Mexico City. They took it and, temporarily, held it.

The attachment reports the letter exchange between the mediators of the ABC powers and Zubarán, Carranza's representative.

The British diplomat believes to have news, according to which the United States supports Villa against Carranza.

Monday, June 22, 1914, Mexico City
Secretary of Finance de la Lama visits and shows me three telegrams:

1. From yesterday morning, [from] the president to the delegates:

"Please mention that the only and actual purpose of the Niagara Falls conference—namely the Tampico incident—has neither been deliberated nor solved; reject the consideration of questions dealing with the internal affairs of Mexico."

2. From the Mexican delegation to the president:

"Argentine diplomat returned from Washington. He is very optimistic, states that United States wishes to avoid break off of negotiations. He talked with Cabrera and suggested direct negotiations of the Constitutionalists with us. Cabrera agreed. We are asking for authorization. The most important factor is that Huerta's troops near Zacatecas are winning. With urgency we recommend advising the *president* to make all efforts so that Zacatecas will be a triumph won with his weapons. The outcome of the battle of Zacatecas is of transcendental importance for the fortunes of Latin America."

3. From the president to the Mexican delegates:

"I approve direct negotiations independently with Constitutionalists, independent of the conference. I have sent orders to win battles near Zacatecas."

De la Lama says that now eight thousand men are stationed near Zacatecas; two thousand have begun to move. Altogether twenty thousand could gather there.

De la Lama regrets that delegation has not followed earlier the advice to negotiate directly with the rebels, which I have repeated for a long time. He thanks me for the preparation of the president.

Ambassador da Gama yesterday cabled the Brazilian diplomat [in Mexico]:

Your efforts in regard to Lascuraín have not been in vain, insofar as you have firmed up our opinion about Carbajál; continue to name names for us. Thanks to the talks of the Argentine diplomat with Bryan the outlook of the mediations is better today. Because the United States has shown itself moving toward leaving the discussion of domestic Mexican questions to direct negotiations between Mexican delegates and Carranza's delegate; perhaps because of the splits between the revolutionaries. What remains to be done by the conference is its original and actual objective: namely, laying to rest the Tampico incident. Tomorrow (that means June 22.) Today we will codify through protocol what we have reached through mutual understanding, which will [also mean] that no indemnification will be asked for.

Huerta's Mexican delegates take control of the direct negotiations because, this way, they hope to eliminate U.S. influence over the revolutionaries.

Carrancistas are considering it while experiencing pressure from internal factional fights. All in all, all participants want to win time through this way out.

Tuesday, June 23, 1914, Mexico City

General Rincon Gallardo told me that the Zapatistas had taken the village of San Francisco on June 19. In the night of July 20-21 the Federales advanced: General Iturbide advanced with mounted police and artillery, also the Twenty-Second Rurales. Furthermore, General Rincon Gallardo approached with his Rurales, on June 21, 2:00 a.m. The fight is supposed to have lasted until the afternoon, 3:00 p.m. of the twenty-first. Two officers and one seargent are dead.

The losses of the Zapatistas are not known. They escaped into the mountains. He estimates their numbers at between eight hundred and one thousand. From General Iturbide's group, I hear different news: that Rincon Gallardo had to escape with his Rurales. In no way did he participate in the encirclement maneuver. Already on the twenty-first, around 3:00 p.m., he took the electrical train back to the capital. This is one of the Zapatista raids into the suburbs of Mexico City that I predicted.

Today we learn that, once again, Zapatistas have penetrated Xochimilco.

Huerta told the Japanese diplomat Adachi—asking about the state of mediation (on June 22): *it* advances too slow for him. He will not make any concessions but will put himself at the head of the troops and, within fourteen days, he will have thrown the United States back into the ocean. It was 6:00 p.m. when Huerta made these statements—too late!

Shortly afterward Adachi talked to Huerta's oldest son, Jorge, who offered his opinion: it is better that the mediation ends in failure. That would be for the good of the country.

Huerta told the British diplomat that his nephew Gen. Joaquin Maas, whom everybody knows is commanding the army near San Luis [Potosí] "is a pretty good boy, but hungry for money beyond measure."

Bryan answered the petition that was passed to him by the Brazilian diplomat. It had asked to lift the double customs taxation of the goods imported to Veracruz and, from there, shipped to Mexican locations.

His answer was: the United States is lifting customs only for the account of the Mexican government. Only the Mexican secretary of finance could decide about the nullification of customs payments. Besides, the German ambassador in Washington has demanded that Veracruz customs income be reserved to pay the interest of the Mexican debt held in German hands. He says he discussed that with de la Lama, who had declared he could not do anything about it. That was the only perspective he could offer. The possible perspective of taxes later, paid a second time, will be returned upon production of the certificates. Several merchants have been able to sell merchandise at good prices—even luxury articles that had been brought on land before or during the occupation. Importing to Mexico has to be rewarded. Puerto México has to arrange for imports to Mexico as long as Veracruz is occupied.

The government these days is reaching the end of its funds. Currently 230 million banknotes are circulating (in addition, paper money issued by revolutionaries: about 76 million). Of these 230 million pesos, nominally 45 million are "covered", using the known and often misused 1913 bonds. The rest—185 million—is supposed to have been deposited at banks, a third of it in cash.

It is doubtful that this is the case: currently the government considers several projects to raise money. Among others: to declare "as cash" the known bonds and to issue paper money in a ratio of three to one, instead of one to one. Another idea is simply to print banknotes without coverage: the nation will pay! For the time being nothing has been decided.

Wednesday, June 24, 1914, Mexico City

The Mexican government holds in its hands only two cables from Niagara Falls:

1. One dated June 21 thanking the president for the latest instructions (direct negotiations with revolutionary representatives). As soon as the appropriate opportunity—which has not been the case so far—presents itself to make use of it.
2. The second one is dated June 22, saying: the change of public opinion in the United States is caused by Huerta's declaration: "his person is not going to be an obstacle for peace" and through the lifting of the blockade of Tampico. The president

should remain in this position and take great pains not to attack the United States about their national pride. Also not to attack Wilson, because for the United States he stands as a symbol of the nation. For several days now the papers have not published caricatures and have offered no insults. In contrast, papers have been critical, some even aggressively, of Wilson's politics.

Thursday, June 25, 1914, Mexico City

Consul Weber, El Paso, cabled that—according to local news—Zacatecas has fallen. Secretary of finance visits and shows me the dispatch of the Niagara Falls [conference] delegates: "Local New York news says that Zacatecas has fallen, is that correct?" This morning he showed the telegram to the president, who expressed himself; he will generalize statements like "Ojala que haya"—May God grant that it has. And the news has not yet been confirmed for the remarks about disease.[63] But he—de la Lama—has taken from the president's statements that, indeed, Zacatecas has been taken by the rebels. One telegram says: in the night of Tuesday to Wednesday ([June] 23-24).

Once again he will ask and inform me. If Zacatecas really has been taken, then almost the entire artillery has been lost at once, and they had no more means to defend themselves: furthermore, it is proof how much the army is exhausted and tired of war. It does not pay anymore to keep on fighting. Everywhere Federales maintain a defensive posture despite strict orders to the opposite. They do not attack a single time and are steadily defeated, with the exception of the one attack on Zacatecas.

As I used to say, quite correctly: the president's mood is that of a desperate person. He has no right to gamble with the nation's interest (simply) because of himself. His inactivity is atrocious. The president must make a decision and, actually, very fast. Otherwise, here in the capital, it will come to a catastrophe. No money is here and troops are tired. A decision is needed. The organization of the revolutionaries in the capital is accomplished.

I asked him: what is the status of negotiations in Niagara Falls? De la Lama replies, the delegates have taken up the issue of Tampico. Taking care of it would depend on Washington. When asked whether the delegates had reported the direction they were taking in the negotiations, the answer is: no.

I'm quite surprised about this because it is their duty to keep the government informed. Even if they have authority to make decisions. Frequently there is the impression that the delegates poorly inform the Huerta government. At the very least they have been unable to get in touch with the delegates of the Carrancistas because they had *not* yet arrived in Niagara Falls. The Brazilian diplomat has *not* received news from Niagara Falls since Sunday. My impression is that the United States and the Carrancistas treat the negotiations dilatorily and that the Mexican delegates are not very committed to working against this.[64] In reality, everybody is waiting on the essential question of how the conflict will be decided here in the capital; that is, the toppling of Huerta—everything pivots around this.

Huerta seems to sense this and, therefore, tries everything to provoke the United States. He prefers to lose as the nation's hero rather than as a representative of a revolutionary faction. Not to be forgotten, with the United States he can be certain of his life and money. Whereas arriving rebels would make both disappear. Finally, this corresponds with his state of mind—as a desperate man—the result of desperate measures, no longer (just) to rescue himself but to spread the apocalypse to everybody.

Ricardo García Granados warns that the capital is full of Zapatistas.

Consul Weber cables: five thousand defeated [enemy] prisoners; twelve cannons; nine railroad trains; six thousand guns; and several wagons [of] ammunition (near Zacatecas).

In confidence I inform de la Lama, whose evaluation is: a complete disaster.[65] The president needs to reach an understanding with the revolutionaries so that they come to the capital not as revolutionaries but as "government." But of course he makes no mention that he is interested in talking to the president about this.

Carden holds a telegram: "Yesterday the peace protocol was signed by the United States and Mexico." The Mexican Foreign Ministry did not receive anything in that regard via the landline. However, de la Lama visits me in the evening and shows me a private telegram mailed by Rabosos, president of the peace delegates. It begins, "Refer to our telegram to *relaciones*" and continues: process means, indirectly, recognition of Huerta government and successor; it means a triumph for us. All domestic issues will be left to the rebels. The only clause that we complained about, and then rejected, was the one that pertains to the evacuation of Veracruz. The United States had written it in vague terms. We propose to leave this out anyway and to deal with the evacuation of Veracruz as a legal consequence of the peace process. Implicitly it is a direct consequence of it and will come into force as soon as the new provisional government has been put in place. And relations between Mexico and the United States have resumed. Please ask President Huerta to make friends with this proposal, the only one we can reach in order not to have the agreement fail.

We propose to accept without change the clauses of all these protocols. Because the United States is weary and flip-flops and we have difficulty in assuring the United States is staying in the game. Cabrera is expected as Carranza's delegate.[66] We are looking forward with hope. A critical hour full of substance!

The Brazilian diplomat calls me at night. I learn from him the following [facts written] in a da Gama telegram that he has just received:

1. Yesterday evening we put in *Protocol* Clause No. 1 problems addressed pertaining to domestic issues reserved for arrangement by Mexicans. For example, the provisional government, amnesty, etc.
2. Mediation [pertaining to questions] that have not been discussed nor decided but that were studied: national economy and who should report on international problems. The two parties involved in the conflict have applauded this clause energetically.
3. The United States and the ABC powers will recognize the provisional government immediately after it is established.
4. [Considered was] neither indemnification whatsoever nor international satisfaction.
5. Amnesty [given to] foreigners who compromised themselves in the civil war.
6. An international commission to settle foreign claims.
7. Indemnification for damages suffered from the civil war.

The telegram says nothing about the evacuation of Veracruz: it closes with words heavy with future meaning: this protocol depends on the accord to be established between Federales and rebels. This addition shows how little the entire draft still means today.

De la Lama asks me: what to do? I advise, as long as this does not affect the entire agreement, not treating Veracruz's evacuation as a legal consequence of the peace agreement. I remind him of the long-lasting occupation after reaching peace. Instead they need to put down a [specific] time. Besides, I'm asking for time to think.

Consul Weber's details about the battle of Zacatecas say a lot: the Federales lost five thousand prisoners, twelve cannons, nine railroad trains, several wagons with cartridges. In confidence the Mexican government informs me that the number of men in the federal army concentrated around and in Zacatecas numbered nineteen thousand men; Generals Medina, Barron, Argumedo, Orozco, perhaps also Joaquin Maas. The high number of prisoners allows the conclusion that there were many who crossed over, just like at Paredon. A sign of the disintegration inside the army. It cannot be determined exactly how strong the rebels had been. In the Foreign Office one only knows that a few days ago Villa had moved twenty thousand men and forty cannons from Torreón . The Federales' loss in artillery is very concerning.

No connection with Zacatecas; a sign that the rebels are already south of it. A telegram from Aguasfrias says: loss of the Federales is a complete rout.

Friday, June 26, 1914, Mexico City

The president apparently takes the case of Zacatecas lightly: "I am already in the process of concentrating troops at Aguascalientes."

De la Lama visits, nine o'clock in the early morning, with the text of the dispatch from the delegates that finally had been received in the Foreign Ministry:

Yesterday evening, from Tuesday to Wednesday, we gathered for a plenary meeting:

1. The federal government to which Protocol No.3 refers will be organized in accordance with the two parties.
2. Once the provisional government has been constituted in Mexico City, the United States will immediately recognize it, which should establish diplomatic relations between the two countries. The United States will not claim war indemnification of any kind nor other international satisfactions. The provisional government will proclaim absolute amnesty for all foreigners and the political actions they committed during the civil war period in Mexico.—The United States will negotiate the staff-

ing of an international commission to determine foreign claims for acts they suffered during the period of civil war. As a consequence of military acts or acts of national authorities.

3. Mediating powers will gather to recognize the provisional government that will organize itself in accordance with Article 1.

Apparently Protocol No. 3 contains the proposals of the Mexican government from June 5 [see diary entry for June 5, 1914]. It has been signed June 8 or 9 [see diary entry for June 10, 1914]. The most essential part of this protocol is that Huerta drop the earlier condition for his stepping down: to have established peace.

De la Lama read the protocol aloud to the president, who declared, "Inadmissible." And as it was read to him he repeatedly exclaimed, "I will not step down until the Veracruz occupation has ended." De la Lama asks me to influence the president so that he accepts the protocol. I explained to him,

1. The protocol has been composed considering that Huerta's resignation is a fact. That hurt Huerta.
2. It would leave out the crucial point: namely the departure from Veracruz. [I ask] if the United States had difficulty with this earlier? In lively fashion de la Lama confirms it: "A lot of resistance!"

In my opinion the delegates should transmit verbatim the text of the U.S. proposal so that Huerta can evaluate it. And so that he could be urged: his personal sacrifice could drive the invaders out of the country. This is the only possibility for persuading him.

3. The question of whether the evacuation of Veracruz should be removed from the peace document and should be treated as a legal consequence does not appear very promising. Because legal conclusions can be extracted from the treaties only when both parties are likely to agree. Which here most likely will not be the case.
4. I do not see a basis for a useful talk with the president as long as we don't have the text of the U.S. proposal pertaining to Veracruz. Right away de la Lama wires for the text. Regardless of what he wants to achieve with his step, I speak with the presi-

dent right away on the telephone. Because by noon he has to cable the answer to the delegates. I don't want to be "holier than thou."

Therefore, I rejected using my previously stated justification and I don't refer again to the evacuation of Veracruz. De la Lama urges me on and asks me also to speak with Blanquet. He keeps in mind, in the background, the report that the president is out of money and does not know how to organize new [money]. [The issue is] an additional tool to pressure the president, even though he thinks he can issue paper money. [For that reason] he is preparing a victory. It is designed to prevent bank robbery. I remain firm and say I am considering having my opinion checked with Carden—if he would not mind—and then I will give him an answer.

Carden, to whom I present the above-stated justification, explained after a long period of consideration, "I agree with you on every point." He believes that, finally, it would become the job of the diplomatic corps to build a professional government. That might be possible and not that difficult—as far as I'm concerned.

Smiling, Carden adds, "I say, wouldn't it be glorious if we got behind the back of the Americans?" I replied that the United States is contributing through influence on the rebels and the conference so that it could remain a purely local affair—to find a peaceful transition to a new provisional government without clashes in and around the capital—and that we need to aim for this peaceful transition in the interest of everyone. Therefore I maintain that it would be premature to approach the president before we have the exact text of the protocol, including the rejected clause about Veracruz. Because this clause, perhaps, could not be entirely acceptable.

De la Lama follows my argumentation and wants to return at once, following the reception of the text of the protocols and the U.S. proposal pertaining to Veracruz.

I visit the government of the Federal District in order to discuss again the measures that need to be taken as far as the threatened uprising in the city is concerned. There I learn that the rebels have occupied San Juan del Rio at the central railroad, about four hours from the capital. They have interrupted the connection of the central railroad as well as threatened the connection of the national railroad. Furthermore, [I learn] that parts of the army of San Luis Potosí have risen against its commander. The commanding general, Maas, has fled with many officers and had already arrived in the capital. From San Luis Potosí, a private telegram arrives saying: all the officers have left. No word from the imperial [German] consul.

Tonight, General Iturbide moves with eighteen hundred men—soldiers and police, no Rurales—to Topilejo near San Francisco, close by Xochimilco but very close to the capital. There have dug in two thousand Zapatistas, whom Iturbide and Gen. Rincon Gallardo had wanted to chase away on June 21. As part of this effort Gen. Rincon Gallardo turned around with his men instead of proceeding from San Francisco—after a few losses, of three dead. Then he took the electrical tramway back to the capital. Therefore the planned concentrated attack failed. This time Rincon Gallardo remained at home.

I see my prediction justified that the most obvious danger is raids by Zapatistas. The two thousand Zapatistas [have been] stationed now for fourteen days in most immediate proximity of the capital and suburbs. Until today the government has not been able to push them away.

Day before yesterday—June 24—rebels or Zapatistas made an energetic attack against the power line of the Mexican Light and Power Co., which supplies Mexico with electric light and power. They destroyed four towers. Fortunately repair began soon thereafter. It can be expected that the attacks will be repeated. If the transmission wires or the plant is destroyed Mexico City will have one reserve—(steam engine plant). But at most it will work for ten days.

The reserves of oil and coal in the capital are coming to an end. If used sparingly they [will] suffice for about ten days. The British diplomat asks me on behalf of the needs of two railroad companies—Mexicano and Interoceanico, both British—for my support. [I should ask] the president to allow oil to be supplied from Veracruz. I promise it to him—since maintenance of the connection with Veracruz is in the interest of the Germans.

Saturday, June 27, 1914, Mexico City

The British diplomat [Carden] visits [and] explains: he has news that a plot has been organized in the capital and that it is ready to start and will take off parallel with the approach of the Villistas. On the same day the Zapatistas will attack the city. Already several revolutionaries living in the capital, whom he knew, have departed to join the Villistas. Furthermore: according to his news, attacks against Necaxa are being repeated. One day the capital will be without electric light. It is the same with the attacks against the water main in Xochimilco. Railroad companies have little fuel left. Therefore trains are running on a very limited schedule: as a consequence, only a few food supplies are reaching the capital. His community shared with him that the local butcher house, in four days, will be out of supplies to process. New supply is not expected due to the sparse railroad connection. He thought about all these points and decided to call together the members of his community who were still residing here and to urge them, *immediately*, to leave the capital. Immediately: because it is only a matter of days. His news from Zacatecas said that little fighting has taken place: two thousand Federalists switched lines, with flying colors, to the rebels. (The Italian diplomat tells me: Gen. Rojas and his people.) Thereupon Ángeles allowed federal general Medina Barron to depart with the troops that have remained loyal to him. Therefore the federal army does not merit trust. He asks me to tell my community to leave the city immediately so that this fact would impress his community.

I reply: Germans have had many opportunities—and comfortable ones, may I say—to leave the capital. And I have advised them of that. Despite that, most remained. They did not want to abandon their interests here, trusting that my duty and power will protect them nevertheless. I see no justification for that but can't change it. I doubt that such warnings will have a different success among my countrymen than panic—even though I recognize them as justified. *In my opinion the terrible situation can be eradicated by attacking its roots. Obviously the Huerta regime is finished. Also, one should make an effort [so] that the transition to another government proceeds without catastrophe. One should leave the formation of another government to the Mexicans. Then we should help—in a friendly way and not an official one—in order to avoid a catastrophe.*

This is a local matter and needs to be dealt with on the local level.

Carden acknowledges these explanations as correct. I add: he spent his entire life in South America. Based on his experience he should tell me if there exists a way other than the one described by me? Sir Lionel replies: indeed, he has spent his entire life among Latino Americans [*sic*], but never has he been in such a difficult, confusing situation. He has acknowledged completely the justification of what I have said. His suggestion with the community could only be "petite work" [*sic*]. In case of unrest in the city, preparations for the defense of the communities could probably be useful. But not in case of an entry of a demoralized federal army or the Villistas or the Zapatistas. Expressly I state that he is limiting his community's capacity of defense [to act] against a mob of uprisings in the capital. (And that nevertheless the British community prepared, participated, and interested itself to an entirely different degree and number for self-defense compared with the German one). We agree right now, today, to discuss the situation with the secretaries of finance and war in the sense that we have outlined.

I asked the board of the rowing club to meet with me. I asked it not to undertake the usual Sunday exercises, considering the Zapatistas that are nearby.

The community defense council and I talk about my negotiations with the government of the Federal District.

De la Lama has a meeting with Carden and me at 5:00 p.m. We are meeting in the house of Mr. Adams—a neutral place that attracts no attention. He hands me the following telegram from Rabasa to read:

> The text of the clause pertaining to the evacuation of Veracruz reads: the time and nature of the evacuation of Veracruz is to be determined in negotiations between the United States and the new interim government. The negotiations that have taken place are a triumph of law that rests on the side of Mexico, presented to the entire world confronting fraud, brutality, and force. It is the only triumph we could expect.
>
> The formula in regard to the evacuation of Veracruz is unacceptable. Nevertheless, we suggest keeping unmentioned in the protocol the time and manner of the evacuation so that the entire agreement is not endangered. [That possibility] has had no influence on the decisions of the United States. In contrast, the demands of the rebels did. The representatives will take [our] remarks to discuss in Washington but will not send an answer to us. We will wait until Monday. But then we will treat the lack of the answer as a rejection and act accordingly.

Once again Huerta remarks in regard to this telegram: he will not leave before the United States has evacuated Veracruz. One can see that the decision remains the same, the reason changed. But today he ordered Gen. Rubio Navarrete—who is stationed with the majority of the troops near San Francisco before Veracruz—to withdraw to the capital. He uses general staff officers to gather intelligence about a position between here and Queretaro.

Rightly so, de la Lama says, "Huerta does not say what he thinks!"—De la Lama describes Huerta's situation as unsustainable. When I asked him expressly if the cabinet shares this opinion, he answers, "The entire cabinet is unanimous."

Something needs to happen, otherwise the coup in the capital will take place. He asks us to present our views to Washington, asking the United States to exercise its influence over the rebels so that they do *not* advance with the goal of military conquest. That is necessary to save citizen life and property. We, in agreement, reply that the United States had given assurances to create equal protection for U.S. citizens as for foreigners. Experience has taught that the United States has not been able to protect its own citizens, nor foreigners. Furthermore, experience teaches that the United States could exercise little influence on the rebels.

Sir Lionel adds: from the very beginning it had been the intention of the United States to accept the conference in order to give enough time for the rebels to gain more territory. Now, after Zacatecas, the rebels are in front of the capital, [and] the United States had decided, as written in the protocol, to refrain from participating in the internal conflicts of Mexico. That could be seen and based on the fact that the rebels had advanced far enough to establish for the United States—without help of the conference—the government that is suitable [to the United States].

De la Lama exclaims, "Then everything is lost. We have no more means to counter violence with violence." I suggest—making clear it is only an idea, subject to critique by both of them—bringing about a *momentary* and temporary pause. Huerta *names a neutral person as secretary of foreign affairs. Then he steps down and thereby, due to the constitution, makes him president.* This way Huerta will rescue himself, as well as his family and his future, by not compromising himself by signing a treaty with the United States—and the successor, therefore, will be able to negotiate easier with the United States and the rebels. Carden adds: only the successor should be allowed to sign the protocol with the United States. In a lively fashion he entertains the idea. The person suited for this is Lascuraín. The Brazilian diplomat has hinted that this will be acceptable to the United States and the rebels. After repeated explorations of consequences of such a Lascuraín appointment, we make the following summary:

1. Today de la Lama and Blanquet will suggest to the president that he should name Lascuraín: time is very short.
2. If they don't get through to the president they will call me and Carden for help.

Today at lunch Carden attempted to talk to the president in order to tell him that he could *not* host Huerta's family (as refugees), as, once, he had arranged it. Huerta did not receive him.

Also, Cardoso has received warnings about the conspiracy in the capital from several sources. These matching threatening reports force me to replenish supplies: foodstuffs, coal, wood, oil, etc., to resupply the house and one automobile and the option for a second one because my food reserves are nearing an end. . . .

Cardoso received a telegram from Ambassador da Gama: "[I] travel to New Jersey for my recuperation." Another source declares that the Chilean diplomat has also left Niagara Falls. That only allows one interpretation! Mediators have decided to consider their mediation finished based on the last protocol.—Perhaps in order to avoid complete failure.

In fact, the mediation has achieved hardly anything. With the exception of working toward Huerta's resignation. From the point of view of many interests, hardly a satisfying result. The capital's streets are steadily being combed by military patrols. At night more than during the day.

Sunday, June 28, 1914, Mexico City

De la Lama visits me, pleading [with me] to persuade the president to resign and to make Lascuraín his successor by appointing him secretary of foreign relations: this is the only possibility to prevent a desaster.

I ask whether he and Blanquet had talked about this with the president, as had been agreed upon yesterday? He says no. These people, due to fear, are completely paralyzed. I repeat to him that most of Huerta's cabinet must give that advice; that I would be willing, in case Huerta pretends to have difficulty hearing, to support the cabinet through amicable and direct influence. However, the cabinet has the right to speak the first word. De la Lama sees the point and prepares himself in my presence to go to the president.

FIG. 36. Chilean diplomat Eduardo Suárez Mujica. Courtesy of the
Library of Congress.

News reports exist that Gen. Velasco has been thrown into prison. Until now he has been commander of the army of San Luis Potosí.

Two thousand men of Gen. Rubio Navarrete's troops have been withdrawn to the capital; also parts of Garcia Peña's army (also near Córdoba).

Cardoso arrives and reports that the federal garrison of Queretaro has switched sides and joined the rebels. This morning he explained to Esteva Ruiz: only one alternative exists to avoid the massacre inside the capital. One [possibility] is that, immediately, Huerta abdicates and puts in Lascuraín to succeed him. The other is to ask the United States to come up from Veracruz as a police corps authorized by the Mexican government.

For both Esteva Ruiz showed complete understanding. Cardoso wants to cable Washington—near capital Zapatistas and rebels, as well as demoralized federal army. Another conspiracy is being prepared inside the capital. The situation is very serious—so that Washington becomes aware of its responsibility and will not be surprised when the possible request comes to march [to the capital]. I agree with this intent, even though I do not trust in Huerta's willingness to ask for it and the United States' willingness to do it.

Tomorrow Cardoso wants to send his family to Veracruz.

Carden asked me to walk with him to meet Huerta when the question of Huerta's resignation has to be dealt with—proof of how profound Huerta's rejection had been, he dished out against him. The talk at Huerta's, together with Carden, darkens the outlook as far as my influence is concerned. But it demonstrates the nature of our local politics that I cannot reject his request.

Carden has received news from San Luis [Potosí] that the rebels concentrate east of the city.

General Salas shares with me that the Federales received orders to evacuate Aguascalientes. Because the path southward is blocked they will withdraw to San Luis [Potosí], eastward. That is not without danger because the rebels also are in Pinos.

The president meets with me in the evening, about eight o'clock. He orders his car stopped. He steps out and, apparently, wants to share something important with me. However, a large crowd of people surrounds us so uncomfortably—certainly not friendly or courteous, nobody removes his hat—that he limits his words to telling me he has important things to say to me on Monday or Tuesday and gets back into the car.

Monday, June 29, 1914, Mexico City

On Saturday, June 27, a military revolt was uncovered. Yesterday thirty-six of the alleged perpetrators were shot to death. Among them eleven officers in the Citadel. Huerta pulls back troops from Veracruz in order to defend the capital against the Zapatistas. Already the latter are in Xochimilco.

Unfortunately neither Rubio Navarrete (near Santa Fé and San Francisco) nor Garcia Peña (near Cordoba) have many men or sufficient ammunition. The positions in front of Veracruz anyway are nothing but a deception.

The British diplomat repeats categorically the demand to his colony to send women and children out of the city; to move them to Puerto México and, from there, on to Jamaica.

The French chargé d'affaires visits me. He urges me to bring sailors here to protect the diplomatic legation and community. Already he has talked with Carden, who was not against it. I explain my position as:

1. I cannot move here sufficient sailors or soldiers for the protection of my community;
2. that a small, insufficient number would only increase the number of fatalities;
3. that for quite some time I have had here two Maxim cannons and four men, but only to calm the nerves of my community.
   [. . .]

Ayguésparse classified as poor the colony's ability to defend itself. Based on 1913 experiences he is right about that. He decides to have about six men come up—simply to calm down the French community. For me, an additional reason that I don't mention is that the [German] imperial government, according to its statements, wants to avoid the landing of troops. It wants to leave extradition to the United States.

The Brazilian diplomat shows me a telegram from Ambassador da Gama (from New Jersey) stating, "Today he returned to Niagara Falls, following pressure from colleagues."[67] He interprets this as resumption of the work of the conference, certainly not without reason.

Yesterday Sir Lionel Carden held a community meeting and asked its members to leave the city. I see in the *Mexican Herald* a fitting description. Thereafter great panic broke out among the British and probably among Germans. I can't wait, because I have consulted [with them] so often and repeatedly made recommendations to them to leave and made available abundant means. Carden wants to charter a ship to accept possible refugees. Last Saturday his satisfaction in regard to the talk with the president was so poor that he called him crazy—the man he once adored—"the only one who can save Mexico." He told Huerta that he cannot *provide shelter in the legation in case of emergency. He intimated to Huerta that if he* sought shelter in the British legation, rarely would he be able to leave it. I don't know how he took it. He didn't look offended. However, the main reason for the differences breaking out between the two is the question of oil transport from Veracruz to here. Carden engages himself in favor of it in a lively fashion, also because of Pearson's interest. Carden considers a joint presentation of the diplomatic corps, asking Huerta to step down. I counter that: first, without the endorsement of our governments, this step is outside our powers, and second, it is most unlikely that he could persuade the diplomatic corps to take such a step.

The last protocol of the conference still has not been answered. The Mexican government was supposed to present it to the Senate. The delegates asked to wait.

Today de la Lama talked with the president about the dire situation. Huerta declared: he did not want to hear anything anymore about the designation of a successor. De la Lama is supposed to compose immediately a telegram to the Mexican delegates saying: if the United States does not give in by Wednesday, July 1, 6:00 p.m., they are supposed to withdraw from the conference. At the same time he will launch an attack against the United States in Veracruz.

Once again Huerta is emboldened by receiving two types of news: one, that Villa and Ángeles are supposed to have returned to Chihuahua in order to fight against the counterrevolution. The other one stating that the mood in the United States is turning in his favor thanks to Hopkins's publication describing Standard Oil's cooperation with the revolution. De la Lama urges me with greatest urgency to talk to Huerta. I ask him if Blanquet, as agreed upon, has already tried his luck.

De la Lama replies: Blanquet visited Huerta this morning. He waited for 1.5 hours but was not received. I declare: first, I need to hear Blanquet before I could undertake steps of my own. De la Lama confirms news of the military revolt of Saturday, June 27, and repeats: no means exist, neither money nor soldiers, to offer resistance. The president has to go.

De la Lama sends me the attached memorandum of the Mexican delegates that had been handed to the United States before the signing of the last protocols.

Secretary of War Blanquet declares to me: it is his opinion that Huerta has to go and to hand the presidency to a neutral person. There exists no other solution. It is not possible for him to assemble another army of fifteen thousand to twenty thousand men to confront the revolutionaries. The army that has been defeated near Zacatecas is so demoralized that it could not be used to fight for another three to four months. Yes, if he wanted to hand over Michoacán, Jalisco, Guanajuato, México, etc., then perhaps he could put together an army. But it is dangerous to give up these states. Rubio Navarrete, near San Francisco (Veracruz), had three thousand men. Of them, two thousand have been pulled back to the capital city. Garcia Peña has three to four thousand men near Cordoba. That is all that he could position against the United States! How could he advance offensively against the United States with that? Rubio's people could do nothing further to guard haphazardly the Interoceanic Railroad.

When the president talks about moving against the United States, then, this makes no sense. I reply to Blanquet that Huerta is supposed to have shown to me troop strength reports. He replies, "On paper you can show anything." I ask him if he enlightened the president about the desperate military situation. Blanquet claims, "In its entirety, but Huerta choses to remain a dreamer in the midst of his wishes." Whether he also talked to Huerta about what he had described as the only possible solution? "No, I am a soldier; that is a matter for the other secretaries. If they move ahead I will follow them but I cannot be the first one." Whether the question has ever been raised in the council of secretaries? A council of secretaries has not met for a long time. I state: if ever, the moment is now to speak in favor of a council of secretaries. Blanquet agrees, but statesmen are afraid and would not gather. The diplomatic corps should say something. In a determined way I declare that this would exceed the powers given to the diplomatic corps, unless Huerta's official advisors speak first. Blanquet needs to influence the council of secretaries to meet first and tell Huerta its opinion.

When I ask him whether news about the military conspiracy from Saturday, June 27, is accurate, he admits it with hesitation.

In Queretaro a mutiny is supposed to have taken place. He [Blanquet] will recapture San Juán del Rio, or he took it again already. I ask him in a clear, direct manner, repeatedly, if he is still in possession of sufficient amounts of heating oil to maintain the operation of the railroad in a haphazard fashion. Blanquet replies emphatically that, for weeks, he has been working toward this goal and now he had collected a large amount of heating oil: therefore concerns are not justified. However he does not have soldiers, or at least not in sufficient number, no leadership, and not enough artillery.

He repeats: the only possible solution would be Huerta's resignation in favor of a neutral person.

As usual, Blanquet impresses me as an excellent noncommissioned officer. He disdains initiative of his own as unsoldierlike and undisciplined, because—in this case—it is directed against his superior. I can only take notice of this opinion and share that with him.

Tuesday, June 30, 1914, Mexico City

De la Lama informs me that yesterday evening Huerta submitted to the delegates the following telegram: "The permanent extension of the negotiations damages Mexico's interest. If on Wednesday, July 1, in the evening you have not been able to reach a satisfactory result, then declare the negotiations finished and withdraw, assuring that Mexico reserves the freedom to act as it sees fit."

Based on his own authority, de la Lama added: the president approves the terms of the last protocols but demands adding an addendum that requires the *immediate evacuation of Veracruz and the withdrawal of U.S. ships from Mexican waters. De la Lama described his impression*: "The president wants to break off the negotiations" and declared this intention as not making sense. He asks me to move Huerta away from this idea. I tell him details from my discussion with Blanquet, the parts I am allowed to share and the program that had been discussed:

1. The cabinet, based on a joint decision, presents Huerta with the seriousness of the situation and the only solution: resigning in favor of Lascuraín so that he reaches an understanding with the rebels and the United States.
2. Friendly advice given by some diplomat, if it [the cabinet] does persuade him, in the sense of point three and when points one and two do not catch on. Then a joint declaration of the situation from the diplomatic corps and inquiry [as to] what he intends to do vis-á-vis the endangerment of life and property of our countrymen.

After I justify the program more, de la Lama accepts the points and drives immediately to the secretary of foreign affairs to urge him to call together the cabinet. De la Lama implores me to move the president immediately to take back the ultimatum. *He* had tried in vain to do so this morning. Supposedly Huerta explained, "Once an order is given, it remains in existence."

I ask de la Lama how he expects success to be the result of my steps when his—de la Lama's—ended in fiasco. He answered: Huerta declared repeatedly that he accepted hints only from me as put forward by the diplomatic corps as a whole. I am the only one who is speaking openly and honestly with him. He has lost trust in Carden.

The expedition against the Zapatistas near Xochimilco has returned: they chased away the Zapatistas from Cuauzin, allegedly suffering three deaths, inflicting twenty-four upon the enemy. This success does not look as if it will last. Near Cuauzin really means "in the mountains." There Zapatistas still remain. My estimation has been confirmed that the most immediate danger would be Zapatista raids into suburbs of Mexico City.

Mexican delegates are sending cables: Carranza's *delegates* are justifying their absence [by] arguing that, first, they had to collect the opinion of various leaders. They consider this opinion to be credible and attribute best intentions to the Carrancistas.

Carden tells me that Necaxa Light & Power has entered into an agreement with the rebels. The company is alleged to have paid a certain sum and, because of that, enjoys immunity—as long as the rebels remain true to the pact. I tell Carden my suggestion about advising the cabinet. He considers it to be the only passable path and the precondition for any kind of activity from our side.

Livestock is supposed to be coming from Oaxaca. It has to be brought here in a drive because rebels destroyed the railroad between Tehuacan and Oaxaca.

The situation is as follows in Morelos:

1. Federales are located near Cuernavaca.
2. Zapata is located in Tepozotlán and Chon Díaz in Zacatepec, each of them with three to four thousand men.[68]
3. In Iguela Figueroa and Lugo there are 10,000 men.
4. The agreement between (2) and (3) is not supposed to be particularly deep.

Alberto García Granados tells me in confidence that Carden expressed the wish to him to make contact with Villistas. He brought Ignacio Rivero to Carden. After long negotiations, during the afternoon of the twenty-seventh, Rivero sent a man to *Villa*, following an order of Carden. He was supposed to ask if Villa would be disposed to mediation through the diplomatic corps and if he was willing to commit to not allowing excesses, as he planned to march into Mexico City. In my opinion this arrangement seemed to have been done with little sense of humor.

Ignacio Rivero, formerly governor of the Federal District and later representative to Argentina, pays me a visit and hands me the attached excerpt of a meeting that he held with the British diplomat during the afternoon of June 27. In my opinion:

1. Carden enlisted the help of the diplomatic corps unnecessarily and apparently without official power.
2. From the very beginning Rivero undertakes too much.
3. He [Rivero] should limit himself to exploring the ideas of revolutionaries about the way they thought they would enter Mexico City if a Huerta government no longer exists here. Whether that be because Huerta has resigned or has withdrawn from the city.

Everything else [will follow] out of that—if the rebels want that.—It is characteristic that Carden makes contact with *Villa* and expressly has rejected establishing ties with Carranza.

Rivero is very grateful and, apparently, takes along my words of criticism, which he did not have an obligation to do. He reacts with a firm denial to my question of whether behind him might be standing an organization; since he was willing to go out on a limb to such a degree.

The British diplomat achieved [what he intended] with his suggestion to his British community to leave Mexico City and to withdraw to a safe place. He repeated on the twenty-eighth that forty-five individuals declared themselves willing to go to Jamaica. Now his community numbers only seven hundred to eight hundred people. It is known that the British community initiated, from the very beginning out of its own free will, the strongest possible emigration. The German community remained behind, more than twice as strong, because of the already repeatedly listed reasons.

On the other hand, [the German community] staffs the defensive corps with only half the number compared to the British. I am not able to change that.

Wednesday, July 1, 1914, Mexico City

Secretary of Finance de la Lama visits me early in the morning. As agreed upon yesterday, he had gathered the cabinet in a spirit of collegiality and all of them agreed unanimously: as soon as Huerta again makes difficulties as far as a resignation is concerned, then they collectively will hand in their resignation and demand his resignation.[69]

Equipped with this pressure, de la Lama visited the president yesterday evening and finally, at 8:00 in the evening, they met in the restaurant
Globo. He told him: this moment is of absolute seriousness and importance. He needed to speak with him. Huerta answered him: well, speak
here, right now!—But de la Lama refused to speak inside the restaurant,
so that finally the president gave in and stepped with him inside his automobile.

There de la Lama impressed him with the seriousness and urgency
of the situation from the political, military, and financial point of view.
Also the unanimity of the cabinet, as far as it evaluates the current situation. Also he submitted to Huerta a long telegram from the delegates
wherein, once again, the peace protocol is being submitted for signature
as everything possible that can be accomplished. At the same time the
protocol is positioned as a triumph of Huerta, and he points at the advantageous circumstances due to the situation of Villa versus Carranza.
Carranza expressed his willingness to negotiate, but first he wanted to
secure the agreement of the different leaders. After a short refusal Huerta caved in, facing the described unanimity. And [he] empowered de la
Lama to cable to the Mexican delegates to Niagara Falls the following
instructions:

The president empowers you to sign the peace protocol of June 24 [...]
under the assumption of the immediate evacuation of Veracruz and the
withdrawal of U.S. warships as the result of signing the peace and that
this precondition is being guaranteed by the mediating powers.

I point out that the delegates, once again, needed to have confirmed
the guarantee of the mediators—which allegedly they have offered. De
la Lama wants to do that in a new telegram. I consider this to be a valuable moral weapon facing the anticipated hesitation of the United States
to leave Veracruz soon.

That Huerta changed his mind within twenty-four hours is emblematic. It is a symptom of a pathological picture. And at the same time it
shows that he—the unbending one—yields—see the unanimity of the
cabinet—only to force.

De la Lama declares: As far as Huerta's resignation is concerned the
cabinet's unanimity also remains in existence for the future; as soon as
he hesitates to keep his word, "his honor is compromised."

He informs me about a financial project:

1. It [the Mexican government] will issue 6 percent of sixty million *titulos de la deuda*.
2. The interest on it will be assured with a stamp tax—*renta del timbre*.
3. The sale of the bond will serve as the payment of interest on the railroads, the 5 percent bond, the budget deficit, and the cost of fighting war to combat the revolution.
4. As long as the bond cannot be sold, it will be deposited, depending on need, at the Commission de Cambio y Moneda, and paper money will be issued in its place.[70] De la Lama expects that the international buyers will accept the loan and doubts that many domestic purchasers will participate.[71]

I explain to de la Lama all [the] reasons that speak for negotiations with revolutionaries as fast as possible. And the only way to preempt U.S. interference is to [exploit] the advantages of fast action. De la Lama asks about my support, which, to his contentment, I promise him, in a tone of friendship and discretion.

One needs to point out, as far as the bill is concerned and its justification for a sixty million 1914 internal bond: the twice expressly stated fact that Mexico is in a state of war.

Thursday, July 2, 1914, Mexico City

Meeting with [Mexican secretary] of state and secretary of finance. The first decodes a telegram that has just arrived from Mexican delegates in Niagara Falls: "The United States and we signed today the final protocol (NS 4 or H2 4) that the president promulgated two days ago. This solves the international conflict, namely as a triumph of the Latin American race and as a protective wall against the advance of the North Americans. We suggest express gratitude to the mediators, etc."

Following my direct questions: has the United States accepted the conscious reservation as far as Veracruz is concerned, and have the mediators agreed to vouch for it? De la Lama and Esteva Ruiz have answered: "Yes."

Esteva Ruiz would like to present the treaty to Congress *immediately*, but he lacks the necessary documents for that; [he has] only the delegates' telegraphed reports. Besides, he states that the last cable talks about four protocols, but he is in possession of only *two*. Once again one sees how poorly the delegates have served the government.

I state my concern that to wait for the original documents—fifteen days—[to arrive] here would create an unbearable tension that could peak in [violent] outbreaks, and I propose to demand that the delegates wire the texts of all protocols immediately and forward them to the Senate without delay.

Both agree fervently and visit the president to present this proposition.

De la Lama, in light of the urgent danger of the situation, asks me to move the president to step down and to hand the presidency to Lascuraín. I counter: do you have proof that the rebels will agree to Lascuraín? De la Lama replies: he is inferring this from the information of the Brazilian diplomat. I do know his sources and, therefore, they are not decisive for me. Therefore I say, it would be better to ask the representatives of the rebels about this through the delegates. Right away de la Lama wants to send a cable.

The peace protocol is a triumph of U.S. policy, a complete defeat of the Huerta policy and a cover for the failure of mediation.

In essence it says:

1. Huerta must go.
2. U.S. citizens will remain in Veracruz an indeterminate time, because leaving, "as legal consequence of the treaty," might also take place simply in a few years. The United States remains on Mexican soil as long as it suits its policy—and now Huerta should be forced to go, from the inside [of the country]. An undertaking that brings with it all dangers and allows the continued existence of all that have threatened the Germans until now.

De la Lama has the news that in San Pedro de la Colonias Villa's and Carranza's delegates are meeting and planning. Secretary of the Interior Alcocer has caved in.[72] On Tuesday he declared Huerta's resignation as urgent and impossible, together with all other members of the cabinet.

Today he explained to de la Lama: he will do whatever president Huerta would order! De la Lama characterizes Alcocer as a vain, ambitious man. But in his opinion, his switching sides would not mean anything. I ask if all members of the cabinet expressly had committed themselves to remain silent about their decision. De la Lama, with certainty, affirms it.

A few leading deputies (Guasque and Rabago) have calculated the odds of the elections that soon will take place. According to them, even under today's circumstances, there will be "elected" close to 180 deputies. In a country where two-thirds have been placed outside of Huerta's control, the reason for this is the old Porfirian census, which grants the border states Chihuahua, Coahuila, and Sinaloa only two deputies each. Territories, for example, Tepic, will receive only one, and the states in the center will have an inappropriate degree [of influence].

Since the total number of deputies is only 245, then 180 at least could establish a quorum. However, these deputies do *not* believe that Huerta will emerge from the elections as elected president. Their reasons are based less on the constitution than on the [prevailing] mood.

The Brazilian diplomat has a telegram from Bryan that recognizes his good reports and asks him to continue to cable about the situation in the capital. *In case of emergency he should request U.S. citizens and other foreigners to leave the city.* About Villa, the telegram reports: his army is located along the railway line between Torreón and Ciudad Juárez.

Da Gama's telegram informs Cardoso that he has left Niagara Falls for Washington. But he does not provide specifics about the peace protocol.

Cardoso evaluates the final protocol

1. as an attempt of the mediators, to save from mediation whatever could be saved;
2. as a triumph of a U.S. bluff;
3. as a defeat of Mexican (Huerta's) policy. Because everything would remain as it had been, *all* dangers of domestic development would continue to exist: with the only difference [being] that the United States' remaining in Veracruz would be legalized and be based on a treaty.

He has no news about it but he takes from the words of Esteva Ruiz that "the mediators are the carriers of the guarantee of the evacuation of Veracruz."

This is or might be correct. Still, the moment to evacuate remains to be decided. And about this the phrase says, "About the evacuation of Veracruz the U.S. government will negotiate with the new provisional government." Such interpretation is, in my opinion, right. The United States has to leave Veracruz due to Huerta's moral and legal promise, and for the reason that it gave an informal promise—when? That has not been determined. Because even if the legal conclusion resulting from the treaty would be that they evacuate Veracruz, this does not define anything about the *point in time*.

Friday, July 3, 1914, Mexico City

Consul Weber cables from El Paso following my request:

1. In Torreón, negotiations are taking place to find agreement between Carranza and Villa.
2. Carranza is in Monterrey and cuts Villa off from the supply of ammunition and coal.
3. Carranza promoted the leaders of the revolutionary army to higher rank, bypassing Villa.
4. Villa tries to obtain ammunition from inside the United States. He wants to reestablish soon the connection with Ciudad Juárez (interrupted due to rain) and to go there.

The British diplomat concluded from the protocols, "Huerta must get out," and he is willing and in the process of doing his part [to see] that Huerta leaves. A curious turn of events after sticking with him through thick and thin so long, and he owes him so much.

Secretary of Finance de la Lama is visiting and regrets that he is still missing Protocol No. 3. The reason is supposed to be that the Mexican delegates have left for New York. A very short while ago, the Brazilian ambassador left for the very location. While the Argentine ambassador returned to Mexico: to protect the execution of the treaty.

Following my renewed question: we do not have any notice that the declaration of the mediators guarantees the evacuation of Veracruz; as a legal consequence, it is supposed to have been made *in writing or to be part of the documents* (i.e., the meeting protocols). He wants to ask for it through telegraph. I ask him for his overall evaluation of the protocols: "It could be worse, but it is bad." I talk encouragingly to him, since the protocol is enough to make it the basis of future steps and to make the best out of it. Furthermore, I explain how untimely it is to speak to the president about his resignation before an agreement has been reached with the rebels about his successor. De la Lama interjects: also to this point, the delegates have not yet answered. De la Lama asks me how I see the coming development.

I tell him openly: the new provisional government more or less will create calm, as far as it can be arranged (here de la Lama states: some time ago the president did commit himself to it, and I counter, how often Huerta has thrown to the wind such commitment); be that with a president who would come from the Constitutionalists or a neutral one. Then a new revolution will, perhaps, bring to the forefront the "strong man" that Mexico needs. De la Lama says in a sad tone: that is also *his* opinion and the opinion of many patriots.

From a talk with Carden I conclude that he has the task of working toward Huerta's resignation. He states that he needs to talk to him but he has no idea how to go about it because he had a falling out with him.

He hints: could we go together? I hint that this would be impractical, in my opinion, to deploy two [forces of] influence. Perhaps Downing Street has decided to do Washington a favor. It would not be the first time and it would not cost more to give the dying lion a kick.

The Austrian diplomat asks me what possibly could be up with Carden. He had visited him twice and asked him to invite Huerta for tomorrow's requiem for Archduke Franz Ferdinand, who has passed into eternity.[73] [Austrian diplomat] Kanya, rightly so, countered that this would be against custom. He had informed the government about the memorial and the government replied that it would send the secretary of foreign affairs and General Corona as representatives of the president. Carden finally asked for the invitation as a personal favor to him—Carden. And thereupon Carden wrote a letter that announced the memorial. The interconnection is clear: Carden has been charged and does want to *influence* Huerta to step down. He has no opportunity to approach Huerta, who would turn him away. He had become gruff (he himself said: I fell out of my role), and thereupon Huerta had replied back in a hearty way. Therefore, he is searching for a neutral reason to meet with Huerta—this following my rejection of joining him and going there.

Saturday, July 4, 1914, Mexico City

General Velasco asks for asylum. For eight days now he has been watched and followed. Huerta is supposed to have mentioned: before he would leave he wants to move out of the way all people who, after his departure, could become a danger to him. Besides, Huerta intends to create an international incident through the murder of a diplomat. The ensuing chaos would allow him to submerge or, even better, to get away. Perhaps even to move up. I state that I could grant asylum only in the most extreme emergency and, according to international law, only in a conditional way. If he would visit my house in an emergency I would appreciate if he could give me his word of honor that he is not guilty in some fashion.

Also, other news indicates that Huerta—before his stepping down, if he decides to do so—still wants to make certain jumps. Therefore, I am forced to maintain my cautious behavior: car, house, the option of a second car, etc. It is only natural that the desperate state of Huerta's soul does reveal itself as particularly sensitive and screams for escape from where he sees himself, at the end, due to the peace protocol—or at least near the end.

The man with power of attorney for Ketelsen and Degetau, for whose claims, as reported, I have managed to be paid in bonds, had entrusted Mr. F. Ritter with their collection. Suddenly he reports, because of customary commissions (bribes) the secretary of finance would not pay. According to his explanation he is at fault. On June 27 the secretary had been willing to pay. Ritter had told me so, personally, at that time. On the twenty-seventh I went to the ministry. The people declared they were willing to pay in order to do me a favor. Mr. Ritter claims he twice went to the ministry but did not receive money. It is not sufficient to show up there twice. Until I produce money for our citizens, I am going there until I have it. The money had been easy to get assured on June 2 because then the people were breaking things down and wanted to spend everything that was still there. Today it is no longer flowing. Today they prepare themselves for a few weeks of extended life. The representative of Ketelsen and Degetau is at fault. I complain to him about this. He excuses himself, saying he personally did not deal with it but had charged a certain Ernesto Christlieb with the "negotiations"—another German Mexican.

These second-rate-quality people are probably a necessity in this country, but I don't have time to deal with them.

The attachment provides the details about the newly issued paper money. Initially the chamber of commerce reacted by wanting to close the stores. Following government pressure they abandoned this intention.

The attached clipping from the July 1 *Mexican Herald* and June 30 described head-on the difficulties of U.S. policy in the current situation.

The *Mexican Herald* from July 1 presents Carranza's rejection of the accusation [that he is] connected financially, and in other ways, with [an unmentioned company].

Sunday, July 5, 1914, Mexico City

The secretaries of commerce and trade and the former foreign secretary, Mohena, escape abroad. Also two of Maas's generals are leaving the country. They are said to be Huerta's relatives. It is reported that they are moving money abroad for him.

Today take place elections for president, vice president, senators, and representatives. In the morning I will visit some polling stations and in the afternoon—a stunning emptiness. In only a single polling station [do] I encounter one voter. He voted for Gamboa.

The chief of General Huerta's staff, General Corona, as well as the inspector of the Rurales, General of the Division Rincon Gallardo, have handed in their resignations: "in order to withdraw to private life."

Huerta turned down both [men's] request: "They enjoyed their time with him during good days, now they should be so kind and stand in his camp during bad days."

Strong military patrols [take place] during the day; apparently the garrison is being mobilized in its entirety. It is known that it has been reinforced significantly by pulling back in large part troops from Veracruz. But such caution is not necessary: the people have completely understood that a farce is taking place and demonstrate this estimation through a strong, publicly displayed indifference.

I talk to the president of the Chamber of Deputies. He calls the election a comedy, expected to end in complete failure. However, he adds, one will help as far as missing votes are concerned. He invites me to a gathering of deputies. I decline, pointing to Huerta's suspicion and his police. It seems to be in need of demonstrating its need to exist by inventing a crime, if it can't find one. In particular conspiracies: every harmless gathering of friends is easily stamped a conspiracy.

Monday, July 6, 1914, Mexico City

Today the description of the election given by *Imparcial*; it is the most explicit and most fanatical tool [for] Huerta [and] is too characteristic to be omitted here.[74]

The government paper emphasizes that 25 percent of polling stations did not function. For the capital this assertion is important. Because, according to law, at least half of "casillas electorales" need to function for the presidential elections to be valid. Even though under today's reign of anarchy all rules of law are beside the point. The law is being treated with contempt. Or applied only where it serves the purposes of those in power.

The secretary of foreign affairs, without much ado, declares the elections to be a farce. In confidence he tells me: in the night from Saturday to Sunday he has received via cable Protocol No. 3. It says (the points, etc., are authentic): "On the day of . . . 1914 one will establish a provisional government in Mexico—" and nothing more!

Esteva Ruiz is highly agitated. Yesterday, on Sunday, he mailed a strongly worded telegram to Rabasa [asking] why Protocols No. 1 and No. 2 continue to be kept from him. Esteva Ruiz summarizes his personal opinion as follows: the delegates have deceived us, a statement that, I believe, is exactly right. Unfortunately very late. I refer to the many places in this diary where I say, based on my incomplete knowledge of events, "The delegates are serving the government in a poor way," and furthermore, referring to the segment where I state on the day of the naming of the three delegates, "The president is no longer deciding based on reason who selected these three delegates." In sum, the protocol says nothing more than "the Huerta government does not exist and did not last. At such and such point in time the provisional government of Mexico will be created."

Protocol No. 4 refers to it, determining: the creation of the provisional government will be brought about by agreement of the parties that are fighting in Mexico.

Yesterday Esteva Ruiz negotiated the entire day with de la Lama *how* they can inform Huerta about this Protocol No.3. They agreed *not to say anything* until they have available all the material, in particular Protocol No. 1 and No. 2.

Esteva Ruiz asks me how he should present *these* protocols for ratification to the Senate. We agree:

A. that the mood of the Senate, the Chamber of Deputies, as well as the people is: "Huerta has to go";
B. accordingly, all should be told the truth, but not the *entire* truth.

For example, the delegates' deception. Perhaps the addition that no treaty exists and that such a treaty is not necessary in view of the very small nature of the conflict. It could be taken care of very well through protocols.

The essential—the pacification of the country—will be accomplished through the yet to be reached agreement between government and rebels.

I advise him to speak to Huerta using the same argument. Esteva Ruiz interrupts in a spirited fashion: time must not be lost, Zapatistas are already at the city's gates. The Villistas, now that unity has been reestablished with Carrancistas, would move very fast to the capital's front side. *Inside* the capital the Carrancistas would probably no longer keep the reins on their impatience.—In short: in spite of all the calm outside, maintained by police and military, "the situation in the capital is extremely critical." In his opinion fast action is absolutely necessary.

The president *must* create an easing of the situation by making his successor secretary of foreign affairs, either Lascuraín or Carbajál. The delegates have cabled; the rebels have not yet answered them stating their positive feelings about Lascuraín.

Esteva Ruiz asks me to speak with the president. I counter: I cannot go to the president without having anything in my hands; based on experiencing his skilled dialectic this would be dangerous. The circumstances force us to await the protocols *and* the answer of the rebels as far as their candidates are concerned. Esteva Ruiz fears that then it will be too late to avoid the eruption inside the capital. But finally he accepts his argument.

The German citizen—Roever—demands that I organize for him again two wagonloads of sugar, which allegedly the Federales have confiscated in San Luis [Potosí]. Following my presentations Esteva Ruiz promises it.

Here the second diary ends. For the admiral a warlike conflict in Mexico City had been resolved, and he resumed writing reports through regular diplomatic channels. The following regular telegrams narrate Huerta's departure from Mexico into Spanish exile.

5

Whisking Huerta into European Exile

BAD GUYS DON'T ALWAYS DIE

July 11, 1914, Mexico City

A REGULAR DIPLOMATIC TELEGRAM

No. 73. Telegram. Top Secret. Hintze to German Consul Veracruz, for *Dresden*. Imperial government empowers me to enlist one of her majesty's ships to take onboard and transport Huerta and his family. As far as I can see, I will have to ask for such requisition in a few days, and [I] report kindly [now] just to inform you.

1. Boarding probably will take place in Puerto México.
2. In Jamaica, leaving the ship.
3. I have reached an agreement with the British diplomat that a small British warship will participate in (1) and (2)
4. I assume that the ship that Your Honor will select will not leave for Puerto México until local departure is certain. Please confirm. **Hintze**

July 12, 1914, Gulf of Mexico

A REGULAR NAVAL TELEGRAM

No. 113. Telegram. *Dresden* to German Legation. Confirm receiving Telegram No. 73. Wish to be informed twenty-four hours before ship is needed in Coatzacoalcos. Signed **Dresden**.

July 12, 1914, Mexico City

A REGULAR NAVAL TELEGRAM

No. 75. Telegram. Top Secret. Hintze to German Consul, Veracruz, for *Dresden* (for your personal information). The United States sees Huerta's

FIG. 37. The *Dresden*, which transported Victoriano Huerta into exile.
Courtesy of the Library of Congress.

transport as a favor that is provided to it. However, the [local] administration in Veracruz is not in on the game. Did not arrive *Karlsruhe* on the
tenth? **Hintze**

July 13, 1914, Veracruz

A REGULAR NAVAL TELEGRAM

No. 76. German Consul, Veracruz, for *Dresden*. Your No. 113 and No. 114
received correctly via land. Back by imperial government power respect-
fully ask for following requisition:

1. From Friday, July 17, on will wait in Puerto México; earlier
   presence there not advisable due to causing attention.
2. There to take President Huerta and Secretary of War Blanquet
   onboard and to transport to Jamaica as soon as possible after
   their embarkation.
3. There both deboard. For your information: already earlier British warship travels to Puerto México to take onboard the president's friends and his friends' families, altogether sixty-one
   souls. Following the president's wish, he wants to embark with
   the secretary of war on Your Excellency's [ship]. It is planned

that both will have lost their official character when they arrive at your [location]. British admiral has calming news about Tampico. Please confirm. Signed **Hintze**

July 14, 1914, Mexico City

A REGULAR NAVAL TELEGRAM

No. 78. Telegram. Top Secret. Hintze to German Consul, Veracruz, for *Dresden*. The departure of both known persons from here has been moved up one day earlier and since circumstances make necessary even earlier departure. I duly send my request that, if possible, *Dresden* possibly should not leave for Puerto México later than the English ship selected to take the family. This is the *Bristol*. Today she will receive order to go to Puerto México and to wait there for the family. Please confirm. **Hintze**

July 15, 1914, Mexico City

A REGULAR NAVAL TELEGRAM

No. 81. Hintze to Consul Aleman, for *Dresden*. Have no confirmation of my telegrams No. 78 and No. 79. But until I hear otherwise [I assume] you have received the same. Top Secret. The known sixty-one people for *Bristol* have left Tuesday night. President and secretary of war depart today, Wednesday evening, to Coatzacoalcos; [they] arrive probably night from Thursday to Friday. Repeat, due to expressed wish of president, that only those two gentlemen are to be carried by *Dresden*. Please confirm. **Hintze**

July 15, 1914, Mexico City

A REGULAR DIPLOMATIC REPORT

No. 132. Hintze, Royal Diplomat, to German Foreign Ministry. I gave up my attempts to push Huerta onto a British warship because his refusal threatened his very departure. Yesterday evening departed Huerta's family and several heavily compromised government officials and officers, including their families, altogether sixty-one souls, in order to embark on the British warship *Bristol*.

This afternoon president will resign during session of Congress and, joined by secretary of war, depart for Puerto México. Only those two will embark on *Dresden*. Secretary of foreign affairs predicts unrest in the capital. I took precautionary measures. **Hintze**

July 16, 1914, Berlin, Germany

A REGULAR DIPLOMATIC TELEGRAM

No. 98. Telegram. Berlin. Secretary of State to His Majesty the Emperor and King. His Majesty's diplomat to Mexico telegraphed:

Congress approved with overwhelming majority Huerta's resignation. Due to power of constitution Carbajál interim president.[1] **Jagow**

July 16, 1914, on the way to Coatzacoalcos

A REGULAR DIPLOMATIC TELEGRAM

Huerta to the German Diplomat, Mexico. I am asking you, as your humble servant, to hand to your Majesty the following message:

Yesterday, on the fifteenth, at 5:00 p.m., I resigned the presidency of the republic and in my place stepped Lic. Francisco Carbajál y Gual.

While I have the honor to report to Your Excellency this event, I ask humbly to share your friendship and support with the new government. I extend all my appreciation and respect to you and remain your dedicated servant.

V. Huerta

July 16, 1914, Coatzacoalcos

A REGULAR NAVAL TELEGRAM

No. 119. *Dresden* to German Legation. *Dresden* and *Bristol* arrived July 16 at eight in the morning in Coatzacoalcos. **Dresden**

July 17, 1914, Coatzacoalcos

A REGULAR NAVAL TELEGRAM

No. 120. Telegram. *Dresden* to German Legation. President expected July 17 around p.m. *Dresden*. No. 82. I received your No. 123. Your No. 122 is missing. Recommend not to wait for *Bristol* but to depart because waiting would increase danger for your two guests and in interest of their departure. Confirm. **Hintze**

July 19, 1914, Coatzacoalcos

A REGULAR NAVAL TELEGRAM

No. 124. Dresden to German Legation. The president does not want to go onboard and depart until departure of all families has been ascertained. He asked about accepting seven generals and two staff officers. I agreed and am asking for your agreement. The *Dresden* cannot accept more [persons]. **Dresden**

July 19, 1914, Mexico City

A REGULAR NAVAL TELEGRAM

No. 83. Top Secret. Hintze to German cruiser, July 19. Answer to your [No.] 123. Top secret. It is negative for our interest to pick up the most heavily compromised sons and friends of Huerta, [speaking] according to the law. Therefore I have expressly limited my request to Huerta and Blanquet and repeated expressly in telegram No. 81 that only those two are assigned to be boarded by *Dresden*.

From here I cannot say if Your Excellency has the possibility to take onboard, in an appropriate way, seven generals and two staff officers beyond my requisition.

I repeat my urgent telegram No. 82 from July 18. I "recommend, because of growing danger in case of waiting for the two guests and in the interest of having them out of office not to wait for *Bristol* and to depart. Confirm." And I advise to hold point No. 1 in front of Huerta in an urgent way. For your own order: probably tomorrow *Bristol* receives order to sail to Jamaica. Ask for immediate confirmation. **Hintze**

July 20, 1914, Coatzacoalcos

A REGULAR NAVAL TELEGRAM

No. 122. Telegram. To German Legation, Mexico. President arrived here without blemish on July 17 at 8:00 p.m. Embarkation on July 18, in the morning. **Dresden**

Note: this telegram has been sent on July 20, 1914.

July 20, 1914, Coatzacoalcos

A REGULAR NAVAL TELEGRAM

No. 127. Telegram (partly in cipher) to German Legation in Mexico. President just asked me for approval to embark, in addition to him and secretary of war, also both of their wives and their four daughters, no male family member or aide. This way they would not have to wait any longer for steamer that is supposed to transport remaining people.

I agreed, just so I can finally leave, and I embarked the named people at seven o'clock and started the trip to Kingston. Arrive approximately July 24.

For a short time and accompanied by *Karlsruhe*, I intend to go to Havana on the return trip, due to reasons resulting from my office service. Approximately arrive in Veracruz on August 2nd. I am asking to be informed in Kingston in case situation requires an accelerated return. **Dresden**

A Postscript: On the Road to the 1917 Zimmerman Telegram

A REGULAR DIPLOMATIC REPORT

No. 886. Madrid. December 6, 1914, 12:45. The Royal Ambassador to the Foreign Ministry. Diplomat Ratibor to Berlin AA, A 33707.

Félix Díaz, currently in New Orleans, communicated through a trusted confidant to the imperial consul in San Sebastian that he intends to rise up and eliminate Mexico's anarchic situation, for which he needed five million dollars. Morgan initially had committed [itself]. Later, due to European war, the commitment had been withdrawn.

Félix Díaz, allegedly certain of the support of his uncle, would like to know if Germany would be disposed to provide the advance amount of money. In return, besides granting concessions that still would remain to be negotiated, would be immediate petroleum export from British wells in Tampico and Túxpam, following his landing in Mexico. The payment needs to be made in New Orleans; Porfirio Díaz is currently in Biarritz [France]. **Ratibor**

December 7, 1914, Berlin

A REGULAR DIPLOMATIC TELEGRAM

No. 362. December 7, 1914. Addendum to 33707, via Norddeich to Embassy for Madrid. Undersecretary of State [Zimmermann]. Answer: No.

Victoriano Huerta remains the only major national Mexican political figure who left the Mexican Revolution alive. In June 1914 he chose the German ship SMS *Dresden* to carry him to Kingston, Jamaica. From there the deposed dictator continued on to Barcelona. Unlike the dictator Porfirio Díaz, who went to Paris, Huerta chose the imperial Spain of Alfonso XIII as place to gather new energy. If he would have stayed in Europe he could have enjoyed a comfortable exile. But he could not leave Mexico forever, nor could he stop fighting.

In 1914 he was again in contact with Porfirian reactionary exile groups living in Paris and the United States. Lore has it that Huerta was approached by German naval intelligence forces while still in Spain. Surviving sources remain open on that question.

By 1915 Huerta returned to the United States on his own decision and will. In New York, now a hotbed of international intrigue related to World War I, he planned a second counterrevolution.

From fall 1914 on, World War I had turned the Mexican Revolution into a profoundly internationalized revolution, mostly because of the question of what role U.S. neutrality would play in deciding world affairs. And U.S. companies were rapidly developing into the military arsenal of imperial Great Britain, France, and Russia.

By then Admiral von Hintze had been reassigned to a European diplomatic post. But suddenly, Emperor Wilhelm II's navy appreciated the subversive potential that Victoriano Huerta's desire to resume revolution offered.

German money in Havana bank accounts, but also personal encouragement in New York through German agent von Rintelen, a resident of the Waldorf Astoria Hotel, encouraged Huerta to hurry his return to Mexico. Ideally, German military intelligence hoped that Huerta would cause a Mexican-U.S. conflict that would absorb weapons and soldiers so that they could not be used to help Great Britain against Germany on European battlefields.

On June 27, 1915, Victoriano Huerta, as political head of a soon-to-be-launched second counterrevolution, took a train from New York, hoping to reach the U.S.-Mexican border and cross from El Paso into Mexico. Fortunately, Huerta was arrested in Newman, New Mexico, shortly before reaching El Paso, by U.S. Treasury agent Zachary Cobb.

For a while he was held at the U.S. Army prison in Fort Bliss. Later he spent time under house arrest before being incarcerated again. There he died on January 13, 1916, due to his deteriorating personal health.

A major antidemocratic, dark figure of the Mexican Revolution had passed away.

Notes

Introduction

1. Paul von Hintze (1864–1941) served until 1911 as rear admiral. Later he served as a German secretary of foreign affairs, from July to October 1918.
2. Wilhelm II (1859–1941), emperor of Germany, crowned 1888. The German Foreign Ministry was located in Berlin in 1911. Diplomats were appointed mostly on the basis of aristocratic origin or financial wealth, not business experience, foreign-language skills, or country expertise.
3. These diary segments are at Bundesarchiv-Freiburg, Paul von Hintze, Teilnachlass I.
4. Politisches Archiv des Auswärtigen Amt, Berlin (hereafter cited as PAAA).

1. Revolutionary Mexico

1. Francisco León de la Barra (1863–1939), Mexican ambassador in Washington, 1909–11; secretary of foreign affairs, April–May 1911 and February–July 1913; interim president, May–November 1911.
2. The diplomatic reports use the term "U.S. Americans," which I have replaced with "U.S. citizens" throughout.

    There is an introductory part to this source that reads,

    I repeatedly, in due form, reported to Your Excellency that on July 19, [1911,] the U.S. ambassador informed me before his departure for vacation that, possibly, he expects to be sent back again [to the United States] (as in December 1910). The solution to the local situation could be found in receiving a mandate for either an armed intervention of the United States or (if the foreign powers could not find common ground about this) to receive a mandate for a protest of the most interested, the United States, Great Britain, Germany and Spain or (if the foreign powers could not find common ground) is alleged to inspire President Taft's Mexican policy. His current perception is expressed in the sentence: "I believe much for the worse."

    Mr. Wilson made similar remarks to the British diplomatic chargé d'affaires. In recent times he received from members of the British colony news that reported a firming up of U.S. intensions in favor of intervention. And the same sources point [to] diplomat Hohler.

U.S. ambassador Mr. Wilson spoke to the fact that the first consequence of an intervention would be the persecution of foreigners. The British diplomat so cabled to London. The Austrian chargé d'affaires presented Mr. Dearing, the first secretary of the U.S. embassy, with the words that in the country anarchy was progressing. U.S. America must intervene and will. Due to my instructions and the constantly arriving orders, and based on my limited observations that I have been able to make here, I have to surmise that a U.S. intervention can only be the very last means to protect Germans interests.

3. In 1898 President William McKinley sent U.S. forces to Cuba and defeated Spain in a ten-week war. Subsequently the United States gained military control over Cuba until 1902. Thereafter the United States, under the Platt Amendment, severely limited Cuban sovereignty in domestic and foreign policy.

4. Ambassador Hintze to German chancellor von Bethmann-Hollweg, Doc. No. 51, Mexico, July 22, 1911, transmitted through courier, A 12597 pr., August 10, 1911, p.m., R 16903, Mexican Relations to North America, PAAA.

5. Felix A. Sommerfeld (ca. 1877-?), President Maderos's chief of secret service; later Pancho Villa's arms-purchasing agent. Occasionally he worked as an informer and spy for Germany.

6. "The Madero family" refers, for example, to individuals such as Gustavo Madero (1875-February 18, 1913), a businessman and the brother of President Francisco Madero. The original document uses "Gegenseitigkeitsvertrag," which I have translated as "treaty of reciprocity."

7. Francisco Indalecio Madero (1873-February 22, 1913), liberal politician, hacienda owner in Coahuila, presidential candidate for the anti-Díaz faction in 1910, and president of Mexico, November 1911-1913.

8. Ernesto Madero, uncle of President Francisco Madero.

9. Sherbourne Gillette Hopkins, a lawyer and representative of U.S. oil companies, advised Central and South American revolutionaries. He advised Gustavo Madero in 1910-11 and Venustiano Carranza in 1913-14.

10. Hintze to Bethmann-Hollweg, No. 118, July 25, 1911, delivered through courier, A 12615 pr., August 10, 1911, R 16903, PAAA.

11. Philander Chase Knox (1853-1921), U.S. secretary of state, March 1909-March 1913.

12. Washington to Foreign Office, No. 27, February 12, 1912, Berlin, following Tel. No. 23, A 2768 priv., R 16903, PAAA. Johann-Heinrich Graf von Bernstorff (1862-1939), ambassador to Washington DC, December 1908-February 1917.

13. To Chancellor Bethmann-Hollweg, No. 80, Mexico, December 4, 1912, delivered through courier, A 23062 pr., December 22, 1912, R 16903, PAAA.

14. U.S. ambassador Henry Lane Wilson (1857–1932), U.S. ambassador to Mexico, December 21, 1909–July 17, 1913. In March 1913, as he followed Howard Taft into the U.S. presidency, Woodrow Wilson appointed John Lind as personal envoy for Mexican affairs. Special envoy Lind often conducted critical negotiations while Ambassador H. L. Wilson was also present in the Mexican capital.
15. William Howard Taft (1857–1930), U.S. president, March 1909–March 1913; U.S. secretary of war, 1904–8.
16. Secret, excerpt from letter no. 25, Hintze to AA, February 28, 1913, Legation Mexiko Stadt, box 33, folder A13d, Revolution: Regierung des Generals Huerta, PAAA.
17. Bernstorff to Chancellor von Bethmann-Hollweg, No. 2, Washington DC, January 2, 1913, delivered through courier, A 908 pr., January 14, 1913, R 16903, PAAA.
18. Pedro José Domingo de la Calzada Manuel María Lascuraín Paredes (1856–1952), Maderista; Mexican secretary of foreign relations, April 10, 1912–December 4, 1912, and January 15, 1913–February 18, 1913.
19. Sir Lionel Edward Gresley Carden (1851–1915), British diplomat in Mexico, October 1913–August 1914.
20. *Deutsche Zeitung von Mexico* was a German-language newspaper in Mexico. Hans Freiherr von Wangenheim (1859–1915), German diplomat in Mexico, 1904–7.
21. Montgomery Schuyler (1877–?), first secretary of the U.S. embassy in Mexico, 1912–March 1913; he served as chargé d'affaires November 1912–January 1913.
22. Hintze to Chancellor Bethmann-Hollweg, "Mexico and the question of a U.S. intervention," January 21, 1913, A 2699 pr., February 8, 1913, R 16903, PAAA.

2. Path to Madero's Assassination

1. The diary reproduced in this chapter is a separate account, stored as part of Hintze's private papers. It is not part of the war diary of Admiral Hintze, which this book refers to as Diary No. 2.
2. Félix Díaz (1868–1945), a Mexican general and the nephew of Porfirio Díaz (Mexican dictator, 1876–1910), on October 16, 1912, revolted with the Veracruz garrison against Madero.
3. Victoriano Huerta (1854–1916), Mexican general who claimed to be president from February 1913 to July 1914.
4. A legation is a diplomatic post below the rank of embassy.
5. Necaxa is the name of a power plant.
6. Zapatistas were followers of the Morelos rebel leader Emiliano Zapata.
7. Throughout the text Hintze refers to himself as "the diplomat." To improve readability, I have used "I" instead.
8. Felipe Ángeles, Mexican general and artillery commander of rebels during the battle of Zacatecas. Later he followed Venustiano Carranza and Pancho Villa.

9. The Zócalo is the central plaza in front of Mexico City's National Palace and cathedral.
10. This refers to the Citadel in Mexico City.
11. Chapultepec is a Park in Mexico City, the location of the presidential residence.
12. Cuernavaca is a city on the southern side of the mountains surrounding Mexico City.
13. Aurelio Blanquet, Mexican general; Mexican secretary of war, June 1913-July 1914.
14. Ricardo García Granados, Mexican positivist. He also represented Mexico in El Paso during negotiation of the treaties to end the Madero revolution.
15. Alberto García Granados (1849–October 1915), governor of the federal district, 1911–12; secretary of government, 1913; executed by Carrancistas.
16. Capitán Hilario Rodríguez Malpica (1889–1914); he served on the ship *Tampico*.
17. G. de Pottere, Austrian-Hungarian diplomat to Mexico, 1912–13.
18. Max Dobroschke, principal of the German school in Mexico City.
19. Julius Carlos Cornelios Bacmeister, merchant of German origin in Mexico City, 1855–1932.
20. Paul Kosidowski, German consul general in Mexico City.
21. Alberto José Pani Arteaga (1878–1955), Maderista; undersecretary of education under Madero; opposed Huerta.
22. The list was misnumbered in the original; the numbering has been corrected here.
23. Casa Veerkamp, German merchant house, Mexico City.
24. Pablo Viau, Mexican artist and printer.
25. General Guillermo Rubio Navarrete (1893–1950), commander of artillery at Tacubaya.
26. Badische Anilin Gesellschaft, a multinational chemical company; today known as BASF.
27. Manuel Mondragón (1859–1922), a major participant in the coup against President Madero; Mexican secretary of war, February–June 1913.
28. Roma and Juárez are districts of Mexico City.
29. William A. Burnside, U.S. military attaché, Mexico City.
30. Bernardo Jacinto Cólogan (1848–?), Spanish diplomat in Mexico, 1907–14.
31. Joaquín Maas Águila (1879–1948), division general in 1914, in charge of recapturing Torreón. Nephew of Huerta.
32. José de la Cruz Porfirio Díaz (1830–1915), Mexican president and dictator (1876–1910), reigned until Mexican Revolution began 1910.
33. Sommer Herrmann & Co. was a German merchant house in Mexico City.
34. Camacho was president of the Mexican Senate.
35. A mitrailleuse is a type of rapid-fire machine gun.
36. The original phrase is, "von ihm aus sei niemals die Frage intervention nach Washington zu eroertert worden" [sic].

37. Hintze uses the term "Massregeln."
38. Fidencio Hernández, Mexican attorney.
39. The doyen is the longest-serving diplomat at a government seat. That gives him special privileges to represent the entire foreign diplomatic corps to the foreign government.
40. In the original the word choice is "fence" (*Zaun*).
41. José María Pino Suárez, governor of Yucatan; vice president of Mexico, 1911–13.
42. It declared him a person who was no longer allowed to remain in the country and was asked to leave.
43. Hintze to Imperial Chancellor von Bethmann-Hollweg, May 19, 1913, Ausw. Amt I, 15076 pm, R 133485, PAAA.

3. Getting to Know the Dictator

1. Querido Moheno (1874–1933), secretary of foreign affairs, October 1913–February 1914.
2. Manuel de Zamacona, temporary Mexican diplomatic envoy to the United States for Huerta.
3. Hintze to Auswärtiges Amt (hereafter AA), Telegram No. 79/Jn 2270, October 7, 1913, A2140 pr., 26 October 1913, R 16863, PAAA.
4. Santiago de Chile to AA Bethmann-Hollweg, No. 50, October 20, 1913, R A 23070 pr., November 19, 1913, R 16864, PAAA.
5. No. 114, October 30, 1913, A 21661 pr., October 30, 1913, a.m., R 16863, PAAA.
6. Command SMS *Hertha*, G 644, Gulf of Mexico, November 4, 1913, Rohardt, captain of Your Majesty's ship *Hertha*, to Your Majesty the emperor and king, "Military Report about Visit of Your Majesty's Ship in Veracruz," October 21 to November 2, 1913, secret, copy of A 24547 priv., December 2, 1913, 13, R 16866, PAAA.
7. "The union" refers to the United States.
8. Hintze to AA, telegram, No. 119, A 22357 pr., November 9, 1913, a.m., R 16864, Allgemeine Angelegenheiten, November 1913–21 November 1913, PAAA.
9. Hintze to AA, No. 121, November 13, 1913, A 22607 pr., November 13, 1913, a.m., R 16864, PAAA.
10. Report about representative of prime minister, Grey, November 11, 1913, 812.00/10438, U.S. National Archives, cited in P. Edward Haley, *Revolution and Intervention: The Diplomacy of Taft and Wilson with Mexico 1910–1917* (Cambridge MA: MIT Press, 1970), 11.
11. Bernstorff to AA, No. 143m November 14, 1913, A 22673 pr., November 14, 1913, R 16864, PAAA.
12. This report (No. 198) was not attached to the original diplomatic report.
13. Military Attaché Report No. 207, November 20, 1913, Content: General Wood about Mexico, Washington DC, copy for report 24099/pr.5.12.13, R 16865, PAAA.
14. Hintze does not explain what incident he refers to.

15. Allgemeine Angelegenheiten Mexico, November 25, 1913, A 24094 pr., 5 A December 1913 a.m., A 156, Durch Dep Kasten am 25. 11. 1913, R 16865, PAAA.

16. Report No. 103 to Chancellor von Bethmann-Hollweg, delivered through courier box, November 27, 1913, A 25625 pr., December 28, 1913, R 16866, PAAA.

17. Military Political Report "Bremen," November 10-November 22, 1913, secret; November 22, 1913, copy to A 627/14 pr., January 10, 1914, R 16867, January 1, 1914-January 31, 1914, PAAA.

18. Bernstorff to AA, No. 154, December 5, 1913, 24081pr., December 5, 1913, a.m., R 16865, PAAA.

19. Hintze, Mexico, to AA, Telegram No. 144, December 18,1913, A 25000 pr., December 18, 1913, a.m., R 16866, PAAA. Another source later contradicts this statement. Regardless, it shows the importance of financial shenanigans in the background.

20. The original text uses the word "folles."

21. No. 2, January 5, 1914, through courier box, to Chancellor Bethmann-Hollweg, A 1700 pr., January 27, 1914, R 16867, Mexico January 1 to 31, PAAA.

22. Hintze to AA, Telegram No. 4, January 11, 1914, A 650 pr., January 11, 1914, a.m., R 16867, PAAA.

23. Thomas Beaumont Hohler (1870-1946), British chargé d'affaires in Mexico, August 1914-1917.

24. Sir Edward Grey (1862-1933), Viscount of Fallodon (as of 1916), undersecretary of state, British Foreign Office, December 1905-December 1916.

25. Nelson Jarvis Waterbury O'Shaughnessy (1876-1934), secretary of U.S. embassy in Mexico, March 1913-April 1914; U.S. chargé d'affaires, July 1913-April 1914.

26. Hintze to Chancellor Bethmann-Hollweg, No. 10, January 13, 1914, through courier bag, A 2077 pr., 1 a February 1914, R 16868, PAAA.

27. Baron Makino Nobuaki (November 24, 1861-January 25, 1949), Japanese secretary of foreign relations, 1913-1914.

28. Tokyo to AA, Doc. A 265, German diplomat signature unreadable, December 29, 1913, delivered through courier bag, A 916 pr., January 15, 1914, R 16867, PAAA.

29. Hintze to Foreign Ministry, No. 8, January 25, 1914, A I 591i pr., January 25, 1914, p.m., R 16867, January 1, 1914-January 31, 1914, PAAA.

30. Hintze to AA, No. 19, March 6, 1914, A 4528 pt, 6A March 1914, R 16869, PAAA.

31. A. No. 6, March 12, 1914, through pouch, A 7056 pr., April 10, 1914, a.m., R 16870, PAAA.

32. Hintze to Chancellor Bethmann-Hollweg, No. 59, March 19, 1914, A 7307 pr., April 14, 1914, p.m., R 16870, PAAA.

33. Pancho Villa, popular name of the Chihuahuan revolutionary José Doroteo Arango Arámbula (June 5, 1978-July 20, 1923). He had led the northern Mexi-

can guerrilla and military forces that helped defeat President Porfirio Díaz and send him into exile. After Huerta's coup Villa participated in the founding of the Constitutionalists to fight Huerta.

34. Bernstorff to AA, March 24, 1914, A 5824 pr., March 24, 1914, a.m., R 16869, PAAA.

35. Romberg to AA, weapon sale to Mexico, Bern, Switzerland, March 24, 1914, A 6030 pr., March 27, 1914, R 16869m, PAAA.

36. Mexiko Report to Chancellor Bethmann-Hollweg, Doc. No. 64, March 25, 1914, A 7312 pr. April 14, 1914, p.m., R 16870, PAAA.

37. No. 29, April 8, 1914, A A 6878 pr., 8A April 1914, a.m., R 16870, PAAA.

38. The U.S. Congress had passed an act that exempted U.S. coastal vessels from paying a toll when traveling through the soon-to-be-opened Panama Canal. President Wilson opposed the measure and intended to reverse it.

39. Confidential, Bernstorff, Washington, to Chancellor Bethmann-Hollweg, No. A 48, Washington DC, April 11, 1914A 7845, April 22, 1914, p.m., R 16870, PAAA.

40. Bernstorff to AA, April 21, 1914, A 7750 pr., April 21, 1914, R 16870, PAAA.

41. Frank Friday Fletcher (1855-1928), U.S. rear admiral, commander of the Fourth Division of the Atlantic fleet. The source does not allow certain identification of the ship's name.

42. Memorandum, addendum to report of imperial embassy to Washington, No. A 55, April 22, 1914, R 16871, PAAA.

43. Koenigliche Preussische Gesandschaft in Mecklenburg und Hansestaedten, Ballin, to Bethmann-Hollweg, J. NO B 981, April 23, 1914, A 8003 pr., April 24, 1914, p.m., R 16870, PAAA.

44. Leaflet, April 22, 1914, A 8172, O.S. 140, R 16870, PAAA.

4. Toppling the Mad Tyrant

1. This entry is the beginning of Diary No. 2.

2. Carl Heynen, assistant commercial attaché to the imperial German embassy at Washington in 1915. In this function he helped organize the supply of war matériel for imperial Germany during World War I, assisting Heinrich F. Albert. This work included economic warfare measures such as the Bridgeport Projectile Project but also war matériel support for anti-British Indian revolutionaries in the Pacific. He knew military attaché Franz von Papen and naval attaché Karl Boy-Ed. He was involved in the Agencia Commercial Marítima Heynen y Eversbusch, a company that supplied warships to the German navy during World War I. He served as chief representative of the Hamburg America Line in Veracruz, Mexico.

3. José López Portillo y Rojas (1850-1933).

4. Mexican nationalists had hoped that the occupation of Veracruz would cause all revolutionary factions to join together against U.S. forces. Such hopes for a nationalist utopia proved profoundly mistaken.

5. Franz von Papen (October 29, 1897–May 2, 1969), imperial German military attaché to Washington DC and Mexico, 1913–16. Von Papen was responsible for German military intelligence in the United States and was involved in economic warfare measures against the Allies during World War I. After most embarrassing revelations he was withdrawn in 1916. Later he became chancellor of Germany and served as Hitler's deputy chancellor for one year.

6. Sir Cecil Arthur Spring-Rice (1859–1918), British ambassador in Washington DC, April 1913–1918.

7. Pánfilo Natera, a brigadier general and Maderista, who later fought in the Central Division of the Constitutionalist Army. He failed to take Zacatecas for Carranza in June 1914; during the Convention of Aguascalientes in November 1914 he was appointed president of the Supreme Military Tribunal. Until August 2, 1915, he served as governor of Mexico City.

8. Christopher George Craddock (1862–1914), British rear admiral, February 1913–November 1914. Commander of British West Indian station.

9. José Maria Lozano (1878–1933), Mexican secretary of public works and communication.

10. Admiral J. Badger (August 6, 1853–September 7, 1932), commander in chief of the U.S. Atlantic Fleet.

11. The SMS *Nürnberg*, a Koenigsberg-class light cruiser. Its home base was Tsingtao until the Mexican Revolution.

12. The word used in the original is "Gesandschaftskanzlei."

13. Pierre Marie Victor Ayguésparse (December 1912–1922), secretary of legation at the French legation in Mexico.

14. José Manuel Cardoso de Oliveira (1865–?), Brazilian diplomat (*Gesandter*) in Mexico, 1912–16. In April 1914 the United States and Mexico broke relations. Oliveira represented U.S. interests in Mexico.

15. Hamburg-Amerika Linie was a German shipping agency of global reach based in Hamburg, Germany.

16. Domicio da Gama, Brazilian ambassador in Washington DC, 1911–19.

17. Doc. No. 67, Bernstorff, Washington, to AA, April 29, 1914, A 8705 pr., April 30, 1914, p.m., R 16870, PAAA.

18. The city of Porfirio Díaz is now called Ciudad Juárez.

19. Hintze to AA, telegram, No. 67, May 7, 1914, A 8900 pr., 7a May 1914, a.m., R 16871, PAAA.

20. Roberto Esteva Ruiz, Mexican secretary of state, May–July 1914.

21. This segment begins with an attached letter that is not translated. It dealt with a technical issue that is not relevant here.

22. Bernardo José Cólogan y Cólogan, Spanish diplomat to Mexico, temporary dean of diplomatic corps in 1913. Previously he served during the Boxer Rebellion.

23. José Ives Limantour (1854–1935), Mexican secretary of finance, 1893–1911.

24. Item C is missing in the original diary entry.

25. In the original this last sentence has been added in handwriting.

26. Mr. Benton was a British hacendado in Mexico who was found murdered after a confrontation with Pancho Villa. His case was unsolved at that time.

27. Downing Street refers to the seat of the British government, located at 10 Downing Street.

28. Federico Gamboa (1864–1939), Mexican secretary of foreign affairs, July–September 1913.

29. Javier De Moure, a general during the Mexican Revolution.

30. Hintze displays the antisemitic attitude characteristic of a German of his social standing and time period.

31. Hintze to AA, telegram, No. 79, May 17, 1914, A 9692 pr., May 18, 1914, a.m., R 16872, PAAA.

32. Bernstorff, Washington, to AA, No. 83, May 6, 1914, 8897 pr., 7a May 1914, a.m., R 16872, PAAA.

33. Hintze to AA, telegram, No. 81, May 19, 1914, A 9779 pr., May 19, 1914, a.m., R 16872, PAAA.

34. An *official mayor* is the equivalent of a second undersecretary of state.

35. "Mi permanencia en el poder ha sido ofrecido por mi solemne y exclusivamente a la nacion como garantia de paz y de orden y que realiza de este proposito deseo que mi personalidad no se tenga en cuenta."

36. This diary segment ends on page 87 in the original. A collection of newspaper clippings follows, which are not reprinted here. The third part of the diary resumes on page 89 in the original manuscript.

37. With this entry the third segment of the diary begins. The page begins with the word "wirken," which does not make sense in this context.

38. Not to be confused with Alvaro Obregón from Sonora.

39. Herr Holste refers to Alexander Holste. He came to Mexico in 1910 as representative of the Martin Schroeder Company, Hamburg. The information originates from Holste's interview with the Bureau of Information during World War I. The Martin Schroeder Company, registered in Hamburg, Germany, owned options in Mexican mines in Zacatecas and Guanajuato. It also imported and exported goods. Because the company served the mining business, its agents were familiar with explosives and, therefore, weapons.

40. Rex to AA, Tokyo, May 4, 1914, A 9722 pr., May 18, 1914, R 16872, PAAA.

41. Mineichiro Adachi (1869–1934), Japanese diplomat to Mexico, July 1913–1915.

42. Hintze to AA, telegram, No. 87, May 26, 1914, A 10289 pr., May 26, 1914, a.m., R 16872, PAAA.

43. On the death of Orozco, see Michael C. Meyer, *Mexican Rebel: Pascual Orozco and the Mexican Revolution, 1910–1915* (Lincoln: University of Nebraska Press, 1967).

44. These numbers are an underestimation.

45. Naval Attaché Boy-Ed, Naval Report No. 83, Washington DC, May 27, 1914, Botschaft Mexiko, packet 33, "Revolution/ Reg Gen. Huerta," copy to A 11422/14, PAAA.

46. Bernstorff [? difficult to determine] to Chief of German Navy Staff, May 30, 1914, A 10632 pr., May 30, 1914, R 16872, PAAA.

47. This statement refers to the issue of the salute between Mexican and U.S. forces with which the Tampico incident had begun on April 9.

48. The original uses "licencia," which I have translated as "permission."

49. The original reads "sobre el Ramo de Hacienda."

50. The attachment is not included.

51. This sentence is the first sentence of the fourth part of the diary.

52. The omitted text reads, "see Naval Report No. 83 of May 27, 1914, consecutively numbered No. 31."

53. The report included a clipping from the *New York Staatszeitung* dated May 29.

54. Here the report adds, "[Also] a large number of newspapers [state this] (forgetting the actual cause for the circumstances) (see attachment 1b, *New York Herald*, May 30, 1914."

55. This funeral cannot be identified from the source.

56. No. 275, Washington DC to Secretary of State of the German Naval Ministry, Naval Report No. 87, folder pp. 45-47, both sides, Botschaft Mexiko, Abschrift zu A 12461/14 pr., June 24, 1914, PAAA.

57. Dated Mexico City, June 3, 1914, copy in PAAA.

58. *Chispazos* are sparks or splinters.

59. The original reads "fatal" rather than "detrimental."

60. The original uses the word "instradiert."

61. Enrique Gorostieta (1889-1929), one of Huerta's youngest generals, played an important role in the defense of Veracruz. On July 14 Huerta promoted him to division general. Later, in 1926, he was named as military commander of the armies during the Cristero Rebellion.

62. This remark refers to an incident in the U.S. Civil War when the U.S. government demanded indemnity when U.S. ships were damaged by privateers suspected to be tolerated by the British government.

63. This reference cannot be explained from the available material.

64. The original says "directing," but that seems to be an error; it seems clear that Hintze meant "direct against" or "work against."

65. Hintze's term is "derrota," translated here as "disaster."

66. Luis Cabrera Lobato (1876-1954), Constitutionalist delegate to the Niagara Fall conference; Carranza's secretary of finance and public credit, 1914-17.

67. The original uses "appelado," which I have translated as "pressure." "Apellar" (infinitive) is a term used in the tanning industry, meaning "to have one's skin softened."

68. "Chon Díaz" was the nickname of General Encarnación Díaz (1893-1916) captain of the cavalry of the Southern Army.

69. Hintze wrote "to demand their resignation," but I believe he meant to write "to demand his resignation" and have used that phrasing in the text.

70. The Commission de Cambio y Moneda was a currency commission.
71. Hintze used "Verzweifelung," which could be translated as "despairs," but I believe he meant "Zweifel" (doubts).
72. Ignacio Alcocer, Huerta's secretary of the interior, 1913–1914. The U.S. State Department, on October 10, 1915, reported him executed, after he was charged with complicity in the killing of former president Madero.
73. Franz Ferdinand was an Austrian prince who was about to become emperor of Austria. His assassination sparked the beginning of World War I.
74. Huerta had scheduled what he insisted was a national election of the president and the Mexican Congress. However, voting on July 5, 1914, was held only where his troops controlled territory. Voter participation was minimal.

5. European Exile

1. Mexican General Affairs, Mexiko, No. 1, July 6, 1914–July 20, 1914, R 16875, PAAA. Gottlieb von Jagow (1863–1935), Secretary of state in AA, January 1913–November 1916.

Additional Reading

The discovery of these diaries hands us a most special treasure. So far, in English or German, there is only one other eyewitness account, and that is by Edith O'Shaughnessy, *A Diplomat's Wife in Mexico* (New York: Harper Brothers, 1916). She focused on the period between the fall of 1913 and early 1914. Hintze's diaries shed light on what happened before and after the activities covered in O'Shaughnessy's account and are the single best description of events by an elite witness in Mexico City during the years covered. It is a find of international importance.

Readers who are looking for a general introduction to the Mexican Revolution should consult the *Oxford History of Mexico* (Oxford: Oxford University Press, 2012) or Michael J. Gonzales's *The Mexican Revolution, 1910–1940* (Albuquerque: University of New Mexico Press, 2002).

In the late 1920s U.S. ambassador Henry Lane Wilson wrote *Diplomatic Episodes in Mexico, Belgium, and Chile* (reprint, Port Washington NY: Associated Faculty Press, 1971), which is his retrospective view of events. Friedrich Katz, *The Secret War in Mexico: Europe, the United States and the Mexican Revolution* (Chicago: University of Chicago Press, 1981) remains the best coverage of international events for the period between 1905 and 1920.

Michael C. Meyer, *Huerta: A Political Portrait* (Lincoln: University of Nebraska Press, 1972) remains the unsurpassed single monograph in English analyzing the terrifying years when dictator Victoriano Huerta intimidated popular political will in Mexico.

Index

Elguero, Luís, 113, 121, 136, 181, 199
elites of Mexico City, 18
Esteva Ruiz, Roberto, 107, 116–17, 134–35, 143, 148–50, 177–78, 210, 212, 235, 244, 246, 251–52, 268n20
ethnic disintegration efforts against the United States. *See* guerilla bands
evacuation, 127; of Veracruz, 225–29, 232, 240, 243, 247

federal troops, 16, 24, 27, 30, 33, 35, 47, 48, 55–56, 63, 69, 90, 100, 112, 133, 147, 160, 169, 171, 176, 201, 206, 215, 217, 222, 224, 227, 231, 235, 236
Fletcher, Frank Friday (U.S. admiral), 84–85, 90, 93, 85, 267n41
France, 79, 104, 122, 138, 165, 258, 259
Franz Ferdinand (archduke of Austria), 248, 271n73
France: French banking syndicate, 77; French community in Mexico, 16, 92; French diplomats, 6, 21, 49, 66, 79–80, 82, 94, 96, 115–16, 120, 131, 140, 142, 151, 174, 202, 236, 237; French legation, 147, 268; French policy in Mexico, 79; French refugees in Mexico, 87, 104, 122, 123, 130, 138; money transferred to Victoriano Huerta by, 121; and José de la Cruz Porfirio Díaz, 258–259; Victoriano Huerta's view of, 181

Gallardo, Rincon (chief of Rurales), 69, 140, 142, 144, 215–16, 222, 230, 250
Gamboa, Federico, 62–63, 136, 250, 269n28
gangs, criminal, 64, 76, 176, 195
Garcia Peña, Ángel (general), 56, 144, 179, 184, 235–36, 238
garrison: of Guadalajara, 25, 136; of Jojutla, 24, 114, 170, 182–83; of Mexico City, 15, 121, 122, 141, 151, 263n2,

182–83; of Queretaro, 235; of Veracruz, 161
German community (Mexico City), 25, 92, 95, 115, 125, 126, 135–36, 140, 231, 232, 237, 242
Germany, 1, 2, 4, 5, 40, 78–79, 92, 102, 104, 112, 115, 138, 187, 219, 257–58, 261n2, 267n2, 268n5; forced loan against Germans in Guyamas, 80–81, 134, 141–42, 149, 156, 177, 182, 209; rejection of Félix Díaz's funding request, 258
González, Pablo, 129
Great Britain, 13, 40, 70, 73–79, 82, 94, 102, 111–12, 122, 149, 165, 188, 259, 261n2
Grey, Edward (foreign secretary, secretary of state), 71, 78, 79, 104, 153, 266n24
Guadalajara, 25, 32, 136, 142, 146, 185, 189, 201, 215
guerilla bands, sent into United States, 70, 76, 140

Hamburg America Line (Hamburg-Amerika Linie), 102, 111, 113, 136, 139, 143, 151, 152, 168, 171–72, 174, 192–93, 267n2, 268n15
Heynen, Carl, 87–88, 111, 152, 169, 174, 187, 267n2
Hintze, Paul von: advising unification and reconciliation (5/15), 135; advising Victoriano Huerta to step down (5/29), 164; antisemitic remarks by, 151, 153; assigned to Mexico, 1; assuming Victoriano Huerta is finished (6/25), 224; diary background explanation, 261; effort to postpone barracks revolt, (5/19), 141; hoping to preempt U.S. interference (7/1), 242; hoping lack of money forces resignation (6/25), 224; meeting Victoriano Huerta

Hintze, Paul von (*cont.*)
    with Lionel Carden to suggest res-
    ignation (6/28), 234; proposing path
    to Huerta's resignation (7/1), 242;
    rejection of Tampico oil region for
    Germany by, 165; replacing Victori-
    ano Huerta with a junta (5/21), 146;
    summary biography of, 18
Hohler, Thomas Beaumont, 78, 80,
    100-102, 262n2, 266n23
Holste, Alejandro, 152, 165, 214,
    269n39
Huerta, Victoriano: acceptance of
    resignation of, by Mexican Con-
    gress (7/16), 256; army support for
    (5/29), 162; and banking circles
    outrage, 143; demanding end to
    Veracruz occupation, 224; and de-
    sire for a fortress Mexico (6/20),
    216; and desire to leave with Blan-
    quet (6/13), 194; embarking on SMS
    Dresden (7/18), 256; and loss of ar-
    tillery (6/25), 224; offering Tampi-
    co oil region to Germany, 165; and
    peace settlement with revolution-
    aries (5/29), 162; preparing for new
    offensive (6/17), 204; resignation of
    (7/15), 255; threatening to end Ni-
    agara Falls conference (6/30), 240;
    threatening to force U.S. into war
    (6/19, 6/20), 214; under threat of
    collective cabinet resignation (7/1),
    242; and views of Great Britain,
    France, and Japan (6/28), 243; and
    vision of Germany (6/19), 214

Ignacio Rivero, 241-42
insurrection in the capital. *See* revolt
intellectuals waiting for the masses to
    turn, 96
intervention, armed, in Mexico, 5-10,
    12, 38, 43, 53, 55, 58, 72-74, 77, 79,
    99, 112, 116, 122, 126, 128, 138, 164,

182, 184, 190, 209, 216, 261n2, 261-
    62n2, 263n22, 264n36, 265n10
Iturbide, General (also governor), 95,
    112, 222, 230
Izumo (ship), 134, 155, 201

Japan, 4, 5, 22, 36, 66, 69, 77, 79, 95,
    109, 134, 149, 151, 153, 154-55, 165,
    174, 201, 222; Ambassador Mineich-
    irò Adachi, 171, 174, 201, 269n41;
    Baron Makino Nobuaki, 79, 266n27;
    Minister President Okuma, 153; pol-
    icy toward United States, 93
Jimenez Castro (governor of More-
    los), 136
junta, 91, 136, 146, 173, 176, 178

Ketelsen and Degetau (company), 182,
    249
Knox, Philander, 24, 26, 262n11

Laredo, 107
Lascuraín Paredes, Pedro, 10, 11, 22,
    23, 29-32, 35, 39-44, 52-56, 59, 109,
    136, 196-97, 203, 205, 207, 208-17,
    210, 221, 233-35, 240, 245
Lazar Banking House, 77
Liberal Party, 61, 62
Limantour, José Ives, 126, 268n23
Lind, John (U.S. envoy), 62, 66-67, 70-
    71, 75-76, 81, 126, 158, 263n14
Lobos (island), 129-30
López Portillo, José, 88-95, 100, 103-7,
    136, 151, 179
Loyola (governor of Queretaro), 63
Lozano, José Maria, 61, 90, 95, 103,
    109, 116, 119, 133, 142, 147, 161,
    162-63, 268n9

Maas, General (Joaquín Maas Áquila),
    33, 88, 111, 141, 147, 160, 177-79,
    194-95, 222, 230, 250, 264n31
Madero, Ernesto, 7, 23, 42, 56

In The Mexican Experience series

To order or obtain more information on these or other University of Nebraska Press titles, visit nebraskapress.unl.edu.

CPSIA information can be obtained at www.ICGtesting.com
Printed in the USA
LVOW12s0313081114

412656LV00003B/3/P